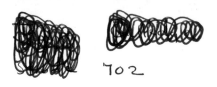

SYMBOLS FOR THEME CORRECTION

(The symbols refer to divisions of Section I of the Appendix.)

A THE COMMA

A 1 Compounds p. 277	**A 2** Compound and compound-complex sentences p. 277	**A 3** Non-restrictive modifiers pp. 277-278	**A 4** Non-restrictive appositives p. 278

A 8 Elements not in normal sentence position p. 278	**A 9** Direct quotations p. 279	**A 10** Dates and addresses p. 279

C THE DASH

C 1 Shifting or interruption of thought p. 279	**C 2** Appositives p. 279	**C 3** Interpolated elements p. 279

F THE COLON   G THE PERIOD

F 1 Direct quotations p. 280	**F 2** Appositives p. 280	**G 1** Declarative sentences p. 280	**G 2** Imperative sentences p. 280

I THE EXCLAMATION POINT

I 1 Exclamatory sentences p. 280	**I 2** Exclamatory elements p. 280	**J 1** Titles p. 280

K THE APOSTROPHE

K 1 Possessives p. 282	**K 2** Contractions p. 282	**K 3** Plurals of letters, figures, and words p. 282

M ITALICS

M 1 Titles p. 283	**M 2** Names of ships, trains, and airplanes p. 283	**M 3** Letters and words used as such p. 283

N CAPITAL LETTERS

N 1 Beginning of sentence p. 283	**N 2** Beginning of quoted sentence p. 283	**N 3** Beginning of line of poetry p. 283	**N 4** Proper nouns and adjectives p. 284

PUNCTUATION AND MECHANICS

A 5 Introductory expressions with appositives p. 278	**A 6** Independent sentence elements p. 278	**A 7** Sentence modifiers p. 278

B PARENTHESES

A 11 To prevent misreading p. 279	**B 1** Appositives p. 279	**B 2** Interpolated elements p. 279

D BRACKETS	**E THE SEMICOLON**	
D Explanatory notes or additions p. 279	**E 1** Compound and compound-complex sentences p. 279	**E 2** Compounds with internal comma punctuation p. 280

H THE QUESTION MARK

G 3 Abbreviations p. 280	**H 1** Interrogative sentences p. 280	**H 2** Interrogative non-sentences p. 280

J QUOTATION MARKS

J 2 Direct quotations pp. 281-282	**J 3** Position of other marks of punctuation p. 282	**J 4** Single quotation marks p. 282

L THE HYPHEN

L 1 Compound words p. 283	**L 2** Divided words p. 283

M 4 Foreign words p. 283	**M 5** Emphasized words p. 283

N 5 Important words in titles p. 284	**N 6** Pronoun I p. 284	**N 7** Words referring to Deity p. 284

OTHER SYMBOLS FOR CORRECTING THEMES

adj *Adjective

adv *Adverb

agr *Agreement

awk Awkward phrasing or construction

cap *Capital letter (See N in Section I of Appendix)

case *Case

coh Coherence

cs Comma splice (See A2, E1, and G1 in Section I of Appendix)

cst Construction; faulty sentence structure

dict Diction

dng *Dangling modifier

frag Fragmentary sentence

inc comp *Incomplete comparison

ital *Italics (See M in Section I of Appendix)

lc Lower case; do not capitalize

mm Misplaced modifier

no ¶ No new paragraph

om Omission of word or words

¶ New paragraph

par cst *Parallel construction

ref *Reference

rep Undesirable repetition

seq tn *Sequence of tenses

shift Shift in tense, person, or number

sp Spelling

sub Subordinate this idea (See Chapter XVI)

tn *Tense

vb fm Verb form

voice *Voice

wd ord Word order

* The asterisk indicates that the entry appears in the Index.

WRITING
GOOD SENTENCES

WRITING GOOD SENTENCES

A FUNCTIONAL APPROACH
TO
SENTENCE STRUCTURE,
GRAMMAR,
AND
PUNCTUATION

CLAUDE W. FAULKNER

PROFESSOR OF ENGLISH
UNIVERSITY OF ARKANSAS

Revised Edition

CHARLES SCRIBNER'S SONS
NEW YORK, N.Y.

ACKNOWLEDGMENTS

I SHOULD like, first of all, to express my obvious indebtedness to all of the students of the English language who have helped to formulate the traditional materials upon which this book is based. More specifically, I owe a debt of gratitude to my wife and to numerous friends who have assisted and encouraged me. I am especially grateful to John Poindexter, Leighton Rudolph, and James L. Jackson of the University of Arkansas. I also wish to express my appreciation to Charles W. Roberts, Mary Kay Peer, and Mildred Goodner of the University of Illinois, William Toran of the University of Kentucky, and Albert Howard Carter, Oliver W. Ferguson, Francis I. Gwaltney, Mozelle Nelson, and Berneace Fitzgerald of the University of Arkansas. Finally, I wish to acknowledge my deep obligation to Atkinson Dymock of Charles Scribner's Sons for his very capable assistance.

C. W. F.

PREFACE TO THE REVISED EDITION

THIS book grew out of the following personal convictions concerning the teaching of composition to college students:

(1) A study of sentence structure is a necessary part of any basic course in composition.

It is true that, in acquiring his native language, everyone learns to speak and write acceptable sentences by imitating what he hears and reads rather than by studying syntax or mastering rules. But, by the time a person reaches college, this imitative process has either slowed down or stopped altogether. No matter whether his level of ability is high or low at this point, if he is to improve his command of the language, he must study the structure of the sentence. A college student can no longer learn verbal skills by imitation.

(2) Such a study should be thorough, not superficial.

Frequently, the attempt is made to simplify the study of sentence structure by eliminating everything except the so-called "minimum essentials," but this sort of simplification inevitably results in throwing out the baby with the bath-water. If anything, we need to *over-teach* sentence structure, since the student is certain to *under-learn* or *over-forget* it. Teaching the student a bare minimum necessarily results in his retaining less than that bare minimum. Teaching him more details than he actually needs to know may result in his retaining at least the essential materials. In writing this text, I have gone into enough detail to make certain that the student will understand and remember the "minimum essentials."

(3) A study of sentence structure can be thorough without being difficult.

This is possible if there is a gradual progression from simple to complex, accompanied by repeated emphasis upon the *function* of sentence elements. This text begins with the basic sentence framework and with simple sentences in which the various functions are performed by single-word elements. As the study proceeds, the student learns that word-groups (compounds, phrases, and dependent clauses) can perform these same functions and that a word-group can perform a function within another word-group. He thus progresses logically and gradually from simple subject-verb sentences to the most complicated compound-complex sentences.

(4) The study of accepted grammatical forms and proper punctuation should go hand in hand with a progressive study of sentence structure.

This is the most effective way to study such matters. Certainly, it does not make good sense to try to master at one time all uses of the

PREFACE

objective case or all types of comma punctuation. In this text, the proper case of the subject of the infinitive is discussed in connection with the syntax of the infinitive phrase, and the comma punctuation used with adverb clauses is treated in connection with the syntax of the adverb clause.

(5) The study of sentence structure, grammar, and punctuation must be directly related to the student's own writing.

The student must somehow bridge the gap between theory and practice. There is, obviously, no substitute for theme-writing, but the teacher needs, in addition, some less time-consuming method of helping the student to apply what he learns to what he writes. Unfortunately, the usual objective-style workbook fails to do the job. It is doubtful that anyone ever improved his own writing by correcting incorrect sentences written by someone else or by analyzing sentences concocted for the purpose. The only way to teach a student to write good sentences is to combine instruction concerning the sentence with actual practice in the writing of good sentences. To give such practice, the exercises in this book require the student to write sentences to fit specified patterns, using correct sentence structure, correct grammatical forms, and correct punctuation. He thus learns to associate proper word-forms and punctuation with the structure of the sentences which he composes, a process which he needs to follow in all of his writing. Furthermore, he may learn to use sentence patterns which he has not previously employed, thereby increasing the variety and effectiveness of his sentences.

This text, then, presents a thorough but simple study of sentence structure, grammar, and punctuation. It uses a functional approach and is designed to achieve a maximum amount of direct and immediate application to the student's own writing.

I am pleased that so many teachers found the first edition of WRITING GOOD SENTENCES pleasant to teach, easy for the student to understand, and, above all, effective in improving the student's writing. And I trust that the revisions in this new edition are changes for the better in all of these respects.

CLAUDE W. FAULKNER

CONTENTS

WRITING
GOOD SENTENCES

CHAPTER I
WORDS AND SENTENCES

LANGUAGE is primarily a means of communicating thoughts from one person to another.[1] Obviously, then, the major concern of the writer or speaker is to use language in such a way that it will communicate to other people the exact meaning which he wishes to convey.

The smallest independent language unit is the *word*—a written or spoken *symbol* which stands for a *concept* or *idea*. The written symbol *sofa,* for example, stands for the *concept* of a particular type of furniture. With reference to words, the primary problem of the writer or speaker is to select that *word*—that *symbol*— which most accurately represents the concept which he has in mind.

How does one select the proper word to fit a concept? Usually one merely imitates whatever use of words he has seen or heard. Since the meaning of a word depends upon usage, this imitative procedure is quite satisfactory—*if* a person is sure that the usage he is imitating is generally accepted. The only way that one can be certain of this, however, is to consult a dictionary whenever he is in doubt about the accepted meaning of a word. A good dictionary—an accurate record of word usage—is an invaluable aid in selecting the exact word to use to convey a particular concept.

A much more difficult process than the selection of a *word* to communicate a *concept* is the construction of a *sentence* to communicate a *thought*. A *sentence* is a *combination of words* which conveys at least one *complete thought* consisting of a *combination of concepts*. Thus the sentence *I saw him* is a combination of three words conveying a complete thought consisting of a combination of three different concepts. With reference to sentences, the primary problem of the writer or speaker is to combine words in such a way that they will accurately communicate the thought which he has in mind.

How does one know how to combine individual words into correct sentences? Like the selection of words, this process is, for the most part, purely imitative. One usually simply patterns his sentences after those he has read and heard. By itself, however, this imitative procedure is not likely to produce an ability to write good sentences. For one can never be certain that the language of the writing and speech which he is imitating is itself acceptable, nor can he be sure that he is imitating it accurately and intelligently. Something more than imitation is necessary. That something is an understanding of sentence structure.

The following chapters present a thorough study of English sentence structure designed to teach the student to construct sentences which will communicate his thoughts accurately. Since the composition of a correct sentence necessarily involves proper word choice, we shall give some attention to the selection of words. However, though the student will be expected to use the utmost care in choosing words when he composes the sentences required by the exercises, the main emphasis of this book is not upon vocabulary but upon the writing of sentences which are constructed and punctuated properly.

---

[1] Language is also a means of communicating emotion or feelings.

1

CHAPTER II

THE SENTENCE: SUBJECTS AND VERBS

THOUGH sentences vary greatly in length and complexity, every sentence—if it is to convey a thought accurately—must contain certain basic elements and must follow certain basic principles of structure. In our study of the sentence, we shall start with sentences which contain only the basic functional elements and which therefore display the basic structural patterns without any elaboration. Then, building upon this foundation, we shall extend our study to include elements, functions, and structural patterns which are not basic and which may or may not appear in any given sentence.

First of all, we shall consider subjects and verbs. Let us examine the following simple, basic sentences:

> *Dogs* bark.
> The *log* burned.
> *We* like music.
> The *child* wrote a letter.
> *Bill* is a reporter.
> *She* seemed graceful.

Each of these sentences has a *subject*—the word which is italicized. In fact, every sentence has a *subject*—a word (or group of words) which names or indicates a person or thing about which something is said. In addition to the subject, every sentence must have a *verb*—a word (or group of words) which says something about the subject, indicating action, possession, or state of being. Note the verbs in the examples already given:

> Dogs *bark*.
> The log *burned*.
> We *like* music.
> The child *wrote* a letter.
> Bill *is* a reporter.
> She *seemed* graceful.

Note: Usually the verb of a sentence is easier to locate than the subject. Once the verb is located, the following method may be used to find the subject of the verb:

1. Form a question by placing *who* or *what* before the verb.
2. The answer to the question is the subject of the verb.

> Children play.
> *Who* play? Children.
> The subject of the verb is *children*.

> The thunder frightens the dog.
> *What* frightens? Thunder.
> The subject of the verb is *thunder*.

> The book seems long.
> *What* seems? Book.
> The subject of the verb is *book*.

> The man was promoted.
> *Who* was promoted? Man.
> The subject of the verb is *man*.

This method of determining the subject is particularly useful when a sentence is complicated or has unusual word order.

2

Sometimes the subject of a verb is *understood* rather than expressed. In the following sentences the subject *you* is understood:

> Stop.
> Shut the door.

Though the subject of a verb may be understood instead of expressed, the *subject* function and the *verb* function are performed in all sentences. Every sentence, then, contains two things:

1. A *subject*—a word (or group of words) which names or indicates a person or thing about which something is said.

> Examples:
>
> The *mayor* consulted the council. (Person)
> The *pencil* was dull. (Thing)

Note 1: In this definition and in the treatment of the substantive which follows, the word *thing* is to be interpreted in a broad sense. It includes inanimate objects (*tree, desk, stone*), animals (*dog, worm, fish*), places (*country, island, Chicago*), activities (*reading, writing, running*), and ideas (*happiness, love. strength*).

Note 2: As indicated in the definition, a *group of words* may serve as the subject of a sentence. In the following examples, note that the *group of words* in the second sentence functions in the same way as the *single word* in the first sentence:

> *Hunting* is fun.   The *outcome* was certain.
> *Hunting rabbits* is fun.   *That he would win* was certain.

Later, we shall make a detailed study of such word groups in the sections on *phrases* and *clauses*. For the time being, it is necessary only to realize that *a group of words, as well as a single word, can perform the subject function.*

2. A *verb*—a word (or group of words) which says something about the subject, indicating action, possession, or state of being.

> Examples:
>
> The plane *flew.* (Action)
> Susie *has* a pony. (Possession)
> The train *is* long. (State of being)

Note: A *group of words* which performs the verb function is called a *verb phrase.* Study the following examples, noting that the *group of words* in the second sentence functions in the same way as the *single word* in the first sentence:

> She *reads* the book.   He *hit* the ball.   The baby *cries.*
> She *is reading* the book.   He *will hit* the ball.   The baby *has been crying.*

A verb which is used with the primary verb to form a verb phrase is called an *auxiliary* (or *helping*) verb. *Have, can, may, be, shall, will, should, would, must,* and *do* are the most common auxiliary verbs. Note the following examples:

> I *have* gone.   I *will* go.
> I *can* go.   I *should* go.
> I *may* go.   I *would* go.
> I *am* going.   I *must* go.
> I *shall* go.   I *do* go.

DO EXERCISE 1

CHAPTER III

SUBSTANTIVES

THE subject, as we have noted, always consists of a word or word-group which names or indicates something.

There is a general term which is applied to the sort of word or word-group which can function as the subject of a sentence. Such a word or word-group is called a *substantive*. This useful term may be defined as follows:

$$\text{A substantive is} \begin{cases} \textit{a noun,} \\ \textit{a pronoun, or} \\ \textit{a word or word-group functioning like a noun.} \end{cases}$$

Note that the word *substantive* does *not* mean *subject,* although every subject is a substantive.

In considering substantives, we shall for the present limit our study to nouns and pronouns.

A. NOUNS

1. DEFINITION

A noun is the name of a person or thing.

Examples: *teacher, desk, cat, Asia, reading, happiness*

Note: As previously stated, the word *thing* is to be interpreted as including inanimate objects, animals, places, activities, and ideas.

2. CLASSIFICATION OF NOUNS

There are two main classes of nouns: (a) common nouns and (b) proper nouns.

a. *COMMON NOUNS*

A common noun is the name of one of a general class of persons or things.

Examples: *child, stick, cow, city, walking, loyalty*

b. *PROPER NOUNS*

A proper noun is the name of a specific and individual person or thing.

Examples: *George Washington, Indiana, the Bureau of Standards*

Note: Proper nouns are capitalized.

B. PRONOUNS

1. DEFINITION

A pronoun is a word which stands for (*pro-*) a noun.

Examples: *I, you, he, it, that, this, who, which*

Note 1: A noun *names* something: *man, woman, book.* A pronoun *indicates* something without giving it a name: *he, she, it.* Both nouns and pronouns are *substantives;* both bring to mind persons and things.

Note 2: If a pronoun refers to a substantive, the substantive is called the *antecedent* of the pronoun.

2. CLASSIFICATION OF PRONOUNS

The nine types of pronouns are the following: (a) personal, (b) demonstrative, (c) indefinite, (d) reflexive, (e) reciprocal, (f) intensive, (g) interrogative, (h) indefinite relative, and (i) relative. Personal, demonstrative, and indefinite pronouns will be treated in this chapter.

C. THREE PROPERTIES OF NOUNS AND PRONOUNS

Both nouns and pronouns may be classified according to certain characteristics which are called *properties*. These are person, number, gender, and case. For the present, we shall consider only the first three properties.

1. PERSON

Person pertains to the relationship of the person or thing named or indicated by the noun or pronoun to the speaking (or writing) of the sentence.

There are three persons:

    a. *First Person*—the person *speaking* (*I, we*)

    b. *Second Person*—the person or thing *spoken to* (*you*)

    c. *Third Person*—the person or thing *spoken of* (*he, she, it, they, tree, basket*)

Note: Nouns are almost always in the third person. However, a noun is in the first person if it names the person speaking and is in the second person if it names the person spoken to.

        Examples:

            I, *James Wilson*, asked the question. (First person)

            John, you received a telegram. (Second person)

2. NUMBER

Number, as the term suggests, pertains to the number of persons or things named or indicated by the noun or pronoun.

a. *SINGULAR AND PLURAL NUMBER*

(1) Singular Number

A noun or pronoun which names or indicates *one* person or thing is *singular*.

    Examples: *girl, ceiling, defeat*

(2) Plural Number

A noun or pronoun which names or indicates *more than one* person or thing is *plural*.

    Examples: *children, leaves, pleasures*

Note: Spelling rules governing the formation of plurals may be found in any good dictionary.

b. *COLLECTIVE NOUNS*

A noun which names a group is called a *collective noun*.

    Examples: *committee, class, audience, crowd, group, squad, team, band*

If the group named by the collective noun is thought of as functioning as a unit, the collective noun is singular. If the group is thought of as functioning as individuals, the collective noun is plural.

    Examples:

        The team is winning the game. (Singular)

        The team are wearing sweaters. (Plural)

Note that a collective noun used with plural meaning does not end in *s* but has the same form as the singular. Of course, the words used as collective nouns can have plural forms ending in *s* (*committees, classes, teams*), but these forms are *not* collective nouns since they name *several groups*, not *a group*. (See the definition given above.)

3. GENERGENDER

    Gender pertains to the sex of the person or thing named or indicated by the noun or pronoun.
    There are four genders: (a) masculine, (b) feminine, (c) neuter, and (d) common.

a. *MASCULINE*

    A noun or pronoun which names or indicates a person or animal of the male sex is of *masculine* gender.

        Examples: *man, rooster, bull, he*

b. *FEMININE*

    A noun or pronoun which names or indicates a person or animal of the female sex is of *feminine* gender.

        Examples: *woman, hen, cow, she*

c. *NEUTER*

    A noun or pronoun which names or indicates a thing which does not have sex is of *neuter* gender.

        Examples: *fence, road, house, it*

d. *COMMON*

    A noun or pronoun which names or indicates a person or animal without showing sex is of *common* gender.

        Examples: *child, person, dog, someone*

D. THREE TYPES OF PRONOUNS

    Of the types of pronouns listed above, the first three—personal, demonstrative, and indefinite—can serve as subjects of simple declarative sentences. Consequently, we shall consider these first of all.

1. PERSONAL PRONOUNS

a. *DEFINITION*

    A personal pronoun indicates the person *speaking,* the person or thing *spoken to,* or the person or thing *spoken of.*
    The personal pronouns are the following:

	Singular	*Plural*
1st Person	I	we
2nd Person	you	you
3rd Person	he, she, it	they

b. *PROPERTIES*

    The personal pronoun varies in form throughout to show person. It also varies in form in the first person (*I; we*) and the third person (*he, she, it; they*) to indicate number, and in the third person singular (*he, she, it*) to indicate gender.

2. DEMONSTRATIVE PRONOUNS

a. *DEFINITION*

    A demonstrative pronoun points out one or more persons or things.
    The demonstrative pronouns are the following:

Singular	*Plural*
this	these
that	those

    A demonstrative pronoun is used as the subject of each of the following sentences:

        That is the library.
        These are expensive.

b. *PROPERTIES*

The demonstrative pronoun is always in the third person. It varies in form to indicate number (*this, that; these, those*), but does not vary in form to show gender.

3. INDEFINITE PRONOUNS

a. *DEFINITION*

An indefinite pronoun refers to one or more persons or things but does not definitely point out which one or ones are meant.

The most common indefinite pronouns are the following:

Singular Indefinite Pronouns: *each, none, some, all, one* (meaning *a person*); *either, neither; anyone, everyone, someone; anybody, everybody, somebody, nobody; anything, everything, something, nothing*

Plural Indefinite Pronouns: *none, both, few, some, several, many, all*

Examples:

One must be brave.
Everybody is present.
Several have finished the exam.

Notice that such indefinite pronouns as *someone, everybody,* and *anything* are written as single words.

Note: When measuring quantity, *none, some,* and *all* are singular; when measuring number, *none, some,* and *all* are plural.

Examples:
None (Some, All) of the soup *was* left. [Soup is measured by quantity.]
None (Some, All) of the marbles *were* under the bed. [Marbles are measured by number.]

b. *PROPERTIES*

The indefinite pronouns are always in the third person. An indefinite pronoun does not vary in form to indicate number or gender.

DO EXERCISE 2

CHAPTER IV

VERBS

A VERB, as we have previously noted, is a word or word-group which says something about the subject, indicating action, possession, or state of being. In this chapter, we shall study the various properties and classes of verbs.

A. PROPERTIES OF VERBS

Verbs have the following *properties*: (1) voice, (2) tense, (3) person, (4) number, and (5) mode. A variation in any of these properties is usually accompanied by a modification in the form of the verb.

1. VOICE

The subject of a verb may be related to the idea expressed by the verb in either of two ways: (a) the subject may be acted upon, or (b) the subject may not be acted upon. This relationship of the subject to the idea of the verb is called *voice*. There are two voices—the *passive* and the *active*—and the form of the verb varies to indicate variation in voice.

a. *PASSIVE VOICE*

A verb in the *passive* voice indicates that the subject is being acted upon. A passive-voice verb always consists of some form of the verb *to be* plus the past participle of the primary verb.

> Examples:
> She *was reprimanded* by the policeman.
> James *will be elected*.

b. *ACTIVE VOICE*

Any verb which does *not* indicate that the subject is acted upon is said to be in the *active* voice. A verb in the active voice may thus indicate that the subject acts, possesses, or is in a state of being.

> Examples:
> The ambassador *speaks* French.
> The terrier *had* a bone.
> The child *was* unhappy.

Note: For the present, we shall be primarily concerned with verbs in the active voice. DO NOT USE THE PASSIVE VOICE IN ANY EXERCISE UNLESS SPECIFICALLY ASKED TO DO SO.

2. TENSE

In addition to indicating voice, verbs show a number of time relationships. This indication of the relative time of the action, possession, or state of being is called *tense* (a term derived from the Latin word for *time*).

Note: Hereafter in this section, to avoid awkwardness, we shall refer simply to the time of the *action*, but all statements are equally applicable to verbs showing *possession* or *state of being*.

a. *THE TENSES*

(1) **The Simple Tenses**

The simple tenses—the present, the past, and the future—show the relationship between the time of the action and the time of the speaking or writing of the sentence.

(a) Present Tense

The *present* tense indicates that the time of the action is identical with the time of the speaking or writing of the sentence.

Example:

He *writes* the letter. [The action is taking place at the time of the speaking or writing of the sentence.]

(b) Past Tense

The *past* tense indicates that the time of the action is in the past with reference to the time of the speaking or writing of the sentence.

Example:

He *wrote* the letter. [The action took place in the past with reference to the time of the speaking or writing of the sentence.]

(c) Future Tense

The *future* tense indicates that the time of the action is in the future with reference to the time of the speaking or writing of the sentence.

Example:

He *will write* the letter. [The action will take place in the future with reference to the time of the speaking or writing of the sentence.]

————————

The following diagram shows the differences between the simple tenses:

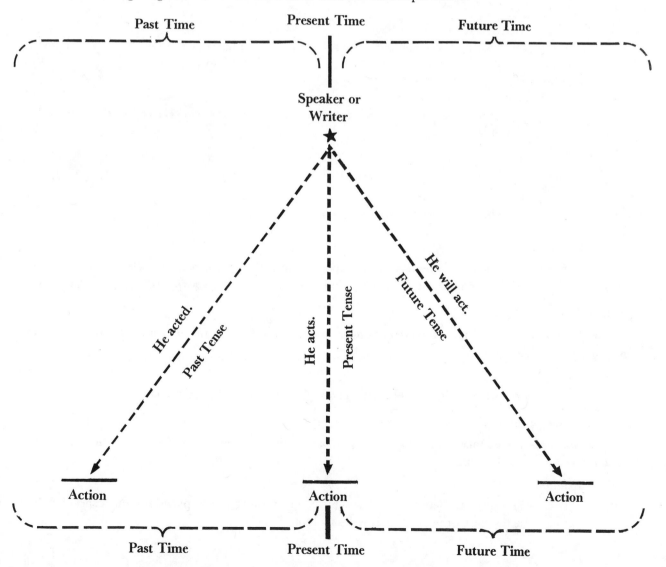

EXPLANATION OF DIAGRAM

Whenever a person speaks or writes a sentence, he must, of course, do so in what is to him the present time. The diagram, therefore, represents the speaker or writer of the sentence as standing at a point designated as the present time. From this point in time he views the action to be indicated by the verb in the sentence which he is composing.

When the speaker or writer looks back in time to an action that occurred at some time in the past, he indicates the relationship of the time of the action to the time at which the sentence is being composed by using the *past* tense; he says, "He *acted*."

When the speaker or writer looks at an action that is occurring at the present time, he indicates the identity of the time of the action and the time at which the sentence is being composed by using the *present* tense; he says, "He *acts*."

When the speaker or writer looks forward in time to an action that will occur at some time in the future, he indicates the relationship of the time of the action to the time at which the sentence is being composed by using the *future* tense; he says, "He *will act*."

Note: The present tense is used to express certain time relationships other than simple present time.

a. *HABITUAL ACTION*

The present tense may be employed to express an action which is habitual.

Example:

He *teaches* chemistry.

b. *HISTORICAL PRESENT*

The present tense may be employed to express actions which happened in the past if it is desired to make them vivid for the reader or listener. (The writer must be consistent; he may not shift back and forth between the past and present.)

Example:

The end *catches* the ball. He *dodges* a tackler. He *sidesteps*. He *crosses* the line. It *is* a touchdown!

c. *FUTURE*

The present tense is sometimes employed to indicate future time.

Example:

The boat *sails* tomorrow.

(2) The Perfect Tenses

The perfect tenses—the present perfect, the past perfect, and the future perfect—select some particular time as a point of reference and indicate that the action was completed (*i.e., perfected*) prior to that time.

(a) Present Perfect Tense

The *present perfect* tense takes the present time as a point of reference and indicates that the action was completed prior to the present.

Example:

He *has written* the letter. [The action was completed prior to the present time.]

(b) Past Perfect Tense

The *past perfect* tense takes some time in the past as a point of reference and indicates that the action was completed prior to that time.

Example:

He *had written* the letter when I saw him. [The action was completed prior to a specified time in the past—the time "when I saw him."]

(c) Future Perfect Tense

The *future perfect* tense takes some time in the future as a point of reference and indicates that the action will be completed prior to that time.

> Example:
>
> He *will have written* the letter by Thursday. [The action will be completed prior to a specified time in the future.]

———————————————

The following diagram shows the differences between the perfect tenses:

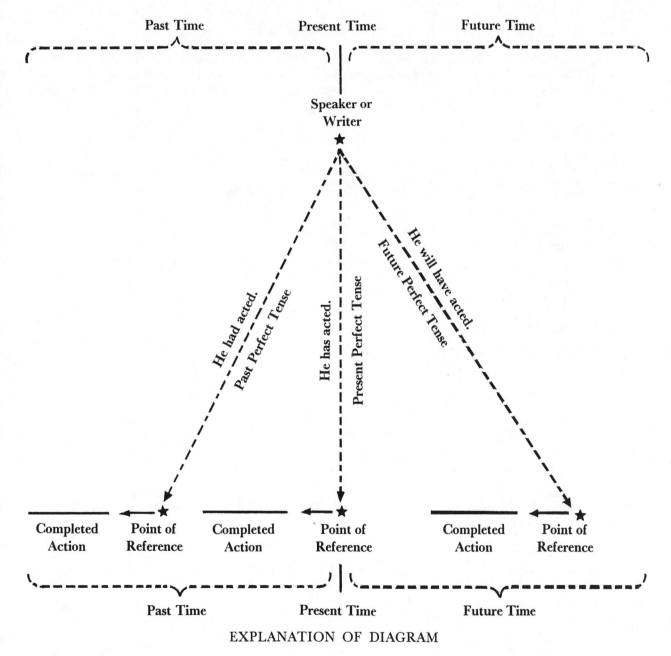

EXPLANATION OF DIAGRAM

As in the diagram of the simple tenses, the speaker or writer is considered to be standing at the point designated as the present time.

When the speaker or writer looks back to a point in the past and sees that an action was completed prior to that time, he indicates the relative position in time of (1) the action, (2) the point of reference, and (3) the composition of the sentence by using the *past perfect* tense; he says, "He *had acted.*"

When the speaker or writer looks at the present time as a point of reference and sees that an action was completed prior to that time, he indicates the relative position in time of (1) the action, (2) the point of reference, and (3) the composition of the sentence by using the *present perfect* tense; he says, "He *has acted*."

When the speaker or writer looks forward to a point in the future and sees that an action will be completed prior to that time, he indicates the relative position in time of (1) the action, (2) the point of reference, and (3) the composition of the sentence by using the *future perfect* tense; he says, "He *will have acted*."

b. *PRINCIPAL PARTS OF VERBS*

Every verb has a limited number of variant forms. The proper form for any tense can readily be determined if one knows the forms used in the *present infinitive*, the *past tense*, the *past participle*, and the *present participle*. These are called the *principal parts* of the verb. The relationship between the forms of the *past tense* and *past participle* and the form of the *present infinitive* depends upon whether the verb is *regular* or *irregular*. The *present participle* of every verb, however, is formed by adding *-ing* to the *present infinitive* form. (Example: *Present infinitive: sleep + -ing = Present participle: sleeping.*)

Note: In classifying verbs according to the nature of their principal parts, grammarians differ both in number of classes given and in terminology used. Some specify two classes: *weak* and *strong*; others give three: *weak, strong,* and *irregular*. But the majority, perhaps, use the classification adopted here: *regular* and *irregular*. It seems to be the most simple and most satisfactory division.

(1) Regular and Irregular Verbs

(a) Regular Verbs

Both the past tense and the past participle of the majority of English verbs are formed by adding *-ed, -d,* or *-t* to the present infinitive form. Such verbs are called *regular* verbs. Note the following examples:

Present Infinitive	*Past Tense*	*Past Participle*
ask	asked	asked
beg	begged	begged
call	called	called
carry	carried	carried
cry	cried	cried
dance	danced	danced
jump	jumped	jumped
kill	killed	killed
love	loved	loved
owe	owed	owed
reply	replied	replied
save	saved	saved
use	used	used
work	worked	worked

Note: Consult any good dictionary for spelling rules which apply when the ending *-ed* or *-ing* is added to the present infinitive form.

(b) Irregular Verbs

Although the majority of verbs are regular, the past tense and the past participle of a number of common verbs are formed in some way other than by adding *-ed, -d,* or*-t*. Such verbs are called *irregular* verbs. Note the following examples:

Present Infinitive	*Past Tense*	*Past Participle*
begin	began	begun
blow	blew	blown
break	broke	broken
choose	chose	chosen
come	came	come
do	did	done

Present Infinitive	Past Tense	Past Participle
drink	drank	drunk
drive	drove	driven
eat	ate	eaten
fall	fell	fallen
freeze	froze	frozen
give	gave	given
go	went	gone
grow	grew	grown
know	knew	known
lie	lay	lain
ride	rode	ridden
run	ran	run
see	saw	seen
sing	sang	sung
sit	sat	sat
speak	spoke	spoken
steal	stole	stolen
take	took	taken
tear	tore	torn
write	wrote	written

Note: See p. 284 for an extensive list of principal parts of troublesome verbs.

(2) Formation of Tenses from Principal Parts

The various tenses are formed from the principal parts of a verb as indicated in the diagram below. Note that the present tense is identical with the present infinitive (except in the verb *to be*).

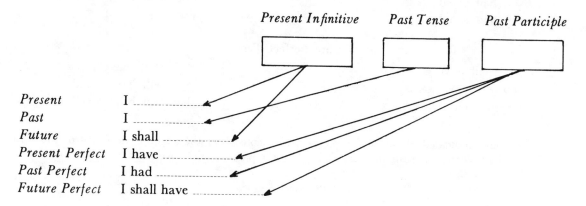

Insertion of the principal parts of any verb (except the verb *to be*) will give the proper tense forms.

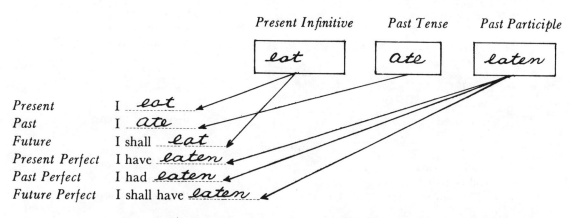

c. *VERB CONJUGATIONS*

(1) **Conjugation of a Typical Regular Verb**

The verb *to love*, a typical regular verb, is conjugated in the active voice in the six tenses as follows:

Singular	*Plural*

Present Tense

I love	we love
you love	you love
he loves	they love

Past Tense

I loved	we loved
you loved	you loved
he loved	they loved

Future Tense

I shall love	we shall love
you will love	you will love
he will love	they will love

Present Perfect Tense

I have loved	we have loved
you have loved	you have loved
he has loved	they have loved

Past Perfect Tense

I had loved	we had loved
you had loved	you had loved
he had loved	they had loved

Future Perfect Tense

I shall have loved	we shall have loved
you will have loved	you will have loved
he will have loved	they will have loved

Note 1: As previously indicated, the passive voice of a verb consists of the appropriate forms of the verb *to be* plus the past participle of the primary verb. Note the passive-voice forms of the verb *to love*:

Passive Voice

Singular	*Plural*

Present Tense

I am loved	we are loved
you are loved	you are loved
he is loved	they are loved

Past Tense

I was loved	we were loved
you were loved	you were loved
he was loved	they were loved

Future Tense

I shall be loved	we shall be loved
you will be loved	you will be loved
he will be loved	they will be loved

Present Perfect Tense

I have been loved	we have been loved
you have been loved	you have been loved
he has been loved	they have been loved

Past Perfect Tense

I had been loved	we had been loved
you had been loved	you had been loved
he had been loved	they had been loved

Future Perfect Tense

I shall have been loved	we shall have been loved
you will have been loved	you will have been loved
he will have been loved	they will have been loved

Compare this conjugation with the conjugation of the verb *to be* on p. 16.

Note 2: In formal writing and speaking, use *shall* in the first person and *will* in the second and third persons to indicate simple futurity. Use *will* in the first person and *shall* in the second and third persons to indicate volition or determination.

Simple Futurity

I shall	we shall
you will	you will
he will	they will

Volition or Determination

I will	we will
you shall	you shall
he shall	they shall

In informal and colloquial discourse, you may use the auxiliary *will* in all three persons for futurity, volition, or determination.

In the exercises in this text, you will be expected to use *shall* in the first person and *will* in the second and third persons, unless otherwise directed.

(2) Conjugation of a Typical Irregular Verb

The verb *to see,* a typical irregular verb, is conjugated in the active voice in the six tenses as follows:

Singular	*Plural*

Present Tense

I see	we see
you see	you see
he sees	they see

Past Tense

I saw	we saw
you saw	you saw
he saw	they saw

Future Tense

I shall see	we shall see
you will see	you will see
he will see	they will see

Present Perfect Tense

I have seen	we have seen
you have seen	you have seen
he has seen	they have seen

Past Perfect Tense

I had seen	we had seen
you had seen	you had seen
he had seen	they had seen

Future Perfect Tense

I shall have seen	we shall have seen
you will have seen	you will have seen
he will have seen	they will have seen

(3) Conjugation of the Verb "to be"

The verb *to be*, the most common of all verbs, is also the most irregular, primarily because its present tense is not based on the present infinitive. It is conjugated in the six tenses as follows:

Singular	*Plural*

Present Tense

I am	we are
you are	you are
he is	they are

Past Tense

I was	we were
you were	you were
he was	they were

Future Tense

I shall be	we shall be
you will be	you will be
he will be	they will be

Present Perfect Tense

I have been	we have been
you have been	you have been
he has been	they have been

Past Perfect Tense

I had been	we had been
you had been	you had been
he had been	they had been

Future Perfect Tense

I shall have been	we shall have been
you will have been	you will have been
he will have been	they will have been

d. *PROGRESSIVE AND EMPHATIC VERB FORMS*

In addition to the simple tense forms which we have studied, there are also *progressive* and *emphatic* forms.

(1) Progressive Verb Forms

The progressive form of a verb shows the continuing or progressive nature of the action indicated. Progressive forms are constructed by adding the present participle to the proper form of the verb *to be*. The following conjugation of the verb *to work* may be used as a model for determining the progressive tense forms of any verb—regular or irregular. (Compare this conjugation with the conjugation of the verb *to be* given above.)

Singular	*Plural*

Present Tense (Progressive)

I am working	we are working
you are working	you are working
he is working	they are working

Past Tense (Progressive)

I was working	we were working
you were working	you were working
he was working	they were working

Future Tense (Progressive)

I shall be working	we shall be working
you will be working	you will be working
he will be working	they will be working

Present Perfect Tense (Progressive)

I have been working	we have been working
you have been working	you have been working
he has been working	they have been working

Past Perfect Tense (Progressive)

I had been working	we had been working
you had been working	you had been working
he had been working	they had been working

Future Perfect Tense (Progressive)

I shall have been working	we shall have been working
you will have been working	you will have been working
he will have been working	they will have been working

(2) Emphatic Verb Forms

The emphatic form of a verb emphasizes the idea stated by the verb. Emphatic forms occur only in the present and past tenses. They are formed by using the verb *to do* plus the present infinitive (without *to*) of the primary verb. The following conjugation of the verb *to study* is typical of both regular and irregular verbs:

Singular	*Plural*

Present Tense (Emphatic)

I do study	we do study
you do study	you do study
he does study	they do study

Past Tense (Emphatic)

I did study	we did study
you did study	you did study
he did study	they did study

Note: Verb forms employing *do* and *did* as auxiliaries are also used in questions and negative statements where emphasis is not involved.

Examples:

Do you know him?
He did not answer.

3. PERSON AND NUMBER

We have seen that verbs vary extensively in form to indicate voice and tense. On a much more limited scale, there is variation in verb form to correspond with changes in the *person* and *number* of the subject of the verb. Thus the verb is said to *agree with* the subject in *person* and *number*.

a. *VARIATION IN BASIC FORMS*

(1) **The Verb "to be"**

The verb *to be* is unique in its variations in form to match the person and number of the subject. Note the forms used in the present and past tenses:

Singular		*Plural*
	Present Tense	
I am		we are
you are		you are
he is		they are
	Past Tense	
I was		we were
you were		you were
he was		they were

(2) **Other Verbs**

With all verbs other than *to be,* the third person singular of the present tense is the only basic form which shows variation because of person and number. Note the present tense forms of *to have, to love, to do,* and *to cry:*

Singular		*Plural*
	Present Tense	
	to have	
I have		we have
you have		you have
he *has*		they have
	to love	
I love		we love
you love		you love
he *loves*		they love
	to do	
I do		we do
you do		you do
he *does*		they do
	to cry	
I cry		we cry
you cry		you cry
he *cries*		they cry

b. *VARIATION IN FORMS CONTAINING AUXILIARIES*

(1) **"To be," "to have," and "to do" as Auxiliaries**

When the verbs *to be, to have,* and *to do* are used as auxiliaries, they vary in form in the same way that they do when used as primary verbs. Note the following examples:

You *were* invited.	He *has* written.
She *is* reading.	He *does* try.

(2) "Shall" and "will" as Auxiliaries

The distinction made in formal writing in the use of *shall* and *will* brings about a variation in verb form according to person in the future and future perfect tenses. See the note on p. 15 above.

4. MODE

Mode (or *mood*) shows the attitude of the speaker toward the statement made by the verb. The form of the verb sometimes varies to indicate mode. There are three modes: (a) the *indicative,* (b) the *subjunctive,* and (c) the *imperative.*

a. INDICATIVE MODE

The *indicative* mode is used when the speaker looks upon a statement as indicating a fact or inquiring about a fact.

> Examples:
>
> The child *lost* the toy.
> *Did* you *buy* a ticket?

Note: The indicative is the most common mode and is the one which you are expected to use in all exercises unless otherwise instructed.

b. SUBJUNCTIVE MODE

The *subjunctive* mode is used when the speaker looks upon a statement as expressing unreality, doubt, uncertainty, desire, possibility, or probability rather than fact.

> Examples:
>
> If I *were* you, I would go.
> Even if that *be* true, he has no excuse.

Since the subjunctive mode usually occurs in a noun clause or an adverb clause, we shall postpone further consideration of it until our study of dependent clauses. (See pp. 112–15.)

Note: The subjunctive is also used to report a command or request in indirect discourse.

> Example:
>
> I requested that he *leave* the room.

c. IMPERATIVE MODE

The *imperative* mode is used when the speaker looks upon a statement as expressing a command, request, or entreaty.

> Examples:
>
> *Stop!*
> *Shut* the door.
> *Save* me!

Note: As indicated by the use of the exclamation point in these examples, an imperative statement is often exclamatory.

DO EXERCISE 3

B. CLASSIFICATION OF VERBS ACCORDING TO RELATIONSHIP TO REST OF SENTENCE

If relationship to the remainder of the sentence is used as a basis for division, verbs fall into three classes: (1) transitive, (2) intransitive, and (3) linking. Each of these classes indicates a different type of verb concept, and it is this variation in concept that gives each class of verb a different relationship to other parts of the sentence.

1. TRANSITIVE

A *transitive* verb indicates action which passes across (*trans-*) from the performer of the action to the receiver of it.

Examples:

The child *smashed* the vase.
I *defeated* him.

In such sentences, the receiver of the action is called the *object* of the verb. Like the subject, the *object* is a substantive—a noun, a pronoun, or a noun equivalent.

Note: The transitive verb is the only type of verb which has a passive voice. In a passive construction the subject of the verb *receives* the action, and there is no object of the verb.

Example:

He *was defeated.*

2. INTRANSITIVE

An *intransitive* verb indicates action which involves only the performer of the action. There is no statement that anything is acted upon.

Examples:

The horse *ran.*
Birds *sing.*

3. LINKING

A *linking* verb links the subject to a substantive or an adjective but does not indicate any action. The substantive or the adjective thus linked to the subject is called the *complement.* The most common linking verb is the verb *to be,* and we shall at first confine ourselves to this linking verb.

Examples:

He *is* a champion.
They *had been* sick.

Note: *Linking* verbs are sometimes called *copulative* verbs.

CHAPTER V

BASIC SENTENCE PATTERNS

THE framework of every normal English sentence will fit one of five basic sentence patterns. We shall first consider the three most simple patterns.

A. THREE SENTENCE PATTERNS

The framework of a simple English sentence will usually fit one of the following basic sentence patterns:

1. *Subject—Verb*

2. *Subject—Verb—Object*

3. *Subject—Linking Verb—Complement*

Normally the sentence elements will occur in the sentence in the order indicated here, but inverted order is also frequently found.

1. SUBJECT—VERB

The basic framework of a sentence may consist of a subject and a verb. The verb may be either active or passive. Such a pattern containing a verb in the *active* voice is indicated in this text as follows:

> *Subject—Verb*

If the verb is *passive,* the pattern is indicated thus:

> *Subject—Passive Verb*

Some examples of these patterns follow:

BASIC PATTERN: *Subject—Verb*

Examples:

> Hornets sting.
> He has resigned.

BASIC PATTERN: *Subject—Passive Verb*

Examples:

> The criminal was punished.
> A candidate has been chosen.

Note: As these examples demonstrate, we shall disregard the articles *a, an,* and *the* in indicating sentence patterns. In the exercises in this text, however, when you write a sentence to fit a pattern, you will be expected to use *a, an,* or *the* wherever one of these articles is needed to avoid primer or telegraphic style.

Example:

Pattern: Subject—Verb

> Girl ran. (Primer or telegraphic style)
> *The* girl ran. (Correct style with article included)

2. SUBJECT—VERB—OBJECT

The basic framework of a sentence may consist of a subject, a verb, and an object. The verb in such a sentence will be a *transitive* verb in the *active* voice.

BASIC PATTERN: *Subject—Verb—Object*

Examples:

I bought a coat.
She invited him.

3. SUBJECT—LINKING VERB—COMPLEMENT

The basic framework of a sentence may consist of a subject, a linking verb, and a complement. This pattern has two subdivisions.

a. *SUBSTANTIVE COMPLEMENT PATTERN*

The complement may be any substantive—a noun, a pronoun, or a noun equivalent.

BASIC PATTERN: *Subject—Linking Verb—Substantive Complement*

Examples:

Wordsworth was a poet.
It was he.

Note: The *substantive complement* is sometimes called the *predicate nominative* or *predicate noun*.

b. *ADJECTIVE COMPLEMENT PATTERN*

The complement may be an adjective.

BASIC PATTERN: *Subject—Linking Verb—Adjective Complement*

Examples:

The horse is black.
They will be happy.
The boy was healthy.

Note 1: The *adjective complement* is sometimes called the *predicate adjective*.

Note 2: In indicating the basic patterns, we have used the normal word-order of English sentences. However, the order of the elements may vary without altering the basic framework. Note the following sentence:

Dreary was the day.

Pattern: Adjective Complement—Linking Verb—Subject

The framework of this sentence fits the third basic pattern even though the word-order is inverted.

B. CASES IN THE THREE PATTERNS

Case is that property of a noun or pronoun which varies according to the function of the noun or pronoun in the sentence. There are three cases in English: (1) the nominative, (2) the objective, and (3) the possessive. At this time, we shall consider the use and forms of the *nominative* and the *objective* cases in the three basic sentence patterns which we have studied.

1. USE OF CASES

a. *THE NOMINATIVE CASE*

In the three basic sentence patterns we have considered, the nominative case is used for the subject of a verb and for the substantive complement of a linking verb. Thus the nominative case occurs in the three patterns as follows:

1. *Subject*   *—Verb*
   (Nominative case)

2. *Subject*   *—Verb—Object*
   (Nominative case)

3. a. **Subject** —*Linking Verb—Substantive Complement*
   (Nominative case)   (Nominative case)
   b. **Subject** —*Linking Verb—Adjective Complement*
   (Nominative case)

b. *THE OBJECTIVE CASE*

The objective case is used for the object of a verb. It will therefore occur in the second basic sentence pattern:

1. **Subject—Verb**
2. **Subject—Verb—Object**
   (Objective case)
3. **Subject—Linking Verb—Complement**

Note: The *objective* case is sometimes called the *accusative* case.

2. CASE FORMS

a. *NOUNS*

Nouns have the same form in both the nominative and the objective cases.

Examples:

The *girl* attended the party. (Nominative case)
I saw the *girl*. (Objective case)

b. *PRONOUNS*

Pronouns often have varying forms in the nominative and the objective cases.

Examples:

I played tennis. (Nominative case)
It is *I*. (Nominative case)
Noise disturbs *me*. (Objective case)

He raised the window. (Nominative case)
That was *he*. (Nominative case)
I dislike *him*. (Objective case)

Of the pronouns we have studied thus far, the following have different forms in the nominative and the objective cases:

Nominative	*Objective*
I	me
he	him
she	her
we	us
they	them

Note: A complete listing of the nominative and objective case forms of personal pronouns follows:

	Singular		*Plural*	
	Nominative Case	*Objective Case*	*Nominative Case*	*Objective Case*
1st Person	I	me	we	us
2nd Person	you	you	you	you
3rd Person	he	him	they	them
	she	her		
	it	it		

DO EXERCISES 4, 5, AND 6

C. TWO TYPES OF PRONOUNS OFTEN USED IN THE SECOND PATTERN

We have already studied the three types of pronouns which can function as subjects of simple declarative sentences. These are the personal, demonstrative, and indefinite pronouns. We shall now consider two additional types of pronouns—reflexive and reciprocal pronouns. These most often appear as objects in the second basic sentence pattern, but they also function in other ways—especially as objects of prepositions.

1. REFLEXIVE PRONOUNS

a. *DEFINITION*

A reflexive pronoun refers to the subject of a verb which expresses an action that affects the subject itself.

Examples:

I hurt *myself*.
He belittled *himself*.

The most common reflexive pronouns are the following:

	Singular	*Plural*
1st Person	myself	ourselves
2nd Person	yourself	yourselves
3rd Person	himself, herself,	themselves
	itself, oneself	

Note: At this point, it will be helpful to read the section on intensive pronouns on page 66.

b. *PROPERTIES*

As is evident in the above list, the reflexive pronoun varies in form to indicate person, number, and gender.

2. RECIPROCAL PRONOUNS

a. *DEFINITION*

A reciprocal pronoun refers to a plural subject of a verb and indicates that each individual person or thing included in the subject performs the verb action upon each of the others named in the subject. (The individual subjects thus perform a mutual or *reciprocal* action.)

Examples:

They dislike *each other*.
We helped *one another*.

The only common reciprocal pronouns are *each other* and *one another*.

b. *PROPERTIES*

Each other usually refers to two; *one another*, to more than two. There are no variations in form to indicate person or gender.

DO EXERCISE 7

D. LINKING VERBS USED IN THE THIRD PATTERN

In addition to the verb *to be*, there are a number of other verbs which may be used as linking verbs. Some of the more common ones are given in the following list:

	Subject —	*Linking Verb* —	*Complement*
act	The man	acts	enthusiastic.
appear	He	appears	young.
become	John	became	a doctor.

	Subject	—	Linking Verb	—	Complement
fall	The boy		fell		sick.
feel	She		felt		unhappy.
get	Mary		is getting		weary.
go	The woman		went		crazy.
grow	Everyone		grows		old.
keep	The girl		keeps		slim.
look	The loser		looks		sad.
prove	The treasurer		proved		dishonest.
remain	The grass		remains		green.
run	The tank		ran		dry.
seem	You		seem		healthy.
smell	The flowers		smell		sweet.
sound	The music		sounds		bad.
stay	The store		stayed		open.
taste	The soup		tastes		salty.
turn	The leaves		turned		brown.

Note that in all of the sentences given above a form of the verb *to be* could be inserted in place of the linking verb used. In fact, all of these linking verbs are closely related in meaning to the verb *to be*. For instance, saying

The milk *tastes* sour.

is practically equivalent to saying

The milk *is* sour.

Note 1: All of the linking verbs can have adjective complements; many of them *cannot* have substantive complements.

The following linking verbs are the ones which are most likely to have substantive complements: *to be, to become, to remain.*

Examples:
The woman is a stenographer.
The athlete will become a coach.
He remained a farmer.

Note 2: Most of the verbs listed in this section may be used in certain meanings as transitive or intransitive verbs. They are *not* linking verbs unless they are *used* as such. In the following sentences the verbs are *not* linking verbs:

The runner *fell.*
She *felt* the cloth.
The child *got* a spanking.
The gardener *grew* potatoes.
I *kept* the watch.

The lawyer *proved* the point.
The man *ran* the race.
The dog *smelled* the meat.
They *tasted* the cake.
The car *turned* the corner.

Note that a form of the verb *to be* could not be inserted in place of the verb in any of these sentences.

DO EXERCISES 8, 9, AND 10

CHAPTER VI

MODIFIERS

IN the previous chapter, we studied three basic sentence patterns. As we proceed from such simple sentences as we have examined to sentences of more complexity, it is important to remember that each of the more complicated sentences is formed upon a framework which fits one of the basic sentence patterns. The framework remains the same no matter what additional elements are hung upon it. With this in mind, let us consider the way in which subordinate elements may be attached to the skeletal framework of a sentence. It will be necessary, first of all, to study the fundamental concepts transmitted by the elements which make up this framework. In the course of our examination of these concepts we shall review and extend our study of the first three basic sentence patterns.

A. FUNDAMENTAL CONCEPTS IN THE FIRST THREE BASIC PATTERNS

With the exception of the pattern containing the adjective complement, all of the sentence patterns which we have considered thus far are combinations of only two types of words: substantives and verbs. Evidently, in the communication of a thought from one mind to another, there are two very basic functions which must be performed within a sentence:

1. The substantive function
2. The verb function

Let us see just how the substantive and the verb perform these functions in the process of transmitting thoughts.

The *substantive* brings to the mind of the reader (or hearer) a mental image or concept of a "substance." [1] The word *tree,* for instance, brings to mind the concept of a certain type of plant. The concept *tree,* however, does not by itself constitute a thought. If someone says, "Tree," we do not feel that he has transmitted a thought to us. We wonder, "What about the tree?" Something must be said about the substantive concept before we feel that a thought has been expressed. This function is performed by the verb.

The *verb* brings to the mind of the reader (or hearer) a concept of action, possession, or state of being and shows it in relation to at least one *substantive* (the particular substantive which is the subject of the verb). If we add to the concept *tree* such a concept of action as *grew,* we have "Tree grew." This is a complete thought in its simplest form—a *substantive* concept plus a *verb* concept.

A sentence consisting of a *substantive* and a *verb* is, of course, a sentence of the first pattern. In such a sentence the verb concept either shows the substantive as simply *acting* without affecting anything else (*active voice*) or shows the substantive as *being acted upon* (*passive voice*).

Examples:

Fish swim. (Active)

Fish are caught. (Passive)

Note: The arrow in the first sentence indicates that the substantive acts; note that there is nothing for it to act upon. The reversed arrow in the second sentence indicates that the action affects the subject. Later we shall study passive-voice verbs with the agent indicated.

Example:

Fish are caught by men.

[1] This term must be interpreted to include not only such tangible "substances" as persons, places, inanimate objects, and animals but such intangible "substances" as activities (*studying, driving*) and ideas (*loyalty, success, goodness*).

In the second sentence pattern there is a *substantive* concept (such as *boy*), plus a *verb* concept involving action which affects something else (such as *hits*), plus the *substantive* concept which is affected (such as *ball*). Thus the complete thought consists of three fundamental concepts—a *substantive*, a *verb*, and a *substantive*.

Example:

The boy h⃗its the ball.

Note: The arrow indicates that the substantive subject acts upon the substantive object.

The third sentence pattern with a substantive complement consists of a *substantive* concept (such as *James*), plus a *verb* concept which is similar in meaning to the equality sign (=) used in mathematics (such as *is*), plus a *substantive* concept (such as *athlete*). The complete thought, like that of the second pattern, consists of three fundamental concepts—a *substantive*, a *verb*, and a *substantive*.

Example:

James īs an athlete.

Note 1:   The equality sign indicates that the substantive subject is equivalent to the substantive complement. Note that the idea of equivalence—though with various modifications in meaning—is present in all linking verbs.

Examples:

James became an athlete.

James remained an athlete.

Note 2:   What has been indicated above concerning the use of symbols to indicate the nature of the verb concept may be summarized as follows:

1st Pattern: **Subject—V⃗erb**

Subject—Passive Verb

2nd Pattern: **Subject—V⃗erb—Object**

3rd Pattern: **Subject—Linking Verb—Complement**

Let us turn now from our study of substantive and verb concepts to a consideration of *modification* of these concepts.

B. MODIFYING THESE FUNDAMENTAL CONCEPTS

Read the following sentences slowly, noting the concept which is brought to your mind by each word:

Snakes crawl.
Children play games.
Flies are insects.

Repeat this process with sentences previously given as examples of the various sentence patterns. Note carefully the way in which a *substantive* produces one type of concept and a *verb* produces an entirely different type of concept.

Now examine the following sentences:

Birds chirp.
Little birds chirp.

What effect does the word *little* have upon the concept given to you by the word *birds?* Obviously, it changes or *modifies* it. A word functioning in this way is therefore called a *modifier*. Since it modifies a substantive, such a word is specifically classified as a *substantive modifier*. Note the effect of the substantive modifier in each of these sentences:

Boys like girls.	Babies cry.	Students work.
Boys like *pretty* girls.	*Some* babies cry.	*No* students work.

Note: Of course, the articles *a, an,* and *the,* which we have been using in writing basic sentences, are substantive modifiers. Note the way in which these articles slightly change or *modify* a substantive concept:

Boys are noisy.	*A* salesman called.
The boys are noisy.	*The* salesman called.

In addition to *substantive modifiers,* we may have *verb modifiers*—modifiers which change or *modify* a verb concept. Usually such modifiers indicate *time, place,* or *manner.* Note the effect of the modifier upon the verb concept in the following sentences:

John ran.	The teacher gave an exam.	She studies Spanish.
John ran *slowly.*	The teacher gave an exam *today.*	*Sometimes* she studies Spanish.

As these examples indicate, the verb modifier is not necessarily near the verb. It may occupy almost any position in the sentence. The only way to tell whether a sentence element is a verb modifier is to determine whether it *modifies* the verb concept. If a word or group of words indicates the exact nature of the verb concept or the circumstances which affect the verb concept, it is a verb modifier, regardless of its position in the sentence.

Throughout the remainder of this text, in indicating the pattern of a sentence we shall use the term *modifier* to refer to both substantive and verb modifiers. An arrow drawn from the notation "Modifier" to the element modified will be sufficient to distinguish between various types of modifiers. Note the method of indicating substantive modifiers in the patterns of the following sentences:

I have a new suit.

Pattern: **Subject—Verb—**Modifier**—Object**

The green cloth covered the table.

Pattern: Modifier**—Subject—Verb—Object**

The brave boy faced the angry bull.

Pattern: Modifier**—Subject—Verb—**Modifier**—Object**

The method of indicating verb modifiers is shown in the following examples:

We swim frequently.

Pattern: **Subject—Verb—**Modifier

The runner won the race easily.

Pattern: **Subject—Verb—Object—**Modifier

In the next two sections, we shall study substantive and verb modifiers in greater detail.

C. MODIFIERS OF SUBSTANTIVES (ADJECTIVES)

All modifiers of substantives are called *adjectives*. The adjective may be defined as follows:

✳ An *adjective* is a modifier of a substantive (a noun, a pronoun, or a noun equivalent).

At this point, it must be emphasized that the term *adjective* (like the terms *substantive* and *verb*) refers to an element which functions in a particular way. Although it is true that certain words are almost always used as adjectives, no word may be positively identified as an adjective unless it is functioning as such.

Note: In general, it may be said that *any* word must be used in a sentence (or at least *used*) before it can be identified as being a particular "part of speech"—*i.e.,* a noun, a pronoun, a verb, an adjective, an adverb, a conjunction, a preposition, or an interjection. For example, the word *tame* cannot be considered to be an adjective unless it modifies a substantive. It is an adjective in this sentence:

I saw a *tame* bear.

But it can function as a verb:

They *tame* lions.

1. TYPES OF SUBSTANTIVE MODIFIERS

Single-word substantive modifiers may be divided into two classes: (a) descriptive adjectives and (b) definitive adjectives. Definitive adjectives may be further divided into seven different types.

a. DESCRIPTIVE ADJECTIVES

A *descriptive adjective* indicates a quality or characteristic of the substantive it modifies. It thus *describes* the substantive. The majority of adjectives are descriptive.

Such words as the following may function as descriptive adjectives:

green, blue, brown; tall, short, fat; smooth, rough; wet, damp, dry; cold, warm, hot; heavy, light; strong, brittle, sturdy; wooden, metallic; fast, slow; intelligent, stupid, serious, witty

Examples:

The *small* boy bought a lollipop.
She ate a *green* apple.
We bought a *brick* house.

Note: Adjectives derived from proper nouns are called *proper adjectives*. Like proper nouns, they are capitalized.

Examples:
That is an *American* ship.
He writes *Byronic* poetry.

b. DEFINITIVE ADJECTIVES

A *definitive adjective* indicates the identity, number, or quantity of a substantive.

Examples:
This essay won the prize. (Identity)
Three boys entered the room. (Number)
He had *much* money. (Quantity)

Definitive adjectives may be divided into seven classes: (1) numeral adjectives, (2) demonstrative adjectives, (3) indefinite adjectives, (4) articles, (5) possessives, (6) interrogative adjectives, and (7) relative adjectives. We shall treat the first five types here; interrogative and relative adjectives we shall consider later.

(1) Numeral Adjectives

Numeral adjectives indicate number or numerical order.
The following words may function as numeral adjectives:

one, two, three, four, etc.; first, second, third, fourth, etc.; single, double, triple, etc.

Examples:

> I have *five* tickets.
> The *third* question puzzled her.
> He had a *single* ambition.

(2) Demonstrative Adjectives

Demonstrative adjectives point out particular persons or things.

The following words may function as demonstrative adjectives:

> *this, that, these, those*

Examples:

> *This* girl reported the fire.
> Everyone enjoys *these* books.

Note: When these words serve as substantives, they are *demonstrative pronouns* (see pp. 6–7); when they serve as substantive modifiers, they are *demonstrative adjectives*.

(3) Indefinite Adjectives

Indefinite adjectives indicate in a general way the identity of persons or things but do not definitely point them out.

Such words as the following may function as indefinite adjectives:

> *each, either, neither, every, much; any, some, no; both, few, several, many, all*

Examples:

> *Each* graduate received a diploma.
> We caught *several* frogs.

Note: Most of the words which function as indefinite adjectives can also be used as indefinite pronouns. Indefinite pronouns function as substantives; indefinite adjectives function as substantive modifiers.

(4) Articles

The adjectives *a, an,* and *the* are termed *articles*. The article *the* is called the *definite* article. The articles *a* and *an* are called the *indefinite* articles.

The article *a* is used before words beginning with a consonant sound; the article *an* is used before words beginning with a vowel sound. (Note that a word having *u* as the initial letter actually begins with a consonant sound: *use, union,* etc.)

Examples:

> *The* lightning struck.
> He wore *a* uniform.
> Marjory wants *a* radio.
> We ordered *an* incubator.

Note 1:   The article *an* is sometimes used before a word beginning with *h* if the first syllable of the word is unaccented.

Examples:

> She gave *an* hysterical laugh.
> This is *an* historic occasion.

Note 2:   The article *the* is closely related to the demonstrative adjective *that*. The articles *a* and *an* are closely related to the numeral adjective *one*.

Note 3:   In indicating sentence patterns we shall continue to disregard the presence or absence of articles. Here are the patterns of two of the examples used above:

> The lightning struck.
> *Pattern:* **Subject—Verb**

Marjory wants a radio.

Pattern: **Subject—Verb—Object**

Note that the articles are not considered in indicating the patterns.

(5) Possessives

Possessive forms of nouns and pronouns identify persons or things by indicating possession. The possessive form of a substantive is said to constitute the *possessive case* of the substantive. However, it is important to remember that the possessives almost always function as adjectives—not as substantives.

Examples:

His attitude irritates me.
This is *someone's* book.
The *farmer's* pig escaped.

We shall first study the possessives of personal pronouns.

Note: When we say that the possessives show "possession," we are using the word in a very broad sense. Note the different relationships indicated by the possessives in the following sentences:

I enjoy *Shelley's* poetry. ["Shelley" *wrote* the "poetry."]
We regretted *Jack's* action. ["Jack" *performed* the "action."]
Susie's dismissal surprised me. ["Susie" *received* the "dismissal."]

(a) Possessives of Personal Pronouns

The possessives of the personal pronouns differ from other possessives in the fact that they have special forms instead of being constructed with the apostrophe and *s*. The following are the possessive case forms of the various personal pronouns:

	Singular		*Plural*	
	Nominative Case	*Possessive Case*	*Nominative Case*	*Possessive Case*
1st Person	I	my, mine	we	our, ours
2nd Person	you	your, yours	you	your, yours
3rd Person	he	his	they	their, theirs
	she	her, hers		
	it	its		

Note 1: Notice that *its,* the possessive form of *it,* does *not* contain an apostrophe. *None* of the possessive forms of personal pronouns contains an apostrophe.

Note 2: The *possessive* case is sometimes called the *genitive* case.

The two possessive case forms listed for some of these personal pronouns differ in function. The first form listed is used when the possessive serves as an adjective preceding the noun it modifies.

Examples:

My father is ill.
Their yard is large.

The second form is used when the possessive serves (a) as an adjective complement or (b) as a substantive.

Examples:

The book is *mine.* (Adjective complement)
The mistake was *yours.* (Adjective complement)
Theirs is lost. (Substantive)
I borrowed *hers.* (Substantive)

(b) Possessives of Indefinite Pronouns

The possessive of an indefinite pronoun is formed by adding an apostrophe and *s* to the pronoun.

Examples:

one	one's
someone	someone's
everybody	everybody's
nobody	nobody's

(c) Possessives of Nouns

The possessives of nouns are formed as follows:

i. Singular Noun Not Ending in "s"

To form the possessive, add an apostrophe and *s*.

Examples:

boy	boy's
student	student's
mayor	mayor's

ii. Singular Noun Ending in "s"

To form the possessive, add an apostrophe and *s* if there is an added *s*-sound in the **possessive**.

Examples:

Morris	Morris's
Tess	Tess's

Add only an apostrophe if there is no added *s*-sound in the possessive.

Examples:

Sophocles	Sophocles'
Carruthers	Carruthers'

Note: With many such possessives, the pronunciation—and hence the spelling—is optional: *Charles's, Charles'*; *Keats's, Keats'*; *Jones's, Jones'*.

iii. Plural Noun Not Ending in "s"

To form the possessive, add an apostrophe and *s*.

Examples:

women	women's
children	children's
salesmen	salesmen's

iv. Plural Noun Ending in "s"

To form the possessive, add only an apostrophe.

Examples:

girls	girls'
players	players'
senators	senators'

Note 1: If you are in doubt about where to place an apostrophe, the following procedure may be helpful.

Let us suppose that you are not sure of the proper position of the apostrophe needed in *boys* in the following sentence:

The boys books are lost.

If the books are owned by *a single boy,* change the sentence to read as follows:

The books of the boy are lost.

Now circle the word naming the possessor:

The books of the (boy) are lost.

The apostrophe in the original sentence will come immediately after the encircled word *boy*:

The *boy's* books are lost.

If the books are owned by more than one boy, the reworded sentence will read:

The books of the boys are lost.

Now the word encircled will be *boys*:

The books of the (boys) are lost.

The apostrophe in the original sentence will come after the encircled word *boys*:

The *boys'* books are lost.

To test this procedure, use it to determine the position of the apostrophe in the following sentences:

The womens candidate lost the election.

A mans home is his castle.

Note 2: The possessive case is not normally used with inanimate objects. Write *the porch of the house* rather than *the house's porch*.

DO EXERCISE 11

2. PUNCTUATION WITH RESTRICTIVE AND NON-RESTRICTIVE SUBSTANTIVE MODIFIERS

In order to punctuate certain sentences properly, a person must be able to distinguish between restrictive and non-restrictive modifiers. At this point, we shall consider the distinction between restrictive and non-restrictive modifiers of substantives and the punctuation used with such modifiers.

a. *RESTRICTIVE SUBSTANTIVE MODIFIERS*

A restrictive substantive modifier *limits* or *restricts* the substantive which it modifies in such a way that the modifier is necessary for the proper identification of the substantive. It is thus so closely connected with the substantive that no punctuation is desirable.

(1) **Restrictive Modifier Preceding the Substantive**

Adjectives functioning as restrictive modifiers usually precede the substantive modified. This is by far the most common construction involving the adjective.

Examples:

We expected *rainy* weather.

He ate *two* eggs.

Pattern: **Subject—Verb—Modifier—Object**

(Restrictive)

(2) **Restrictive Modifier Following the Substantive**

Adjectives functioning as restrictive modifiers may follow the substantive modified. Only descriptive adjectives are used in this construction. Note that the modifier is *not* set off by commas.

Examples:

A day *lost* will upset the schedule.

A man *overboard* delayed the ship.

Pattern: **Subject—Modifier—Verb—Object**

(Restrictive)

b. *NON-RESTRICTIVE SUBSTANTIVE MODIFIERS*

A non-restrictive substantive modifier gives added information about a substantive which is presumed to be sufficiently identified without the modifier. Since it is loosely connected with the substantive, it is set off by commas.

Note 1: Only descriptive adjectives can be used as non-restrictive substantive modifiers.

Note 2: Most non-restrictive substantive modifiers are compound adjectives or adjective phrases. However, as shown by the examples below, single-word adjectives are sometimes used in this construction.

(1) Non-Restrictive Modifier Preceding the Substantive

Adjectives functioning as non-restrictive modifiers may precede the substantive. If the substantive is modified by an article, the non-restrictive modifier precedes the article. Note the comma punctuation.

Examples:

> *Unhurt,* the driver examined the wreck.
>
> *Overconfident,* he refused help.

Pattern: MODIFIER —Subject—Verb—Object

(Non-restrictive)

(2) Non-Restrictive Modifier Following the Substantive

Adjectives functioning as non-restrictive modifiers usually follow the substantive. Note the comma punctuation.

Examples:

> Billy, *delirious,* shouted threats.
>
> The experimenter, *unheeding,* mixed the solutions.

Pattern: Subject—MODIFIER —Verb—Object

(Non-restrictive)

DO EXERCISE 12

3. ADJECTIVE–NOUN COMBINATIONS

A restrictive adjective and the noun it modifies often combine to function as a unit with **reference to** an element which modifies the adjective-noun combination or an element which is modified by such a combination. The adjective-noun combination always *is modified* or *serves as a modifier.*

The adjective-noun combination, therefore, may function in the following ways:

a. As a substantive modified by an adjective

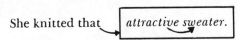
She knitted that *attractive sweater.*

b. As an adjective modifying a substantive

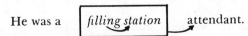
He was a *filling station* attendant.

c. As an adverb modifying a verb

I mailed the letter *last night.*

d. As an adverb modifying an adjective

The tape is *two inches* wide.

e. As an adverb modifying another adverb

The bus came *several minutes* early.

Note: In connection with the last two functions indicated, study the section on modifiers of modifiers, pp. 38–39.

An adjective-noun combination may be what is sometimes called a "compound noun" (*e.g.,* a successful *football coach,* a red *bathing suit,* a *tennis racket* cover), but such a "compound noun" is *not* an adjective-noun combination unless it functions in one of the ways specified above.

In indicating the pattern of a construction containing an adjective-noun combination, we shall enclose the combination within a box to show that it functions as a unit.

Examples:

My new roommate arrived this morning.

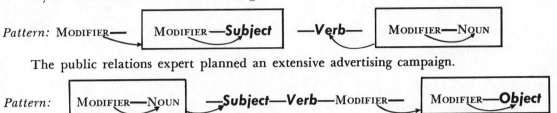

Pattern: MODIFIER— | MODIFIER—**Subject** | —**Verb**— | MODIFIER—**NOUN**

The public relations expert planned an extensive advertising campaign.

Pattern: | MODIFIER—NOUN | —**Subject—Verb**—MODIFIER— | MODIFIER—**Object**

An adjective modifying an adjective-noun combination frequently functions as part of an enlarged combination in relation to still another adjective.

Example:

She dented your silver serving tray.

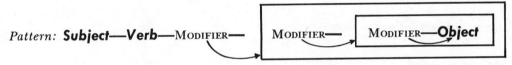

Pattern: **Subject—Verb**—MODIFIER— | MODIFIER— | MODIFIER—**Object**

Note that a descriptive adjective and the noun it modifies are always modified as a unit by any immediately preceding definitive adjective. Example: *He had collected many old guns.* The descriptive adjective *old* and the noun *guns* function as an adjective-noun combination in relation to the definitive adjective *many.*

Note: See p. 56 for tests which are useful in distinguishing certain adjective-noun combinations from constructions involving coordinate adjectival modifiers.

DO EXERCISE 13

4. THE ADJECTIVE COMPLEMENT

The adjective complement, like any other adjective, functions as a substantive modifier. The substantive modified is the subject of the linking verb.

Examples:

The man is tall.

The song was beautiful.

Pattern: **Subject—Linking Verb—Adjective Complement**

Note that *tall* modifies the concept *man* and that *beautiful* modifies the concept *song.*

Note: Henceforth, in indicating sentence patterns, we shall omit the arrow with the adjective complement as we have previously been doing.

D. MODIFIERS OF VERBS (ADVERBS)

All modifiers of verbs are called *adverbs*. However, the term *adverb* is not limited to verb modifiers, as is shown by the following definition:

> An *adverb* is any modifier which does not modify a substantive. An adverb usually modifies a verb, an adjective, or another adverb.

Like the term *adjective,* the term *adverb* refers to an element which *functions* in a particular way. To be classified as an adverb, a word must be functioning as a modifier of something other than a substantive.

1. TYPES OF VERB MODIFIERS

Single-word modifiers of verbs may be divided into three classes: (a) adverbs of time, (b) adverbs of place, and (c) adverbs of manner.

a. *ADVERBS OF TIME*

Adverbs of time modify the verb concept by indicating *when* or *how frequently.*
Such words as the following may function as adverbs of time:

> *now, today, before, often, seldom, again*

Examples:
> The repairman called *yesterday.*
> We failed *twice.*

Pattern: **Subject—Verb**—MODIFIER

b. *ADVERBS OF PLACE*

Adverbs of place modify the verb concept by indicating *where.*
Such words as the following may function as adverbs of place:

> *here, there, down, up, in, out*

Examples:
> We climbed *down.*
> She stayed *there.*

Pattern: **Subject—Verb**—MODIFIER

Note: In the following sentence, *home* is an adverb of place:
> We are going *home.*

c. *ADVERBS OF MANNER*

Adverbs of manner modify the verb concept by indicating *how.*
Such words as the following may function as adverbs of manner:

> *well, badly, quickly, slowly, easily*

Examples:
> The boy swam *slowly.*
> Margaret sings *well.*

Pattern: **Subject—Verb**—MODIFIER

Note 1:   The adverb *not* does not fit conveniently into any of the above classifications. It is an unusual adverb in the fact that it *completely* modifies concepts by negating them.
     When used as a verb modifier, it is also rather unusual in its position in relation to the verb. In modern English, it is normally inserted within the verb phrase.

Note 2: A large number of adverbs are formed by adding the suffix *-ly* to an adjective: *hasty, hastily; beautiful, beautifully; careful, carefully;* etc. However, many adverbs have two forms (*slow, slowly; quick, quickly;* etc.); many adjectives and adverbs are identical in form (*fast, fast; leisurely, leisurely;* etc.); and many adjectives end in *-ly* (*lovely, lonely, slovenly,* etc.). Consequently, the only way to be sure whether a particular word may be used as an adverb is to consult your dictionary.

DO EXERCISE 14

2. VERB–ADVERB COMBINATIONS

A verb and an adverb which modifies it often combine to function *as a unit* with reference to the *subject* of a sentence. Such a *verb-adverb combination* also functions *as a unit* with reference to an *object,* a *complement,* or an *adverbial modifier* when the sentence contains these elements.

Examples:

The man *gave up.* [The verb-adverb combination *gave up* functions as a unit with reference to its subject *man.*]

The student *handed in* the paper. [The verb-adverb combination *handed in* functions as a unit with reference to its subject *student* and its object *paper.*]

The plan *turned out* a failure. [The verb-adverb combination *turned out* functions as a unit with reference to its subject *plan* and its substantive complement *failure.*]

The salesman *stopped by* often. [The verb-adverb combination *stopped by* functions as a unit with reference to its subject *salesman* and its adverbial modifier *often.*]

Note: It is frequently very difficult to decide whether a verb and its modifying adverb function as a unit with reference to a subject if none of the other elements listed is present. The primary question is this: Does the meaning of the verb and its modifying adverb differ from the total meaning derivable from the conjoined meanings of the separate elements? In other words, does the verb in combination with the adverb have an idiomatic meaning? If so, the subject is the subject of a verb-adverb combination instead of being the subject of the verb alone. A helpful test is to move the adverb to the beginning of the sentence. If the resulting construction retains the meaning, the original construction is *not* a verb-adverb combination.

> The man gave *generously.*
> *Generously* the man gave. (This is awkward but possible.)
> The man gave *up.*
> *Up* the man gave. (This is meaningless. The original construction is therefore a verb-adverb combination.)

The following words are frequently used as adverbs in verb-adverb combinations: *across, after, away, back, by, down, in, off, on, out, over, through, under, up, with.*

Examples:

> The winner *gave away* the money.
> The janitor *pulled down* the shade.

Pattern: **Subject— | Verb—**MODIFIER **| —Object**

The adverb in a verb-adverb combination is often separated from the verb:

The winner | gave | the money | away.

Note: The verb-adverb combination which takes an object may be confused with an intransitive verb which is modified by a prepositional phrase (see pp. 78–83). This problem is complicated by the fact that a sentence may have more than one possible meaning:

He *ran down* the highway. [If the meaning is that he *criticized* the highway, the construction is a verb-adverb combination.]

He ran [down the highway.]   [If the meaning is that he *raced* down the highway, the construction

is a verb modified by a prepositional phrase.]

Even when the general meaning of a sentence is clear, there may be varying shades of meaning or emphasis which must be considered in determining which of the two·constructions is present. Example: *He walked on the fresh paint.*

There are several tests which are helpful, but not always conclusive, in distinguishing these two constructions:

a. Shift the word following the verb to a position just after the object. If the meaning of the sentence remains the same, you may be sure that you have a verb-adverb combination.

> Example:
>> He *picked up* the ball.
>> He *picked* the ball *up.*

Note that many verb-adverb combinations cannot be shifted in this way. Thus, failure of this test does not necessarily prove that a construction is *not* a verb-adverb combination.

> Example:
>> He *ran through* his inheritance. [This is a verb-adverb combination, even though it cannot be shifted.]

b. Change the sentence to the passive voice. If the passive-voice sentence makes good sense, the construction is a verb-adverb combination.

> Example:
>> She *turned down* the job.
>> The job *was turned down* by her.

c. Assume that the construction is an intransitive verb modified by a prepositional phrase, and move the supposed phrase to a position preceding the subject. If the resulting sentence makes sense (even though it is less smooth than the original), the element moved must actually be a prepositional phrase.

> Example:
>> The child played *in the yard.*
>> *In the yard* the child played.

d. Assume that the construction is an intransitive verb modified by a prepositional phrase, and determine whether the supposed phrase answers one of the common adverbial questions—*Where?*, *When?*, *Why?*, or *How?* If it does, the element must actually be a prepositional phrase.

> Examples:
>> The man was working *in the garden.* [Answers question *Where?*]
>> The girl swam *with difficulty.* [Answers question *How?*]

DO EXERCISE 15

E. MODIFIERS OF MODIFIERS (ADVERBS)

In addition to modifiers of substantives and modifiers of verbs, there are words which modify the concepts presented by such modifiers. Note the function of *very* and *exceedingly* in ·the following sentence:

> The *very* tall boy plays basketball *exceedingly* well.

Pattern: MODIFIER—MODIFIER—*Subject—Verb—Object*—MODIFIER—MODIFIER

As the arrows indicate, the substantive *boy* is modified by *tall*, which is in turn modified by *very*, and the verb *plays* is modified by *well*, which is modified by *exceedingly*. Note that in both instances the modifier of a modifier indicates *degree*.

Modifiers of modifiers come under the general classification of adverbs. (See the definition of an adverb given on p. 36.) They are usually *adverbs of degree*, showing the extent or degree of the quality indicated by the adjectives or adverbs they modify.

Some of the words which may function as modifiers of modifiers are the following:

> *very, exceedingly, extremely, unbelievably, extraordinarily, unusually, rather, tremendously, exceptionally, quite*

Classified according to function, modifiers of modifiers are of two types: (1) modifiers of substantive modifiers (such as *very* in the example) and (2) modifiers of verb modifiers (such as *exceedingly* in the example). All of the words listed above may function in either of these ways.

1. MODIFIERS OF SUBSTANTIVE MODIFIERS

The following sentences contain modifiers of substantive modifiers:

> A *very* cold wind swept the valley.
> An *extremely* high mountain blocked the way.

Pattern: MODIFIER—MODIFIER—*Subject—Verb—Object*

> We saw an *unusually* good game.
> The mayor gave a *rather* long speech.

Pattern: *Subject—Verb*—MODIFIER—MODIFIER—*Object*

Note: Words indicating colors may be either nouns or adjectives:

> Dark *green* is my favorite color. (Noun)
> The **grass** is very *green*. (Adjective)

The modifier of such a word may thus be either an adjective or an adverb. In the sentences above, *dark* is an adjective; *very,* an adverb.

Note that in the following sentence *dark green* is an adjective-noun combination:

> Karen bought a *dark green* sweater.

2. MODIFIERS OF VERB MODIFIERS

The following sentences contain modifiers of verb modifiers:

> She wrote *rather* poorly.
> The boat sails *quite* well.

Pattern: *Subject—Verb*—MODIFIER—MODIFIER

> Bill hit the ball *exceptionally* hard.
> A millionaire makes friends *very* easily.

Pattern: *Subject—Verb—Object*—MODIFIER—MODIFIER

DO EXERCISE 16

F. MODIFIERS OF SENTENCES (ADVERBS)

Some modifiers comment upon or qualify the entire sentence rather than a single element within the sentence.

Examples:

> *Unfortunately,* he had left the university.
> *Frankly,* I do not believe you.
> *Apparently* a thief had broken the lock.

In these sentences it is fairly obvious that the adverb modifies the entire sentence. However, it is not always easy to tell whether a particular adverb is a sentence modifier (sometimes called a *sentence adverb*) or a verb modifier. Fortunately, when such identification is difficult, mere realization that the word is an adverb is usually sufficient for purposes of writing correct sentences.

Note: The words *yes* and *no* are frequently used as sentence modifiers. As such, they qualify the entire sentence affirmatively or negatively.

Examples:

>*Yes,* you left your hat here.
>*No,* I am not going.

Note the comma punctuation used to set off these words.

G. COMPARISON

Most adjectives and adverbs have the property of expressing degrees of comparison.

1. THE THREE DEGREES OF COMPARISON

Adjectives and adverbs may have three degrees of comparison: (a) *positive,* (b) *comparative,* and (c) *superlative.*

a. POSITIVE DEGREE

The *positive degree* simply indicates a positive quality. No comparison with any other element is involved.

Examples:

>*cold*
>*beautiful*
>*difficult*
>*carefully*

b. COMPARATIVE DEGREE

The *comparative degree* indicates a quality of greater or less intensity than that possessed by another element. The comparative degree thus deals with a comparison between two persons, things, actions, or qualities. It is normally formed by adding *-er* to the positive degree or by using *more* or *less* to modify the positive degree.

Examples:

>*colder*
>*more beautiful*
>*less difficult*
>*more carefully*

c. SUPERLATIVE DEGREE

The *superlative degree* indicates a quality of greater or less intensity than that possessed by any of two or more other elements. The superlative degree thus deals with a comparison involving three or more persons, things, actions, or qualities. It is normally formed by adding *-est* to the positive degree or by using *most* or *least* to modify the positive degree.

Examples:

>*coldest*
>*most beautiful*
>*least difficult*
>*most carefully*

2. COMPARISON OF ADJECTIVES

a. ADJECTIVES WHICH CAN BE COMPARED

Most of the adjectives which can be compared are descriptive adjectives: *tall, smooth, strong,* etc. However, a few indefinite adjectives can also be compared: *much, many, few.*

Note: Some descriptive adjectives cannot logically be compared. For example, a thing may be described as either "unique" or "not unique"; it cannot be said to be "more unique" or "most unique." Other adjectives of this sort are *perfect, straight, round, square.* One should say that one thing is "more *nearly* perfect" than another—not "more perfect."

b. *FORMING THE COMPARATIVE AND SUPERLATIVE DEGREES*

Comparison involving degrees of greater intensity may be divided into three categories: (1) comparison using *-er* and *-est*, (2) comparison using *more* and *most*, and (3) irregular comparison. All comparison involving degrees of less intensity is accomplished by use of *less* and *least*.

(1) Comparison Involving Degrees of Greater Intensity

(a) Comparison Using *-er* and *-est*

The comparative and superlative degrees of adjectives of only one syllable are usually formed by adding *-er* and *-est* to the positive degree.

Positive	Comparative	Superlative
cool	cooler	coolest
fat	fatter	fattest
hard	harder	hardest
hot	hotter	hottest
sweet	sweeter	sweetest

The comparative and superlative degrees of some adjectives of two syllables are formed by adding *-er* and *-est* to the positive degree.

Positive	Comparative	Superlative
happy	happier	happiest
healthy	healthier	healthiest
lovely	lovelier	loveliest
naughty	naughtier	naughtiest

Note: Consult any good dictionary for spelling rules which apply when the *-er* or *-est* ending is added.

(b) Comparison Using *more* and *most*

The comparative and superlative degrees of many adjectives of two syllables are formed by using *more* and *most* before the positive degree.

Positive	Comparative	Superlative
agile	more agile	most agile
boastful	more boastful	most boastful
eager	more eager	most eager
recent	more recent	most recent

The comparative and superlative degrees of adjectives of more than two syllables are usually formed by using *more* and *most* before the positive degree.

Positive	Comparative	Superlative
beautiful	more beautiful	most beautiful
convenient	more convenient	most convenient
deplorable	more deplorable	most deplorable
objectionable	more objectionable	most objectionable

(c) Irregular Comparison

Some adjectives have irregular forms in the comparative and superlative degrees.

Positive	Comparative	Superlative
bad	worse	worst
good	better	best
little	less	least

Positive	Comparative	Superlative
many	more	most
much	more	most

(2) Comparison Involving Degrees of Less Intensity

Comparative and superlative degrees of less intensity are always formed by using *less* and *least* before the positive degree of the adjective.

Positive	Comparative	Superlative
pure	less pure	least pure
friendly	less friendly	least friendly
respectable	less respectable	least respectable

3. COMPARISON OF ADVERBS

a. *ADVERBS WHICH CAN BE COMPARED*

Most adverbs of manner and many adverbs of time and place have degrees of comparison. Obviously, though, such adverbs as *here, there, now, then,* and *not* cannot have comparative or superlative degrees.

b. *FORMING THE COMPARATIVE AND SUPERLATIVE DEGREES*

(1) Comparison Involving Degrees of Greater Intensity

(a) Comparison Using -er and -est

The comparative and superlative degrees of some adverbs, particularly those of one syllable, are formed by adding *-er* and *-est* to the positive degree.

Positive	Comparative	Superlative
fast	faster	fastest
hard	harder	hardest
soon	sooner	soonest

(b) Comparison Using *more* and *most*

The comparative and superlative degrees of the majority of adverbs, particularly those ending in *-ly,* are formed by using *more* and *most* before the positive degree.

Positive	Comparative	Superlative
boldly	more boldly	most boldly
effectively	more effectively	most effectively
hastily	more hastily	most hastily
slowly	more slowly	most slowly

(c) Irregular Comparison

Some adverbs have irregular forms in the comparative and superlative degrees.

Positive	Comparative	Superlative
badly	worse	worst
little	less	least
much	more	most
well	better	best

(2) Comparison Involving Degrees of Less Intensity

Comparative and superlative degrees of less intensity are always formed by using *less* and *least* before the positive degree of the adverb.

Positive	*Comparative*	*Superlative*
comfortably	less comfortably	least comfortably
rapidly	less rapidly	least rapidly

Note 1: The above general comments on the forming of the comparative and superlative degrees of adjectives and adverbs should be helpful in determining proper forms. However, you should always consult a dictionary if you are in doubt.

Note 2: For the time being, in order to avoid incomplete comparisons, we shall not use comparative or superlative degree forms in sentences. We shall use such forms only after our study of adverb clauses of degree.

DO EXERCISE 17

H. USE OF MODIFIERS IN THE FIRST THREE BASIC SENTENCE PATTERNS

In this chapter we have studied the single-word modifiers which are used to modify substantives, verbs, other modifiers, and entire sentences.

Obviously, a very large number of different combinations can be formed by adding various modifiers to the three basic sentence patterns which we have studied. However, it should be kept in mind at all times that, no matter how many modifiers are used in a sentence, the *framework* will still fit one of the basic sentence patterns. The modifiers are merely attached to the framework.

Furthermore, although the number and arrangement of modifiers in sentences may vary widely, the function performed by each modifier is basically the same—the modifying of a concept expressed by another element. Actually, to the substantive and verb functions used in the basic sentence framework we have added only one other—the modifying function. Thus far, then, we have studied only three functions:

1. The substantive function
2. The verb function
3. The modifying function

All of the sentences we have considered have been composed of elements performing one of these three functions.

DO EXERCISES 18 AND 19

CHAPTER VII

VERBALS

THE verb-forms which we have been studying thus far—those which are capable of serving as main verbs in the basic sentence patterns—are called *finite* verb-forms. In addition to these, there are certain *infinite* verb-forms. Such a verb-form may constitute *part* of a finite verb-form, but may not, by itself, serve as a main verb in a sentence.

There are three types of infinite verb-forms: (a) the infinitive, (b) the participle, and (c) the gerund. We have already studied the use of infinitives and participles in the formation of finite verb phrases. In addition to their function in verb phrases, the infinite verb-forms have the ability to function as substantives or modifiers (either adjectives or adverbs). When they function thus, they are termed *verbals*.

Though no verbal can function as the main verb in any of the basic sentence patterns, verbals do have some of the characteristics of verbs, as we shall note particularly in our later study of verbal phrases.

A. THE INFINITIVE

An infinitive is a verb-form which, in addition to its use in certain tenses of verbs (see pp. 12–13), can function as a substantive, an adjective, or an adverb. In these functions it is usually (though not always) preceded by *to,* the "sign of the infinitive."

Examples:

He plans *to return.*
John is the man *to see.*
She was eager *to go.*

1. FORMS OF THE INFINITIVE

There are two tenses of the infinitive: (a) the present and (b) the present perfect. In addition to the simple forms, there are progressive forms for both of these tenses in the active voice.

Transitive verbs have both active and passive forms of the infinitive. Intransitive and linking verbs have only the active forms.

		ACTIVE		PASSIVE
		Simple	*Progressive*	
TRANSITIVE	*Present*	to choose [1]	to be choosing	to be chosen
	Present Perfect	to have chosen	to have been choosing	to have been chosen
INTRANSITIVE	*Present*	to sleep	to be sleeping	
	Present Perfect	to have slept	to have been sleeping	
LINKING	*Present*	to be	——————————— [2]	
	Present Perfect	to have been	——————————— [2]	

[1] The active form of the infinitive is often used with passive meaning.
    Examples:
        I have a house *to rent* (= *to be rented*).
        This is a book *to enjoy* (= *to be enjoyed*).
[2] With some linking verbs, progressive forms of the infinitive may be used.
    Example:
        He expected *to be feeling good.*

2. FUNCTIONS OF THE INFINITIVE

In addition to its function in forming certain tenses of verbs, an infinitive can function as (a) a substantive, (b) an adjective, or (c) an adverb.

a. *INFINITIVE AS SUBSTANTIVE*

An infinitive can perform any substantive function that a noun can perform.

Examples:

To fail is disheartening.

Pattern: **Subject—Linking Verb—Adjective Complement**
(Infinitive)

He intends *to explain*.

Pattern: **Subject—Verb—Object**
(Infinitive)

His impulse was *to resist*.

Pattern: Modifier—**Subject—Linking Verb—Substantive Complement**
(Infinitive)

b. *INFINITIVE AS ADJECTIVE*

An infinitive can perform an adjective function. When functioning as an adjective, it follows the substantive which it modifies.

Examples:

The soldier has money *to spend*.
She collected the clothes *to be washed*.

Pattern: **Subject—Verb—Object**—Modifier
(Infinitive)

c. *INFINITIVE AS ADVERB*

An infinitive can perform an adverbial function. It may serve as a modifier of a verb, adjective, or adverb.

Examples:

Modifier of verb

Mary played *to win*.

Pattern: **Subject—Verb**—Modifier
(Infinitive)

Modifier of adjective

He will be able *to come*.

Pattern: **Subject—Linking Verb—Adjective Complement**—Modifier
(Infinitive)

Modifier of adverb

The boy was too nervous *to talk*.

Pattern: **Subject—Linking Verb**—Modifier—**Adjective Complement**—Modifier
(Infinitive)

My brother looks old enough *to enlist*.

Pattern: **Subject—Linking Verb—Adjective Complement**—Modifier—Modifier
(Infinitive)

3. SOME SPECIAL NOTES ON THE INFINITIVE

a. *SEQUENCE OF TENSES WITH INFINITIVES*

(1) Use of Present Tense of Infinitives

The present tense of the infinitive is used to indicate (a) an action taking place *at the same time* as the action expressed by the main verb or (b) an action which is *in the future* with reference to the action expressed by the main verb.

Examples:

She is walking *to exercise.* [The act of *exercising* is taking place at the same time as the act of *walking.*]

He wanted *to relax.* [The act of *relaxing* is in the future with reference to the time the act of *wanting* took place.]

(2) Use of Present Perfect Tense of Infinitives

The present perfect tense of the infinitive is used to indicate an action taking place at a time *prior* to the action expressed by the main verb.

Example:

I was eventually delighted *to have been chosen.* [The act of *choosing* took place prior to the act of *being delighted.*]

b. *PUNCTUATION WITH INFINITIVES*

The infinitive constructions we have studied do not, for the most part, require any punctuation. However, when an infinitive functioning as an adverb precedes the element it modifies, it is set off by commas.

Examples:

The senator, *to be nominated,* must campaign vigorously.

To be hired, an applicant must pass the exams.

c. *USE OF THE INFINITIVE WITHOUT "TO" AFTER AUXILIARY VERBS*

As has been previously stated, the infinitive is often used without being preceded by *to,* the "sign of the infinitive." The most common construction containing this sort of infinitive is the verb phrase made up of an auxiliary verb and an infinitive. Of the auxiliaries we have considered thus far, *shall, will, do,* and *did* are used with the infinitive without *to.*

Examples:

I shall *come.*
You will *work.*
They do *study.*
He did *report.*

Note: All of these are present infinitives, but other infinitive forms without *to* are also used with *shall* and *will* to form various verb phrases.

Examples:

I shall *have left.* (Present perfect infinitive)
He will *be sleeping.* (Present progressive infinitive)
She will *be elected.* (Present passive infinitive)

The infinitive without *to* is also used after the following auxiliaries: *should, would, may, can, might, could,* and *must.*

Examples:

We should *rest.*
She may *win.*
He can *sing.*
They must *learn.*

Verb phrases formed by use of *should, would, may, can, might, could,* and *must* are called *potential verb phrases.*

Note 1: Such verb phrases are sometimes said to constitute the *potential mode,* and these seven auxiliaries are often called the *modal auxiliaries.*

Note 2: The examples given above show the use of the present infinitive. The other tense forms of the infinitive may also be used with these auxiliaries.

> Examples:
>
> They should *have called.* (Present perfect infinitive)
> He must *have been joking.* (Present perfect progressive infinitive)
> You might *have been hurt.* (Present perfect passive infinitive)

In every sentence containing an auxiliary verb followed by an infinitive without *to,* the infinitive is originally the *object* of the auxiliary verb. However, since the auxiliary has lost its ability to express independent meaning, the infinitive is felt to be the main verb as far as expressing a verb concept is concerned. In indicating the pattern of a sentence containing such an auxiliary, we shall therefore consider the *entire* verb phrase to be the verb-unit.

> Examples:
>
> The letter *may arrive.*

Pattern: **Subject—Verb**

> They *should consult* a lawyer.

Pattern: **Subject—Verb—Object**

Later, in our study of infinitive phrases, we shall consider other instances of the use of the infinitive without *to.*

Note: Besides the auxiliary verbs which are followed by the infinitive without *to,* there are a number of auxiliaries which are followed by the infinitive with *to.*

> Examples:
>
> He ought *to stay.* [*Compare:* He should stay.]
> I am going *to resign.* [*Compare:* I shall resign.]
> We have *to remain.* [*Compare:* We must remain.]

In these constructions the entire verb phrase (auxiliary and infinitive) must be interpreted as the verb-unit. Note the pattern for the following sentence:

> The diplomat *ought to succeed.*

> *Pattern:* **Subject—Verb**

With verbs *other than auxiliaries,* however, the infinitive must be considered to be the object:

> The diplomat *wanted to succeed.*

> *Pattern:* **Subject—Verb—Object**
> (Infinitive)

Note that the auxiliary verbs do not carry a meaning by themselves but merely serve as "helping" verbs. With this in mind, compare *ought* and *wanted* in the sentences above.

DO EXERCISE 20

B. THE PARTICIPLE

A participle is a verb-form which, in addition to its use in certain tenses of verbs (see pp. 12–17), can function as an adjective.

> Examples:
>
> *Hurrying,* I overtook the postman.
> The girl had a *scratched* finger.
> The team, *having won,* celebrated boisterously.

1. FORMS OF THE PARTICIPLE

There are three tenses of the participle: (a) the present, (b) the past, and (c) the present perfect. In addition to the simple forms, there is a progressive form of the present perfect tense in the active voice.

Transitive verbs have both active and passive forms of the participle. Intransitive and linking verbs have only the active forms.

		ACTIVE		PASSIVE
		Simple	*Progressive*	
Transitive	*Present*	choosing		being chosen
	Past	chosen [3]		chosen [3]
	Present Perfect	having chosen	having been choosing	having been chosen
Intransitive	*Present*	sleeping		
	Past	slept [3]		
	Present Perfect	having slept	having been sleeping	
Linking	*Present*	being		
	Past	been [3]		
	Present Perfect	having been	---------------- [4]	

Note: Many pure adjectives look like participles; and, in fact, a number of words now considered to be pure adjectives were once participles. However, such words as *afraid* and *dead,* whatever their origins, are not now construed as participles. When in doubt, consult your dictionary.

2. FUNCTION OF THE PARTICIPLE

Except when used to form verb tenses, the participle normally functions as an adjective. (However, see Appendix, Section VI.)

Examples:

The *greased* pig eluded the boys.

Pattern: Modifier   **—Subject—Verb—Object**

(Past passive participle)

We heard a *crying* baby.

Pattern: **Subject—Verb**—Modifier   **—Object**

(Present participle)

Having been warned, the spy escaped.

Pattern: Modifier   **—Subject—Verb**

(Present perfect passive participle)

[3] The past *active* participle usually functions as a part of an active verb phrase—not as an adjective.

Examples:
     He had *chosen* his vocation. (Active)
     I had *slept* late. (Active)
     She had *been* ill. (Active)

The past *passive* participle is the past participle which is usually used as an adjective. It may also function as a part of a passive verb phrase.

Examples:
     That is his *chosen* profession. (Passive)
     He was *chosen* by the committee. (Passive)

[4] With some linking verbs, a progressive form of the present perfect participle may be used.

Example:
     Having been feeling bad all day, he retired early.

The fender is *dented*.

Pattern: **Subject—Linking Verb—Adjective Complement**

(Past passive participle)

3. SOME SPECIAL NOTES ON THE PARTICIPLE

a. *SEQUENCE OF TENSES WITH PARTICIPLES*

(1) Use of Present Tense of Participles

The present tense of the participle is used to indicate an action taking place *at the same time* as the action expressed by the main verb.

Example:

> *Trembling,* I approached the haunted house. [The act of *trembling* took place at the same time as the act of *approaching.*]

The present tense of the participle may also be used to indicate an action taking place at a time *just before* the action expressed by the main verb. This usage is confined to non-restrictive participial constructions.

Example:

> *Slipping,* he grabbed the limb. [The act of *slipping* took place just before the act of *grabbing.*]

Note: When the present participle indicates present time, the main verb may indicate past, present, or future action.

> Examples:
>
> The woman talking *opposed* the measure. (Past)
> The woman talking *is* an attorney. (Present)
> The woman talking *will support* your views. (Future)

(2) Use of Past and Present Perfect Tenses of Participles

The past and present perfect tenses of the participle are used to indicate an action taking place at a time *prior* to the action expressed by the main verb.

Examples:

> We ate *toasted* marshmallows. [The act of *toasting* took place prior to the act of *eating.*]
> *Having resigned,* the manager left town. [The act of *resigning* took place prior to the act of *leaving.*]

b. *PUNCTUATION WITH PARTICIPLES*

Participles which modify substantives may be either restrictive or non-restrictive. The rules we have already studied for punctuating restrictive and non-restrictive adjectives also apply to participles serving as adjectives.

Examples:

> *Restrictive modifier preceding the substantive*
> *Barking* dogs never bite.

> *Restrictive modifier following the substantive*
> The dog *barking* is Rover.

> *Non-restrictive modifier preceding the substantive*
> *Sobbing,* she left the room.
> *Having been discharged,* John drew his pay.

> *Non-restrictive modifier following the substantive*
> My father, *relenting,* gave his permission.
> The student, *having overslept,* was very late.

DO EXERCISE 21

C. THE GERUND

A gerund is a verb-form which usually functions as a substantive.

Examples:

Hiking is healthful.   She studied *typing*.   Her *singing* was mediocre.

1. FORMS OF THE GERUND

There are two tenses of the gerund: (a) the present and (b) the present perfect. In addition to the simple forms, there is a progressive form of the present perfect tense in the active voice, but this form is rarely used.

Transitive verbs have both active and passive forms of the gerund. Intransitive and linking verbs have only the active forms.

		ACTIVE		PASSIVE
		Simple	*Progressive*	
TRANSITIVE	*Present*	choosing		being chosen
	Present Perfect	having chosen	having been choosing	having been chosen
INTRANSITIVE	*Present*	sleeping		
	Present Perfect	having slept	having been sleeping	
LINKING	*Present*	being		
	Present Perfect	having been	.... [5]	

2. FUNCTION OF THE GERUND

The gerund can perform any substantive function that a noun can perform.

Examples:

Reading is enjoyable.

Pattern: **Subject—Linking Verb—Adjective Complement**
(Gerund)

The children dislike *working*.

Pattern: **Subject—Verb—Object**
(Gerund)

Her hobby is *weaving*.

Pattern: MODIFIER—**Subject—Linking Verb—Substantive Complement**
(Gerund)

The basic distinction between the gerund and the participle lies not in form but in function. The gerund usually functions as a substantive; the participle, as an adjective:

The *winning* car passed the line. (Participle)
Winning is pleasant. (Gerund)

Having failed, he tried again. (Participle)
Having failed did not discourage him. (Gerund)

In certain constructions the gerund does function as an adjective; see Appendix, Section VI.

Note: A gerund may be modified by a possessive which indicates the performer of the action expressed by the gerund. Note the following sentences:

His resigning was a surprise.
We ignored *Mary's* pouting.

DO EXERCISE 22

[5] With some linking verbs, a progressive form of the present perfect gerund is possible, but it would almost never be used.

CHAPTER VIII

COMPOUNDS

IN the preceding chapters we have studied three functions of words within the sentence:

1. The substantive function
2. The verb function
3. The modifying function

More specifically, we have considered ten sentence elements and five parts of speech:

Functions	Sentence Elements	Parts of Speech
Substantive function	1. Subject 2. Object 3. Substantive complement	Nouns Pronouns
Verb function	4. Verb	Verbs
Modifying function	5. Adjective complement 6. Modifier of substantive	Adjectives
	7. Modifier of verb 8. Modifier of adjective 9. Modifier of adverb 10. Modifier of sentence	Adverbs

In every instance, we have dealt with an element composed of a single unit—usually, a single word. However, any of the elements which we have studied may be *compound—i.e.,* consist of more than one unit.

1. Compound subject

    The salesman and the customer were talking.

2. Compound object

    She enjoys *reading, sewing, and dancing.*

3. Compound substantive complement

    The winner will be *Harvard or Princeton.*

4. Compound verb [1]

    I *bought and read* the book.

5. Compound adjective complement

    The girl was *beautiful but dumb.*

6. Compound modifier of substantive

    He gave a *long and tiresome* speech.

7. Compound modifier of verb

    The champion swam *smoothly and rapidly.*

[1] In a verb phrase, either the auxiliary or the primary verb may be compound.
Examples:
I *can and do* cook my own meals. (Compound auxiliary verb)
He had *mowed and raked* the lawn. (Compound primary verb)

51

8. Compound modifier of adjective

She was *really and truly* beautiful.

9. Compound modifier of adverb

The challenger played *extraordinarily and unexpectedly* well.

10. Compound modifier of sentence

Truthfully and frankly, I do not believe you.

It must be emphasized that each compound element, considered as a whole, functions in exactly the same way as its single-unit counterpart. The compound does not have any new functions; it performs one of the functions we have already studied. However, there is a new function *within* the compound—that performed by the coordinating conjunction.

A. COORDINATING CONJUNCTIONS

The units composing a compound are often joined by connecting words called *conjunctions*. Since the units of compounds are of equal rank, these connecting words are specifically designated as *coordinating conjunctions*. The coordinating conjunction, then, is *a word which joins sentence units of equal rank*. The common coordinating conjunctions are *and, but, or, nor,* and *for*.

Examples:

He bought a drum *and* a whistle.
The chauffeur drove rapidly *but* carefully.
I prefer coffee *or* tea.

The coordinating conjunction—like the preposition and the subordinating conjunction, which we shall study later—performs a *connecting* function. This brings our list of functions to four:

1. The substantive function
2. The verb function
3. The modifying function
4. The connecting function

B. TWO-UNIT AND MULTIPLE-UNIT COMPOUNDS

Classified according to structure, there are two types of compounds:

(1) **Those composed of two units—"two-unit compounds"**

Examples:

I read *the book and the magazine.*
The vacationists *hiked and fished.*

(2) **Those composed of three or more units—"multiple-unit compounds"**

Examples:

Apples, oranges, and peaches were available.
We need *nails, screws, nuts, and bolts.*

The two types of compounds are punctuated as follows:

1. TWO-UNIT COMPOUNDS

a. *UNITS CONNECTED BY A CONJUNCTION*

If the two units are connected by a conjunction, no punctuation is used.

Examples:

Mother ironed *the skirts and the blouses.*
The team practiced *blocking and tackling.*

Punctuation pattern of compound: _____ and _____

b. *UNITS NOT CONNECTED BY A CONJUNCTION*

If the two units are not connected by a conjunction, they are separated by a comma.

Examples:

A *steep, rugged* climb lay ahead.
The queen was *tall, beautiful.*

Punctuation pattern of compound: _____, _____

2. MULTIPLE-UNIT COMPOUNDS

a. *LAST TWO UNITS CONNECTED BY A CONJUNCTION*

If only the last two units of a multiple-unit compound are connected by a conjunction, commas are used to separate all units. The comma separating the last two units is placed before the conjunction.

Examples:

We consulted *the mayor, the judge, and the sheriff.*
The girl is *intelligent, talented, and pretty.*

Punctuation pattern of compound: _____, _____, and _____

Note: There is a tendency—particularly in newspaper writing—to omit the comma before the conjunction in this construction. However, since this comma is often necessary for clarity, it is best to use it in all such compounds.

b. *ALL UNITS CONNECTED BY CONJUNCTIONS*

If all units of a multiple-unit compound are connected by conjunctions, no punctuation is used.

Example:

The children *shouted and screamed and yelled.*

Punctuation pattern of compound: _____ and _____ and _____

c. *NO UNITS CONNECTED BY CONJUNCTIONS*

If none of the units are connected by conjunctions, commas are used to separate all units.

Examples:

They *whistled, shouted, screamed.*
The boy wanted *a football, a kite, a train.*[2]

Punctuation pattern of compound: _____, _____, _____

Note: These punctuation rules apply to the conjunctions *but* and *or* as well as to the conjunction *and.*

C. INDICATING THE PATTERN OF A SENTENCE CONTAINING A COMPOUND

To indicate the pattern of a sentence containing a compound, we shall use the following method:

(1) **In showing the elements which make up the sentence, we shall place the word "Compound" before the name of any element which is compound.**

Example:

He raises hogs, chickens, and Jersey cows.

Partial pattern: **Subject—Verb—Compound Object**

(2) **Immediately below the name of the compound, we shall indicate its pattern by using a blank for each unit of the compound and inserting the punctuation and conjunctions used between the units.**

Example:

He raises hogs, chickens, and Jersey cows.

Partial pattern: **Subject—Verb—Compound Object**
(_____, _____, and _____)

[2] In such a list as this, the omission of the conjunction implies that the list is incomplete.

(3) **Finally, beneath each blank we shall show the composition of each component unit by noting the part of speech to which each unit belongs and by indicating in the usual manner any modifiers of the individual units of the compound.**

Example:

He raises hogs, chickens, and Jersey cows.

Complete pattern: **Subject—Verb—Compound Object**

$$(\underline{\hspace{2cm}},\ \underline{\hspace{2cm}},\ \text{and}\ \underline{\hspace{2.5cm}})$$

Noun   Noun   Modifier—Noun

The following are some additional examples of this method of notation:

The minister and I will come.

Pattern: **Compound Subject —Verb**

$$(\underline{\hspace{1.5cm}}\ \text{and}\ \underline{\hspace{1.5cm}})$$

Noun   Pronoun

The snake coiled and struck.

Pattern: **Subject—Compound Verb**

$$(\underline{\hspace{1.5cm}}\ \text{and}\ \underline{\hspace{1.5cm}})$$

Verb   Verb

My friend tried but failed miserably.

Pattern: Modifier—**Subject—Compound Verb**

$$(\underline{\hspace{1.5cm}}\ \text{but}\ \underline{\hspace{2cm}})$$

Verb   Verb—Modifier

He will become a doctor or a dentist.

Pattern: **Subject—Linking Verb—Compound Substantive Complement**

$$(\underline{\hspace{1.5cm}}\ \text{or}\ \underline{\hspace{1.5cm}})$$

Noun   Noun

The tramp was wearing a torn and dirty coat.

Pattern: **Subject—Verb**—Compound Modifier   **—Object**

$$(\underline{\hspace{2cm}}\ \text{and}\ \underline{\hspace{2cm}})$$

Adjective   Adjective

A slim, beautiful brunette entered the room.

Pattern: Compound Modifier   **—Subject—Verb—Object**

$$(\underline{\hspace{2cm}},\ \underline{\hspace{2cm}})$$

Adjective   Adjective

This method of indicating the pattern of a sentence has many advantages over the diagraming method often employed. The essential framework of the sentence stands out clearly in the top line with no distortion of word-order, and notations beneath the top line indicate the precise structure of all parts of the sentence. Furthermore, functions are indicated by words rather than by position. All of these characteristics make it possible to use this method of indicating a pattern not only as a means of analysis of sentences already composed but as a means of showing the structure to be incorporated in sentences to be written by the student.

D. COMPOUNDS USING VARIOUS COORDINATING CONJUNCTIONS

In compounds of the type we have been examining, either single conjunctions or pairs of conjunctions may be used to connect the units of the compound.

1. SINGLE CONJUNCTIONS

The single conjunctions *and, or,* and *but* are frequently used to connect units of a compound.

a. THE CONJUNCTION "AND"

The conjunction *and* is used to connect the parts of compounds consisting of *added* units.

Examples:

Grass and flowers covered the hillside.

Pattern: **Compound Subject—Verb—Object**

(........... and ....)
 Noun   Noun

The engine *coughed and sputtered.*

Pattern: **Subject—Compound Verb**

(........... and ....)
 Verb   Verb

Compounds consisting of added units are the most common of all compounds. Besides the compounds with *and,* all compounds containing no conjunction are made up of added units.

Examples:

We heard *shouts, cheers, screams.*
My uncle is an *old, feeble* man.

In compounds of this sort, the conjunction *and* may always be inserted without changing the meaning. However, insertion of *and* always alters the effect of the compound somewhat:

We heard *shouts, cheers, and screams.*
My uncle is an *old and feeble* man.

Note the difference in effect when the conjunction is used.

(1) Agreement of Verb with Compound Subject Composed of Added Units

A compound subject composed of added units is *plural* in number. Therefore, the verb is *plural* to agree with the subject.

Examples:

The baby and the puppy *were* playing.
Mary, Jean, and Lucille *are* the winners.

Note:　An exception to this rule is the compound subject which stands for a single unit.

Example:

The secretary and treasurer is Johnson.

(2) Compound Substantive Modifier Preceding a Substantive

At this point, it is necessary to give special consideration to constructions involving the use of compound substantive modifiers preceding the substantive modified.

As with all other such compounds, the units of a compound substantive modifier containing no conjunction are separated by commas.

Examples:

An *intelligent, energetic* boy will get the job.

Pattern: COMPOUND MODIFIER —Subject—Verb—Object

       (‒‒‒‒‒‒‒, ‒‒‒‒‒‒‒)
       Adjective   Adjective

A *large, gruff, red-faced* man opposed me.

Pattern: COMPOUND MODIFIER —Subject—Verb—Object

     (‒‒‒‒‒‒, ‒‒‒‒‒‒‒, ‒‒‒‒‒‒)
     Adjective   Adjective   Adjective

It is important to distinguish this construction with the compound modifier from the following construction with an adjective-noun combination. (Note the difference in punctuation.)

Examples:

The best football team will win.

Pattern: MODIFIER— | MODIFIER—Subject | —Verb

Her black cocker spaniel bit him.

Pattern: MODIFIER— | MODIFIER— | MODIFIER—Subject | —Verb—Object

The basic difference between the two constructions lies in the fact that in the compound modifier the adjectives are coordinate whereas in the construction with the adjective-noun combination the adjectives are *not* coordinate. A simple test to determine which structure is present in a sentence is to try to insert the conjunction *and*. Note that the conjunction can be inserted in place of the comma between the units of the compound modifier:

    An intelligent *and* energetic boy will get the job.
    A large *and* gruff *and* red-faced man opposed me.

The conjunction *and* cannot be inserted between the adjectives in the other construction. Note the absurd sentences that would result:

    The best [and] football team will win.
    Her [and] black [and] cocker spaniel bit him.

Note 1: Another test is to change the order of the adjectives. This can be done with the units of a compound modifier but not with the construction involving an adjective-noun combination.

Note 2: It is possible to have a construction which contains both a compound modifier and an adjective-noun combination. Study carefully the structure of the following sentences:

The company wants good, efficient bus drivers.

Pattern: Subject—Verb—COMPOUND MODIFIER — | MODIFIER—Object |

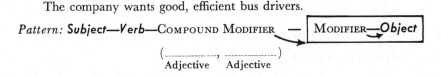
       (‒‒‒‒‒‒, ‒‒‒‒‒‒‒)
       Adjective   Adjective

My squat, ugly bulldog won the prize.

Pattern: MODIFIER— | COMPOUND MODIFIER —Subject | —Verb—Object

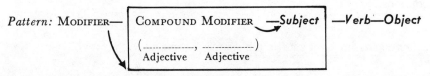
       (‒‒‒‒‒‒, ‒‒‒‒‒‒)
       Adjective   Adjective

b. *THE CONJUNCTION "OR"*

The conjunction *or* is used to connect the parts of compounds consisting of *alternative* units. The various units indicate two or more possibilities.

Examples:

The girls will wear *roses or gardenias.*

Pattern: **Subject—Verb—Compound Object**

(............. or ....)
     Noun   Noun

We will serve *pie, cake, or pudding.*

Pattern: **Subject—Verb—Compound Object**

(............., ..., or ....)
     Noun   Noun   Noun

When a compound composed of units joined by *or* is the subject of a sentence, the following rules determine the number of the verb:

1. If the individual units are singular, the verb will be singular.

   Example:

   The president or the secretary *presents* the awards.

2. If the individual units are plural, the verb will be plural.

   Example:

   The fans or the officials *were* mistaken.

3. If the compound consists of a mixture of singular and plural units, the verb agrees with the nearer unit.

   Examples:

   My cousins or my uncle *is* coming. (Singular)
   My uncle or my cousins *are* coming. (Plural)

All three of these rules are included in the following one:

When the units of a compound subject are connected by the conjunction *or*, the verb agrees in number with the nearer unit.

The verb also agrees in *person* with the nearer unit.

Examples:

You or he *is* guilty.
You or I *was* wrong.

c. *THE CONJUNCTION "BUT"*

The conjunction *but* is used to connect the parts of compounds consisting of *contrasted* units. It often joins verbs, adjectives, or adverbs in two-unit compounds.

Examples:

The forward *shot but missed.*

Pattern: **Subject—Compound Verb**

(............. but ....)
     Verb   Verb

Our host was *polite but reserved.*

Pattern: Modifier—**Subject—Linking Verb—Compound Adjective Complement**

(............................. but ....)
      Adjective   Adjective

They live *comfortably but not expensively.*

Pattern: **Subject—Verb—**Compound Modifier

(_____ but _____)
   Adverb   Modifier—Adverb

2. PAIRS OF CONJUNCTIONS (CORRELATIVE CONJUNCTIONS)

There are a number of pairs of conjunctions which are used to connect the units of a two-unit compound. The first conjunction precedes the first unit; the second joins the two units. These pairs of conjunctions are called *correlative conjunctions.*[3] The most common ones are the following: *both . . . and, either . . . or, neither . . . nor, not . . . but, not only . . . but also* (or *but*).

Examples:

The councilman was *both* young *and* energetic.

Pattern: **Subject—Linking Verb—Compound Adjective Complement**

(both _____ and _____)
       Adjective   Adjective

Either the engine *or* the propeller failed.

Pattern: **Compound Subject   —Verb**

(Either _____ or _____)
     Noun   Noun

Neither varnish *nor* paint was satisfactory.

Pattern: **Compound Subject   —Linking Verb—Adjective Complement**

(Neither _____ nor _____)
      Noun   Noun

That was *not* silver *but* nickel.

Pattern: **Subject—Linking Verb—Compound Substantive Complement**

(not _____ but _____)
   Noun   Noun

The lecture was *not only* dull *but also* disorganized.

Pattern: **Subject—Linking Verb—Compound Adjective Complement**

(not only _____ but also _____)
       Adjective   Adjective

When the units of a compound subject are joined by *both . . . and,* the verb is plural in number.

Example:

Both the book and the movie are excellent.

When the units of a compound subject are joined by *either . . . or, neither . . . nor, not . . . but,* or *not only . . . but also* (or *but*), the verb agrees in number and person with the nearer unit.

Examples:

Neither he nor the children were awake.
Not the speeches but the food was the attraction.
Not only the doughnuts but also the coffee was good.

---

[3] There is also one common set of three correlative conjunctions used to connect units of a multiple-unit compound: *either . . . or . . . or.*

Example:

I will work *either* Monday *or* Wednesday *or* Friday.

E. A SPECIAL NOTE ON COMPOUNDS

Generally speaking, the units of a compound element should be parallel in form as well as function:

> *Incorrect:* I like *hunting* and *to fish*.
> *Correct:* I like *hunting* and *fishing*.
> *Correct:* I like *to hunt* and *to fish*.

Note that a gerund and an infinitive cannot be used as basic units of the same compound.

Compounds may be formed from the elements we have studied as indicated in the following list of possible combinations:

1. Noun + Noun
2. Pronoun + Pronoun
3. *Noun + Pronoun*
4. Verb + Verb
5. Adjective + Adjective
6. Adverb + Adverb
7. Infinitive + Infinitive
8. Participle + Participle
9. *Adjective + Participle*
10. Gerund + Gerund
11. *Noun + Gerund*

Note that only nouns and pronouns, adjectives and participles, and nouns and gerunds may be used together as basic units in the same compound.

> Examples:
>
> *John* and *I* painted the barn. (Noun + Pronoun)
> He was *tired* and *hungry*. (Participle + Adjective)
> She enjoys *golf* and *fishing*. (Noun + Gerund)

Any other combination of these elements in a compound (*e.g.*, Adjective + Adverb, Infinitive + Participle, *etc.*) constitutes faulty parallelism.

Note: Although absolute parallelism is often desirable for effect, units of a compound do not necessarily have the same number of modifiers.

> Example:
>
> He bought a notebook and a fountain pen.
>
> *Pattern:* **Subject—Verb—Compound Object**
> (‑‑‑‑‑‑‑ and ‑‑‑‑‑‑‑‑‑‑‑‑‑‑‑)
> Noun   Modifier—Noun

If the basic units of a compound are properly parallel, the pattern of modifying elements may vary in any conceivable way.

DO EXERCISE 23

CHAPTER IX

THE COMPOUND PREDICATE—A FOURTH SENTENCE PATTERN

A. FORM OF THE COMPOUND PREDICATE

THUS far, we have studied three basic sentence patterns:

1. *Subject—Verb*
2. *Subject—Verb—Object*
3. *Subject—Linking Verb—Complement*

Each of these patterns may be divided into two parts: a *subject*—a substantive about which something is said—and a *predicate*—that which is said (*predicated*) about the subject (including the verb and its object or complement, if it has one).

	Subject	*Predicate*
1.	*Subject*	*—Verb*
2.	*Subject*	*—Verb—Object*
3.	*Subject*	*—Linking Verb—Complement*

We have, therefore, *three basic types of predicates:*

1. *Verb*
2. *Verb—Object*
3. *Linking Verb—Complement*

We have already seen that, without changing the basic pattern of the sentence, we can use a compound subject instead of a simple subject, a compound verb instead of a simple verb, a compound object instead of a simple object, a compound complement instead of a simple complement. It is also possible to have a *compound predicate* instead of a *simple predicate*. The sentence containing a compound predicate, however, does not fit any of the three basic patterns we have studied. It constitutes a fourth basic sentence pattern:

Subject—Compound Predicate

In such a sentence, the *compound predicate* is made up of two or more simple predicates. It is, thus, either a two-unit or multiple-unit compound. The simple predicates may all be of the same basic type, or they may consist of any mixture of types.[1] The punctuation of the compound predicate is the same as that used with any other compound. (See pp. 52–53.)

Examples:

The woman *played the piano and sang.*
The cook *broiled the steak and fried the potatoes.*
The guests *sang songs, played games, and danced.*

B. FUNCTION OF THE COMPOUND PREDICATE

A compound predicate functions in the same way as any of the three basic types of predicates. *It says something about the subject.*

---

[1] Of course, two or more predicates of the first type—consisting of the *verb* alone—will merely be a compound verb, and we will not consider this to be a compound predicate.

C. INDICATING THE PATTERN OF A SENTENCE CONTAINING A COMPOUND PREDICATE

To indicate the pattern of a sentence containing a compound predicate, we shall use the following method:

(1) **We shall use the notation "Compound Predicate" in listing the primary elements of the sentence.**

> Example:
>
> The frightened burglar dropped his gun and ran.
>
> *Partial pattern:* MODIFIER—*Subject—Compound Predicate*

(2) **Immediately below the words "Compound Predicate," we shall indicate the pattern of the predicate by using a blank for each simple predicate and inserting the punctuation and conjunctions used between the simple predicates composing the compound.**

> Example:
>
> The frightened burglar dropped his gun and ran.
>
> *Partial pattern:* MODIFIER—*Subject—Compound Predicate*
> (_____ and _____)

(3) **Then, beneath each blank we shall show the composition of each simple predicate ("Verb," "Verb—Object," "Linking Verb—Substantive Complement," or "Linking Verb—Adjective Complement"). Modifiers will be indicated in the usual manner.**

> Example:
>
> The frightened burglar dropped his gun and ran.
>
> *Complete pattern:* MODIFIER—*Subject—Compound Predicate*
> (_____ and _____)
> Verb—Modifier—Object   Verb

The following are additional examples of this method of indicating the pattern of a sentence with a compound predicate:

> The photographer inserted the holder, focused the camera, and took the picture.
>
> *Pattern:* **Subject—Compound Predicate**
> (_____, _____, and _____)
> Verb—Object   Verb—Object   Verb—Object

> The boy exercised diligently and became strong.
>
> *Pattern:* **Subject—Compound Predicate**
> (_____ and _____)
> Verb—Modifier   Linking Verb—Adjective Complement

> He and I sorted the letters and delivered them.
>
> *Pattern:* **Compound Subject —Compound Predicate**
> (_____ and _____)   (_____ and _____)
> Pronoun   Pronoun   Verb—Object   Verb—Object

Note 1: The sentence with a compound predicate, like all others that we have considered thus far, is a simple sentence.

Note 2: In a compound predicate, as in a compound verb, a single auxiliary verb often serves as auxiliary for more than one primary verb.

> Example:
>
> She *has* washed the woodwork and swept the rugs.

D. COMPOUND PREDICATES USING VARIOUS COORDINATING CONJUNCTIONS

In the examples given above, we have used the conjunction *and* throughout. However, the units of a compound predicate may be joined by other coordinating conjunctions.

Examples:

The murderer wore gloves *or* removed his fingerprints.

Pattern: **Subject—Compound Predicate**

(_____ or _____)

Verb—Object   Verb—Modifier—Object

He studied hard *but* failed the course.

Pattern: **Subject—Compound Predicate**

(_____ but _____)

Verb—Modifier   Verb—Object

My sister *either* forgot the meeting *or* missed the bus.

Pattern: MODIFIER—**Subject—Compound Predicate**

(either _____ or _____)

Verb—Object   Verb—Object

She *not only* composes music *but also* writes poetry.

Pattern: **Subject—Compound Predicate**

(not only _____ but also _____)

Verb—Object   Verb—Object

E. A SPECIAL NOTE ON COMPOUND PREDICATES

The units of a compound predicate must be parallel in one way—each unit must be a *predicate*:

Incorrect: He not only *was energetic* but also *brilliant.*

This sentence is incorrect because the second unit of the compound is not a predicate. The sentence may be corrected by using a compound predicate or a compound adjective complement:

Correct: He not only *was energetic* but also *was brilliant.*
Correct: He was not only *energetic* but also *brilliant.*

Note the parallel construction in both sentences.

DO EXERCISE 24

CHAPTER X

APPOSITIVES

AN *appositive* is a sentence element which provides a supplementary explanation of another sentence element.

Examples:

Frankfort, the *capital,* is a beautiful city.
Pratt, the *banker,* will be present.
The word *athlete* is often misspelled.

The element with which the appositive is in apposition normally precedes the appositive and is called its *antecedent.* Thus, *Frankfort* is the antecedent of *capital, Pratt* is the antecedent of *banker,* and *word* is the antecedent of *athlete.*

A. FORM OF THE APPOSITIVE

Usually, the *form* of the appositive is basically the same as that of the antecedent. In other words, a noun is usually in apposition with a noun, and so on.

Example:

The *musician,* a *violinist,* gave a concert.

However, the appositive and the antecedent may vary in form.

Examples:

He discovered a new *pastime, skiing.*
You, the *inventor,* should know its purpose.

In the first sentence, a gerund is in apposition with a noun; in the second, a noun is in apposition with a pronoun. But in both sentences the appositive and its antecedent are elements which can perform the same function—the substantive function.

An appositive is quite frequently compound.

Examples:

The two boys, *Jim and Billy,* gathered the apples.
I enjoy three sports: *tennis, swimming, and boating.*

Any element in the appositive, of course, may have modifiers of its own.

Examples:

We visited Tinian, a *small* island.
He wanted two things—a *hot* bath and a *clean* bed.

Note: A predicate of one type may be in apposition with a predicate of another type.
Example:
Last year they retrenched (reduced expenses).

B. FUNCTION OF THE APPOSITIVE

1. THE DUAL FUNCTION OF THE APPOSITIVE

Like a modifier, an appositive changes or modifies the concept presented by the element to which it is added. Thus, the appositive *terrier* gives more specific information about the concept *dog* in the following sentence:

> My dog, a terrier, won a blue ribbon.

Because of this characteristic, the appositive is sometimes classified as a modifier.

However, there is an important difference between appositives and pure modifiers. An appositive, in addition to performing a modifying function, always duplicates the function of its antecedent. (In most instances, both elements serve as substantives.) Because of this duplication of function, the appositive—unlike the pure modifier—can usually be substituted for the element to which it is attached.

> Example:
>
> Louise, *my cousin,* went home.
> *My cousin* went home.

Let us examine a similar sentence containing a pure modifier instead of an appositive:

> Louise, *discouraged,* went home.

Note that in this sentence the modifier *discouraged* cannot possibly be substituted for the substantive *Louise.*

The appositive, then, performs two functions at the same time:

(1) **It modifies the element with which it is in apposition.**

(2) **It performs the same function as that performed by the element with which it is in apposition.**

Note 1: A single element performing more than one function is, as we shall see, a common phenomenon in English.

Note 2: If an appositive is a noun or a pronoun, it is in the same case as its antecedent.

2. RESTRICTIVE AND NON-RESTRICTIVE APPOSITIVES

a. *RESTRICTIVE APPOSITIVES*

Some appositives perform their modifying function in such a way that they are *restrictive—i.e.,* they are necessary for the proper identification of the element they modify. With such appositives no punctuation is used.

> Examples:
>
> My brother *Bill* will row the boat.
> William *the Conqueror* ruled England.
> We *boys* built the cabin.

Note 1: In such combinations as *Peter the Great, Richard the Lion-Hearted, Henry the Eighth,* and *Charles the Victorious,* the appositive looks like an adjective, but it actually functions as a substantive as is shown by the modifying article *the.*

Note 2: A combination composed of a substantive and a restrictive appositive functions as a unit in much the same way that a single-word substantive does. Note the possessives of the following combinations:

> my cousin Sarah   my cousin Sarah's house
> Catherine the Great   Catherine the Great's reign

b. *NON-RESTRICTIVE APPOSITIVES*

Most appositives perform their modifying function in such a way that they are *non-restrictive—i.e.,* they give added information about an element which is presumed to be sufficiently identified without the appositive. Such an appositive is set off from the rest of the sentence by punctuation.

> Examples:
>
> My nephew, *Donald,* wants a bicycle.
> We have a new car, *a sedan.*

The punctuation marks used to set off a non-restrictive appositive depend upon the nature of the relationship between the appositive and the remainder of the sentence.

(1) **If there is a rather close connection between the non-restrictive appositive and the rest of the sentence, it is set off by commas.**

Examples:

Larry, my neighbor's boy, raked our yard.

We called Henderson, the plumber.

Note: Comma punctuation is also used to set off one type of introductory appositive:

A distinguished scholar, he has received many honorary degrees. [*Compare:* Since he is a distinguished scholar, he has received many honorary degrees.]

Such an appositive is practically equivalent to an adverb clause and thus has an adverbial function in addition to those functions normally performed by an appositive.

An introductory appositive preceding a summarizing word or word-group is set off by a dash:

To be entirely worthy of his father's faith in him—that was what he wanted most of all.

(2) **If the non-restrictive appositive is loosely connected with the rest of the sentence (that is, if it is parenthetical), it is set off by parentheses or dashes.**

Examples:

His sister—a singer of great promise—won the talent contest.

Substantive modifiers (adjectives) have an important grammatical function.

Note: As the last example illustrates, parentheses are normally used to set off an appositive which explains the meaning of the word or word-group serving as its antecedent.

(3) **If the non-restrictive appositive is placed at the end of the sentence and serves as the climax of the idea, it may be set off by either a dash or a colon.**

Examples:

We beat only one team—the Tigers.

Three things were missing: a clock, a vase, and a bowl.

Note: As the last example illustrates, the appositive does not always immediately follow its antecedent.

(4) **If the non-restrictive appositive contains internal comma punctuation, it is set off by strong punctuation—usually parentheses or dashes. A colon may be used when the appositive is at the end of the sentence.**

Examples:

The three boys—John, Bill, and Jerry—built the clubhouse by themselves.

A few counties (Prairie, Lamar, and Revere) have begun re-assessment of property.

C. INDICATING THE PATTERN OF A SENTENCE CONTAINING AN APPOSITIVE

To indicate the pattern of a sentence containing an appositive, we shall use the following method:

(1) **We shall use the word "Appositive" to designate all appositional sentence elements (thus distinguishing appositives from pure modifiers), and we shall draw an arrow from the appositive to its antecedent (thus symbolizing the modifying function of the appositive).**

Example:

Sally, a good loser, congratulated Mary, the winner.

Partial pattern: **Subject**—Appositive—**Verb**—**Object**—Appositive

(2) **If it is desired to show whether the appositive is restrictive or non-restrictive, we shall make a notation to this effect immediately below the word "Appositive." (This step may be omitted.)**

Example:

Sally, a good loser, congratulated Mary, the winner.

Partial pattern: **Subject**—Appositive —**Verb**—**Object**—Appositive

(Non-restrictive)   (Non-restrictive)

(3) **If the appositional element consists of more than a single word (that is, if the basic appositive word is connected with one or more modifiers or other elements), in a box below the word "Appositive" we shall indicate the exact composition of the appositional element.**

Example:

Sally, a good loser, congratulated Mary, the winner.

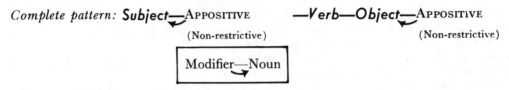

Some additional examples of this method of notation follow:

My friend Rudolph called me.

Pattern: MODIFIER—**Subject**—APPOSITIVE—**Verb**—**Object**
(Restrictive)

He found two clues—a pistol and a knife.

Pattern: **Subject**—**Verb**—MODIFIER—**Object**—COMPOUND APPOSITIVE

(_____ and _____)
   Noun   Noun

D. SOME SPECIAL NOTES ON THE APPOSITIVE

1. INTENSIVE PRONOUNS

An *intensive pronoun* intensifies or emphasizes the identity of the substantive with which it is in apposition. It usually serves as a restrictive appositive.

The following words may function as intensive pronouns:

	Singular	*Plural*
1st Person	myself	ourselves
2nd Person	yourself	yourselves
3rd Person	himself, herself, itself, oneself	themselves

Examples:

I *myself* saw the signals.
The governor *himself* awarded the prize.

The reflexive pronouns and the intensive pronouns are identical in *form;* the distinction between them is one of *function.*

Note 1: The intensive pronoun is a somewhat unusual appositive. It is the only appositive which cannot be substituted in a sentence for its antecedent. Furthermore, its restrictive nature is peculiar. It is not actually necessary for the identification of the substantive to which it refers, but rather *emphasizes* that identification.

Note 2: The intensive pronoun and its antecedent are sometimes separated.

Example:

You heard him *yourself.*

Pattern: **Subject**—**Verb**—**Object**—APPOSITIVE
(Intensive pronoun)

2. ANTICIPATORY *IT* AND THE DELAYED SUBJECT

The pronoun *it* may function as the grammatical subject of a sentence in which the subject concept is specified by a restrictive appositive at the end of the sentence. The appositive in such a construction is called the "delayed subject," even though it does not, of course, function as the grammatical subject of the verb.

Example:

It is advisable *to go*. [Note that the appositive *to go* can be substituted for its antecedent *it:* *To go is advisable.*]

Pattern: **Subject—Linking Verb—Adjective Complement—**APPOSITIVE

(Delayed subject)

Note 1: As we shall see later, this construction is also used with a phrase or a noun clause as the delayed subject.

Note 2: The "anticipatory" *it* may perform a substantive function other than that of subject. In the following sentence, *it* is the object of the verb, *advisable* is an objective complement (see p. 288), and *to go* is a "delayed object" in apposition with *it: I believe it advisable to go.*

3. USE OF INTRODUCTORY WORDS

An appositive may be preceded by an introductory expression which serves as an independent sentence element (see Chapter XI) and which therefore has no effect upon the grammatical function of the appositive.

A restrictive appositive may be introduced by *of* or *such as*. In such instances, there is no punctuation either following the introductory element or setting off the entire appositive.

Examples:

We visited the state of Illinois.

Books such as that one are a waste of time.

Note: Some grammarians would consider *that one* to be the subject of an elliptical clause rather than an appositive.

A non-restrictive appositive may be introduced by one of the following introductory expressions: *or, such as, namely, specifically, that is, for example, viz. (videlicet,* namely), *i.e. (id est,* that is), and *e.g. (exempli gratia,* for example). The expressions *or* and *such as* are usually not followed by any punctuation. A non-restrictive appositive containing one of these as an introductory expression is normally set off from the rest of the sentence by commas unless internal comma punctuation elsewhere within the appositive makes it necessary to use dashes or parentheses. The other introductory expressions are usually followed by comma punctuation, and a non-restrictive appositive containing one of these expressions is normally set off by dashes or parentheses because of this internal comma punctuation.

Examples:

The Indian turnip, or jack-in-the-pulpit, is a common wild flower.

Many occupations—such as dentistry, medicine, and law—demand long professional training.

He was a somnambulist (*i.e.,* a sleepwalker).

The house needs many improvements—for example, painting and papering.

Note 1: If the appositive is particularly long, a colon is sometimes used after an introductory expression.

Note 2: The introductory expressions *such as, for example, for instance,* and *e.g.* introduce examples, or *incomplete appositives.* In the last sentence above, note that only two of the *many improvements* are listed.

Note 3: In a sentence pattern, we shall use the notation "[Introductory Element]" to indicate any expression serving to introduce an appositive:

Example:

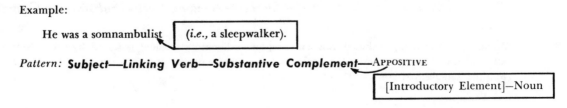

He was a somnambulist   (*i.e.,* a sleepwalker).

Pattern: **Subject—Linking Verb—Substantive Complement—**APPOSITIVE

[Introductory Element]—Noun

DO EXERCISE 25

CHAPTER XI

INDEPENDENT SENTENCE ELEMENTS

AN independent sentence element is one which has no grammatical relationship with any other element of the sentence in which it occurs.

The most important independent sentence elements are the following: (a) exclamatory elements, (b) interpolated elements, (c) vocatives, and (d) the expletive *there*.

A. EXCLAMATORY ELEMENTS

Exclamatory elements include interjections and similar words or word-groups.

An *interjection* is a word used to convey emotion or feeling. Usually it is followed by an exclamation point.

Examples:

Oh! you surprised me.
Ouch! I hit my finger.
Hurrah! he intercepted the pass.

Other words or word-groups may be used in a similar manner.

Examples:

Horses! I hate horses.
Poor old John! the boss fired him.

A mild exclamatory expression is often set off from the rest of the sentence by a comma rather than an exclamation point.

Examples:

Well, I must get some groceries.
Oh, he will be here eventually.

To indicate an exclamatory expression in a sentence pattern, we shall use the notation "[Exclamatory Element]." The brackets symbolize its independent grammatical status.

Examples:

Ah! that is the solution.

Pattern: [EXCLAMATORY ELEMENT]—*Subject—Linking Verb—Substantive Complement*

Note: Often, instead of being included in a sentence, an exclamatory element is set off by itself. Note that capitalization of the word *he* indicates the beginning of a new sentence and thus excludes the exclamatory element from the sentence pattern.

Example:

A carpenter! He can't even drive a nail.

B. INTERPOLATED ELEMENTS

An interpolated element is one inserted in a sentence as an additional remark. Such an element is normally a complete sentence in itself. Because of its extraneous nature, an interpolated element is set off by strong marks of punctuation—either parentheses or dashes.

Examples:

Their cocker spaniel—it's pedigreed—won a blue ribbon last year.

George (you should remember him) sends his regards.

To indicate an interpolated element in a sentence pattern, we shall use the notation "[Interpolated Element]."

Example:

My roommate—he's very smart—made an *A.*

Pattern: MODIFIER—*Subject*—[INTERPOLATED ELEMENT]—*Verb—Object*

Note: The term "interpolated element" is used in this text to distinguish such independent sentence elements from parenthetical elements which are grammatically connected with the sentences in which they occur. The following parenthetical expressions, for instance, are not independent sentence elements. They are adverbial sentence modifiers. (See pp. 39–40.)

Examples:

Dogs, *as you know,* are friendly animals.

Frankly, I don't remember the reason.

James, *we feel sure,* will be a good president.

C. VOCATIVES

A vocative is a word or word-group used to name the person or persons addressed. Such expressions are always set off by commas.

Examples:

My main concern, *George,* is the price.

Ladies and gentlemen, this is a very great honor.

You received a letter, *Mary.*

To indicate a vocative in a sentence pattern, we shall use the notation "[Vocative]."

Examples:

Your delay, Jackson, has cost money.

Pattern: MODIFIER—*Subject*—[VOCATIVE]—*Verb—Object*

D. THE EXPLETIVE "THERE"

The word *there* is often used as an expletive or "filler-word" before the verb in a sentence in which the verb precedes the subject. Usually the verb in such a sentence is a form of *to be.*

Examples:

There is only one possible objection.

There are several books here.

As these sentences illustrate, the verb must agree with its subject; *there* is not the subject.

To indicate the expletive *there* in a sentence pattern, we shall use the notation "[Expletive]."

Examples:

There must be a window open.

Pattern: [EXPLETIVE]—*Linking Verb—Subject—Adjective Complement*

There will be five jobs.

Pattern: [EXPLETIVE]—*Verb*—MODIFIER—*Subject*

Note 1: Very frequently, as in the last example, the verb *to be* in a sentence containing the expletive *there* is not a linking verb but an intransitive verb meaning "to exist." One can test a sentence by omitting the expletive and reversing the verb and subject:

There will be five jobs.

Five jobs will be (= *exist*).

However, note the structure of the other example:

There must be a window open.

A window must be open.

Here, we have a linking verb.

Note 2: The expletive *there* must not be confused with the adverb *there*. The adverb *there* indicates a place. Note the difference between the following sentences:

There is the mistake. (Adverb)

There was a mistake. (Expletive)

DO EXERCISE 26

CHAPTER XII
TYPES OF SENTENCES

SENTENCES vary according to the intention of the speaker or writer. A person may compose a sentence in order to make a statement, set forth a command or request, ask a question, or convey strong feeling. There are, therefore, four types of sentences: (a) *declarative,* (b) *imperative,* (c) *interrogative,* and (d) *exclamatory.*

In this chapter, we shall examine these four kinds of sentences, paying particular attention to the word-order of the various types. It must be emphasized that in spite of any variations in word-order every sentence has a framework which fits one of the basic sentence patterns.

A. DECLARATIVE SENTENCES

A *declarative* sentence is one which states or asserts a fact. A period is used to close such a sentence. This is, of course, the type of sentence with which we have been primarily concerned thus far.

The word-order of the declarative sentence is usually that which we have used in indicating the basic sentence patterns.

Examples:

He is singing.
Pattern: **Subject—Verb**

The car hit the pole.
Pattern: **Subject—Verb—Object**

She is a typist.
Pattern: **Subject—Linking Verb—Substantive Complement**

However, occasionally we have inverted word-order in declarative sentences. As we have noted, the construction with the expletive *there* involves inverted order. (See pp. 69–70.) Some other examples of inverted word-order are the following:

Nearby stood a tree.
Below roared the torrent.
Here comes the bride.

Note: If you have difficulty in determining the subject in a sentence containing inverted word-order, you may use the previously suggested method of forming a question by placing *who* or *what* before the verb. (See p. 2.)

Example:

Here comes the bride.
Who comes? Bride.
The subject of the verb is *bride.*

B. IMPERATIVE SENTENCES

An *imperative* sentence is one which sets forth a command or a request. A period is used to close such a sentence unless the sentence is also exclamatory.

The word-order of the imperative sentence is normally the same as that of the declarative sentence, but the subject is usually understood rather than expressed.

Examples:

(You) Stop.

Pattern: **(Subject)—Verb**

(You) Open the door.

Pattern: **(Subject)—Verb—Object**

(You) Be quiet.

Pattern: **(Subject)—Linking Verb—Adjective Complement**

With the understood subject *you* supplied, each of these imperative sentences fits one of the basic sentence patterns, and the word-order of each sentence is the same as that of a similar declarative sentence.

The verb forms of the imperative mode (see p. 19) are quite easy to learn, since only the *second person* and the *present tense* are involved. The simple form of the imperative is the same as that of the present infinitive (without *to*). The progressive form is constructed by adding the present participle to the imperative form of *to be*. The emphatic form is made up of the imperative form of *to do* plus the present infinitive of the primary verb.

Imperative of *to study*

Present Tense

	Singular	*Plural*
	Simple	
2nd Person	study	study
	Progressive	
2nd Person	be studying	be studying
	Emphatic	
2nd Person	do study	do study

Note: The simple imperative of the verb *to be* is *be;* the emphatic is *do be.*

Examples:

Be a man.
Do be serious.

C. INTERROGATIVE SENTENCES

An *interrogative* sentence is one which asks a question. A question mark is used to close such a sentence.

There are two types of interrogative sentences. In one kind, the question is asked by varying the subject and predicate of a declarative sentence—either in tone of voice alone or in word-order.[1] Such a question usually will be answered by *yes* or *no*.

Examples:

Will you bring your camera? (*Answer: Yes* or *No*)
Did he pass the test? (*Answer: Yes* or *No*)

In the other kind of interrogative sentence, the question is asked by using an interrogative word. This type of question cannot be answered by *yes* or *no*.

Examples:

Who broke the vase?
Where did he go?

---

[1] Along with the variation in word-order, there will usually be a variation in tone of voice; but a shift in word order, when it occurs, is a more significant interrogative characteristic by far than the variation in voice inflection.

1. TYPES OF INTERROGATIVE SENTENCES

a. *QUESTION ASKED BY VARIATION IN TONE OF VOICE OR WORD-ORDER*

(1) **Variation in Tone of Voice Alone**

A sentence may have the same word-order that a similar declarative sentence would have and yet ask a question by means of the tone of voice used in speaking it. (The only indication in a written sentence of this "questioning tone of voice" is the question mark at the end.) Compare the following interrogative sentences with the declarative sentences given as examples above:

> He is singing?
> The car hit the pole?
> She is a typist?

Note: Of course, almost any interrogative sentence is spoken with a "questioning tone of voice." However, in such sentences as these examples, the tone of voice is the only characteristic which makes them questions instead of statements.

(2) **Variation in Word-Order**

Most interrogative sentences which do not contain interrogative words ask questions by means of a shift in word-order.

The variation in word-order can best be understood by changing declarative sentences to interrogative sentences and observing the shifting which must take place to accomplish the change. The exact nature of such shifting depends upon the verb in the declarative sentence. If the verb is a verb phrase, the sentence is changed to a question by shifting the auxiliary verb to the beginning of the sentence.[2]

> Examples:
>
> He was reading.
> Was he reading?
>
> She has refused the job.
> Has she refused the job?
>
> They had been sick.
> Had they been sick?

If the verb is a single word, it usually is first expanded to a verb phrase containing a form of the verb *to do* as the auxiliary, and the auxiliary verb is then shifted as noted above.

> Examples:
>
> His sister teaches (= *does teach*).
> Does his sister teach?
>
> The team lost (= *did lose*) the game.
> Did the team lose the game?
>
> He became (= *did become*) a farmer.
> Did he become a farmer?

The verb *to be* is an exception to this last rule.

> Examples:
>
> He is a chef.
> Is he a chef?
>
> She was unhappy.
> Was she unhappy?

Note that these forms of the verb *to be* cannot be expanded to verb phrases without extreme awkwardness.

---

[2] Only the first auxiliary is moved to the beginning of the sentence if the phrase contains two or more auxiliaries.
> Example:
> They will be working.
> Will they be working?

Note 1: The verb *to have* may or may not follow this rule.

> Examples:
>
> > Does he have a watch?
> > Has he a watch?

Note 2: If a question asked by variation either in tone of voice or in word-order contains a compound connected by the conjunction *or*, the answer will not be *yes* or *no* but will usually specify one of the units of the compound.

> Example:
>
> > Did she marry Tom or Harry? (*Answer: Tom* or *Harry*)

b. *QUESTION ASKED BY USING INTERROGATIVE WORDS*

Many interrogative sentences ask questions by means of interrogative words. These words are of three types: (1) interrogative pronouns, (2) interrogative adjectives, and (3) interrogative adverbs. We shall examine sentences introduced by each of these types.

(1) Sentences Introduced by Interrogative Pronouns

An *interrogative pronoun* is one which is used to ask a question.[3] The interrogative pronouns are the following: *who (whom), which,* and *what. Who* has the objective case form *whom; which* and *what* do not change in form in the objective case.

Nominative:	who	which	what
Objective:	whom	which	what

> Examples:
>
> > *Who* told you?   (Subject)
> > *Whom* did he invite?   (Object)
> > *Which* is correct?   (Subject)
> > *Which* do you want?   (Object)
> > *What* hit him?   (Subject)
> > *What* did you say?   (Object)

Note: Since both *who* and *whom* come at the beginning of an interrogative sentence, some students have difficulty in determining which form of the pronoun is proper in a given sentence. One way to test a sentence is to change it from interrogative to declarative and substitute *he/him, she/her,* or *they/them* for the interrogative pronoun. Let us suppose, for example, that you are in doubt about whether to use *who* or *whom* in the following sentence:

> *Who/Whom* did you see?

This would be changed to read:

> You did see *he/him.*

Obviously, the objective case form *him* is correct. Therefore, the objective case form *whom* is correct in the original sentence:

> *Whom* did you see?

(2) Sentences Introduced by Interrogative Adjectives

An *interrogative adjective* is one which is used to ask a question.[4] The interrogative adjectives are the following: *whose* (the possessive of *who*), *which,* and *what.*

> Examples:
>
> > *Whose* dog bit you? (Modifier of subject)
> >
> > *Which* plan did the council accept? (Modifier of object)
> >
> > *What* books did she buy? (Modifier of object)

---

[3] We shall see later that an interrogative pronoun may be used in indirect as well as direct questions. (See p. 109.)
[4] Like the interrogative pronoun, the interrogative adjective may be used in both direct and indirect questions. (See p. 109.)

(3) Sentences Introduced by Interrogative Adverbs

An *interrogative adverb* is one which is used to ask a question.[5] The interrogative adverbs are the following: *when, where, why,* and *how.*

> Examples:
>
> > *When* will the boat arrive?
> > *Where* are they going?
> > *Why* did the policeman arrest him?
> > *How* will you go?
> > *How* tall is he?

Note: It may be difficult to see that these words are adverbs. If so, an examination of the first example will be of help. If we change this sentence to the declarative and substitute *tomorrow*—another time word—for *when,* we have the following sentence:

> Tomorrow the boat will arrive.

Here *tomorrow* obviously is an adverbial modifier. Since it is a substitute for *when,* the word *when* must be an adverb in the original sentence.

Note that an interrogative adverb which modifies a verb *inquires concerning the circumstances surrounding the verb action.*

(4) Word-Order in Questions Asked by Interrogative Words

With regard to word-order, the primary characteristic of interrogative sentences based on interrogative words is that the interrogative word almost always comes at the beginning of the sentence. As a result, there are two types of word-order.

If the interrogative word is the subject or is a modifier linked with the subject, the word-order of the interrogative sentence is the same as that of a similar declarative sentence.

> Examples:
>
> > *Who* did it? [*Compare:* He did it.]
> > *Which* team won? [*Compare:* Our team won.]

With any other construction, the interrogative word (with any elements directly connected to it) comes first and is followed by the same sort of inverted word-order that is normally used in questions not containing interrogative words.

> Examples:

Interrogative word and connected elements	Auxiliary	Subject	Verb
Whom	did	she	select?
Which	does	he	like?
What	do	you	need?
Whose umbrella	do	I	have?
Which magazine	do	you	prefer?
What procedure	shall	we	use?
When	did	he	leave?
Where	do	you	live?
Why	is	she	crying?
How	can	he	win?
How well	does	she	play?

Note: Here, too, the verb *to be* is an exception:

> How tall is your father?

[5] An interrogative adverb, like the other interrogative words, may be used in both direct and indirect questions. (See p. 109.)

2. INDICATING THE PATTERN OF AN INTERROGATIVE SENTENCE

In indicating the pattern of an interrogative sentence, we shall do the following things: (a) place at the end of the pattern a question mark enclosed in brackets, (b) use a separate notation for the auxiliary when it is separated from the primary verb, and (c) indicate below the function of an interrogative word its exact nature—*i.e.*, *interrogative pronoun*, *interrogative adjective*, or *interrogative adverb*.

Examples:

You lost your wallet?

Pattern: **Subject—Verb—**Modifier**—Object**[?]

Did he buy the car?

Pattern: Auxiliary**—Subject—Verb—Object**[?]

Who brought that box?

Pattern: **Subject**   **—Verb—**Modifier**—Object**[?]
　　　(Interrogative pronoun)

Whom does she want?

Pattern: **Object**   **—**Auxiliary**—Subject—Verb**[?]
　　　(Interrogative pronoun)

Which dinner did he order?

Pattern: Modifier   **—Object—**Auxiliary**—Subject—Verb**[?]
　　　(Interrogative adjective)

When does the game start?

Pattern: Modifier   **—**Auxiliary**—Subject—Verb**[?]
　　　(Interrogative adverb)

How long was the play?

Pattern: Modifier   **—Adjective Complement—Linking Verb—Subject**[?]
　　　(Interrogative adverb)

D. EXCLAMATORY SENTENCES

An *exclamatory* sentence is one which conveys strong feeling. An exclamation point is used to close such a sentence.

1. WORD-ORDER IN EXCLAMATORY SENTENCES

Since any declarative, imperative, or interrogative sentence may be exclamatory if it is expressed with strong feeling, the word-order of the exclamatory sentence may duplicate that of any of the other types.

Examples:

He dropped the ball! (Declarative order)
Grab the ladder! (Imperative order)
Is that true! (Interrogative order)

There is, however, one type of exclamatory sentence which has its own characteristic word-order. In sentences of this type the exclamatory adjectives *what* and *such* and the exclamatory adverb *how* are used as introductory words. These words and the elements they modify come at the beginning of the sentence; the remainder of the sentence follows in normal declarative order.

Examples:

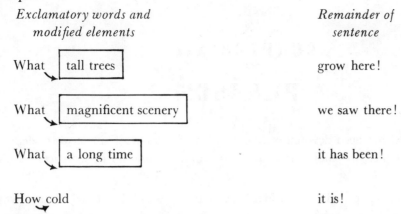

Exclamatory words and modified elements	Remainder of sentence
What ↳ tall trees	grow here!
What ↳ magnificent scenery	we saw there!
What ↳ a long time	it has been!
How cold ↳	it is!

Note: Often the remainder of the sentence is omitted in such a construction, leaving an exclamation which is not a sentence.

Examples:
What nonsense!
How horrible!

There is no objection to this sort of incomplete (or *elliptical*) sentence.

2. INDICATING THE PATTERN OF AN EXCLAMATORY SENTENCE

In indicating the pattern of an exclamatory sentence, we shall do the following things: (a) place at the end of the pattern an exclamation point enclosed in brackets and (b) indicate below the function of an exclamatory word its exact nature—*i.e., exclamatory adjective* or *exclamatory adverb.*

Examples:

He has a gun!

Pattern: **Subject—Verb—Object**[!]

What wonderful pies your mother makes!

Pattern: MODIFIER ⟶ — MODIFIER—*Object* — MODIFIER—*Subject—Verb*[!]
    (Exclamatory adjective)

How beautiful she is!

Pattern: MODIFIER ⟶ —**Adjective Complement—Subject—Linking Verb** [!]
    (Exclamatory adverb)

DO EXERCISES 27 AND 28

CHAPTER XIII

PHRASES

OUR study up to now has been devoted primarily to the functions of single-word elements and compound elements. In this chapter, we shall deal with the functions of *phrases* in sentences. A phrase may be defined as follows:

> A *phrase* is a group of related words which does not have a subject and verb and which functions in the sentence as a single unit.

Note: The phrase may contain a *verb form* (an infinitive, a participle, or a gerund) but not a *finite verb*—*i.e.*, a verb which is capable of serving as a main verb in one of the basic sentence patterns.

It is important to note that phrases—like compounds—perform the same functions that single words perform. The phrase does not have any new functions; it is merely a word-group which performs one of the functions we have already studied. It functions as a verb, a substantive, an adjective, or an adverb.

Classified according to their composition, there are five types of phrases:

1. The verb phrase
2. The prepositional phrase
3. The gerund phrase
4. The participial phrase
5. The infinitive phrase

We shall consider each of these separately.

Note: The adjective-noun combination and the verb-adverb combination could be considered phrases, since they are groups of related words which do not contain subjects and verbs and which function as single units. However, we shall retain the conventional classification and limit the term *phrase* to the five types of phrases listed above.

A. VERB PHRASES

A verb phrase is a group of two or more words used as a verb. It includes the primary verb and all of its auxiliaries. A verb phrase always functions as a verb.

> Examples:
>
> We *had gone*.
> He *had been swimming*.

Since we have already studied such verb forms in detail, no further treatment is necessary here. (See pp. 8–19)

Note: The verb phrase differs from the other four types of phrases in the fact that all of its elements are alike —*i.e.*, they are all verbs. It therefore lacks many of the structural characteristics of the other types of phrases. It might be well to use some other name instead of "verb phrase." Certainly the term *phrase* usually brings to mind the characteristics of prepositional, gerund, participial, and infinitive phrases rather than those of the verb phrase. However, in this text the traditional terminology for the verb phrase is employed.

B. PREPOSITIONAL PHRASES

1. FORM OF THE PREPOSITIONAL PHRASE

A prepositional phrase is a group of words consisting of a preposition and its object, plus any modifiers of the preposition or the object.

FORMULA: Preposition + Object (+ Modifiers)

Examples:

on the street
in the front yard

Like the conjunction, the preposition performs a *connecting* function. A preposition connects its object with another element and shows at the same time the relationship between them.

Example:

He owns the book on the table. [The preposition *on* connects *table* with *book* and shows the relationship between them.]

The object of the preposition is always a substantive. It is normally in the objective case.

Examples:

I gave it to *him*.
He sat beside *her*.

Either the preposition or its object may have a modifier.

Examples:

We stood *very* near the door. (Modifier of preposition *near*)
He ran through the *tall* grass. (Modifier of object *grass*)

Note 1: An infinitive or a gerund may serve as the object of a preposition.

Examples:

He was willing to do anything except *to work*.
She was tired of *walking*.

Note 2: An interrogative pronoun may serve as the object of a preposition. Such a pronoun will be in the objective case.

Examples:

To *whom* did you give the note?
For *whom* is he looking?

A list containing the common prepositions follows:

Preposition	*Prepositional Phrase*
about	about the game
above	above the stream
according to	according to the paper
across	across the mountain
after	after school
against	against the wall
along	along the shore
among	among the spectators
around	around the house
at	at the corner
because of	because of his illness
before	before noon
behind	behind the sofa
below	below the surface
beneath	beneath notice
beside	beside the tree
between	between the two men
but (meaning *except*)	but my father

Preposition	*Prepositional Phrase*
by	by the tower
concerning	concerning the assignment
despite	despite my warning
down	down the drain
during	during vacation
except	except my father
for	for money
from	from my friend
in	in the room
in front of	in front of the building
inside	inside the house
in spite of	in spite of his injury
instead of	instead of my brother
into	into the yard
like	like a storm
near	near the door
notwithstanding	notwithstanding his objections
of	of the book
off	off the subject
on	on the chair
out of	out of the car
outside	outside the fence
over	over the hill
past	past the store
since	since the flood
through	through the forest
throughout	throughout the year
till	till morning
to	to the library
toward	toward home
under	under the porch
underneath	underneath the rug
until	until June
up	up the ladder
upon	upon the platform
with	with a stick
within	within the town
without	without a reason

Note: As indicated by this list, a number of prepositions consist of more than one word. Often such prepositions contain a prepositional phrase which has lost some of its independent meaning.

   Example:

   in spite of

Any group of words functioning as a preposition may be termed a "group" preposition.

Since a preposition *always* has an object and usually is followed immediately by its object, the prepositional phrase is a unit which is rather easy to recognize.

Note: In direct questions and subordinate clauses, the object of the preposition often precedes the preposition and is separated from it:

   Examples:

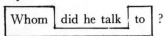

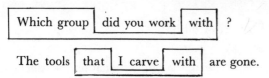

Which group | did you work | with | ?

The tools | that | I carve | with | are gone.

See page 100 for a similar separation of the parts of an infinitive phrase.

Either the entire prepositional phrase or any part of it may be compound. (The punctuation of such compounds is the same as that of other compounds. See pp. 52–53.)

Examples:

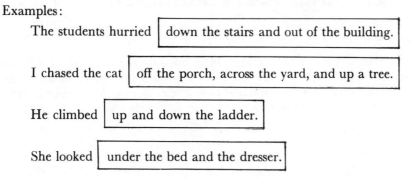

The students hurried | down the stairs and out of the building.

I chased the cat | off the porch, across the yard, and up a tree.

He climbed | up and down the ladder.

She looked | under the bed and the dresser.

When the object of the preposition is compound, both units must be in the objective case.

Examples:

Between *you and me,* he is a fake.
The pup barked at *him and me.*

The prepositional phrase may contain any elements which can serve as substantives or substantive modifiers or which can be attached to either of these elements—for example, adjective-noun combinations, infinitives, gerunds, participles, modifiers of modifiers, appositives. Nevertheless, the basic formula is always the same: Preposition + Object (+ Modifiers).

2. FUNCTIONS OF THE PREPOSITIONAL PHRASE

The prepositional phrase usually performs the function of an adjective or an adverb:

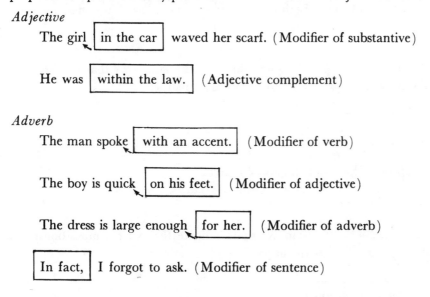

Adjective

The girl | in the car | waved her scarf. (Modifier of substantive)

He was | within the law. | (Adjective complement)

Adverb

The man spoke | with an accent. | (Modifier of verb)

The boy is quick | on his feet. | (Modifier of adjective)

The dress is large enough | for her. | (Modifier of adverb)

In fact, | I forgot to ask. (Modifier of sentence)

In some constructions a prepositional phrase functions as a substantive:

Substantive

Over the fence | is out. (Subject)

| In the library | is the best place to study. (Subject)

Note 1: In some sentences it is difficult to decide whether there is a prepositional phrase functioning as the object of a preposition or whether there is simply a two-word preposition:

> Example:
>
> The child crawled *from beneath the porch.*

Note 2: A prepositional phrase after the verb *to be* may sometimes be interpreted in either of two ways.

> Example:
>
> The woman was *on the steps.*

Here, if the verb *was* is interpreted as a linking verb, the prepositional phrase *on the steps* must be considered to be an adjective complement. However, if the verb *was* is interpreted as an intransitive verb (meaning *existed* or *was standing*), the prepositional phrase may be considered to be an adverbial construction modifying *was.* In some instances, only one interpretation is possible.

> Examples:
>
> He is *beyond help.*
> She was *at ease.*

These are clearly adjective complements.

Note 3: There is a very close connection between prepositions and adverbs. Many words can serve in either function. Note the way in which an adverb and an adverbial prepositional phrase perform the same function in the following examples:

> She came *up.*
> She came *up the hill.*
>
> He ran *across.*
> He ran *across the bridge.*

3. INDICATING THE PATTERN OF A SENTENCE CONTAINING A PREPOSITIONAL PHRASE

To indicate the pattern of a sentence containing a prepositional phrase, we shall use the following method:

(1) **We shall indicate the function of the prepositional phrase in the same way that we show the function of a single word. Nearly always, the prepositional phrase is a modifier.**

> Example:
>
> I saw a boy | with a red wagon.

Partial pattern: **Subject—Verb—Object—**MODIFIER

(2) **Then, in a box below the name of the function, we shall indicate the exact composition of the phrase, including modifiers of the preposition or the object.**

> Example:
>
> I saw a boy | with a red wagon.

Complete pattern: **Subject—Verb—Object—**MODIFIER

Prep.—Modifier—Object

Some additional examples of this method of notation follow:

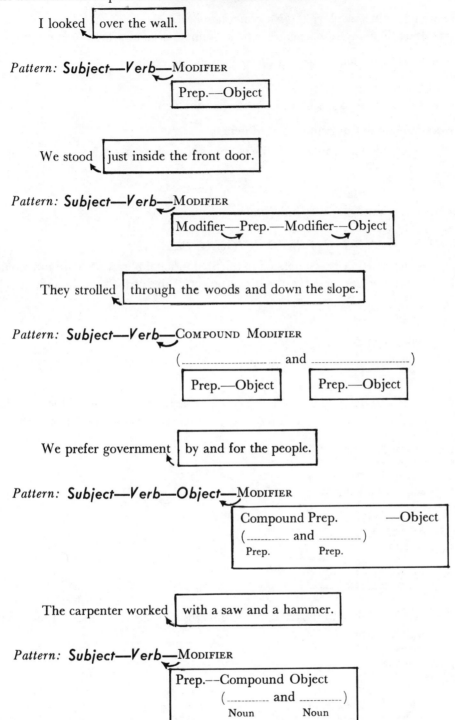

4. SOME SPECIAL NOTES ON THE PREPOSITIONAL PHRASE
a. *PUNCTUATION WITH PREPOSITIONAL PHRASES*

Most prepositional phrases are not set off by punctuation. Certain introductory prepositional phrases and prepositional phrases functioning as sentence modifiers are exceptions to this general rule.

(1) Introductory Prepositional Phrases

A short introductory prepositional phrase is not set off by punctuation unless there is danger of misreading the sentence. If the sentence might otherwise be misread, the introductory phrase is set off by comma punctuation.

Examples:

> On the porch a child was playing. (No punctuation)
> Across the street, lights were burning brightly. (Punctuation to prevent misreading)

Long introductory prepositional phrases are set off by comma punctuation.

Example:

> In spite of overwhelming opposition, he continued the fight.

(2) **Prepositional Phrases Functioning as Sentence Modifiers**

Prepositional phrases functioning as sentence modifiers are almost always set off by comma punctuation.

Examples:

> In short, the firm is bankrupt.
> Cats, on the other hand, are very independent.

b. *THE INDIRECT OBJECT AND THE PREPOSITIONAL PHRASE*

The *indirect object* is a construction closely related to the prepositional phrase. A word functioning as an indirect object is in the objective case and precedes the direct object of the verb. Note the indirect objects in the following sentences:

> They gave *me* a tie.
> She offered *the winner* a prize.
> He paid *them* the money.
> The carpenter made *us* a table.

All of these indirect objects—in fact, *all* indirect objects—can be restated as prepositional phrases based upon the preposition *to* or the preposition *for*. (Such phrases, however, will follow the object of the verb.)

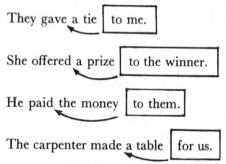

These prepositional phrases modify verbs and thus function as adverbs. Similarly, the indirect objects to which they are equivalent function as adverbs:

> They gave | (.to) me | a tie.
>
> The carpenter made | (for) us | a table.

In fact, the function of the indirect object may perhaps be best understood by considering it to be the object of the "understood" preposition *to* or *for*.

Note: Actually the indirect object did not develop through ellipsis of a prepositional phrase but is a survival of a dative case construction.

The following verbs are among those which may be accompanied by indirect objects: *give, grant, award, offer, allow, leave, furnish, present, pay, lend; hand, throw, pass, toss, bring, send; buy, sell, get; assign; prepare, make, cook, fix; read, tell, write, teach, sing.*

Since the indirect object is actually a verb modifier, we shall indicate it in a sentence pattern just as we do any other verb modifier, noting beneath the word "Modifier" that it is an indirect object:

Example:

    She baked me a cake.

Pattern: **Subject—Verb—**MODIFIER   **—Object**

                     (Indirect object)

Note: A construction somewhat similar to that involving the indirect object is that with the double object:

        I asked him a question.

        Pattern: **Subject—Verb—Object—Second Object**

    Here, the verb *asked* takes each of the substantives following it as a direct object. The meaning is that *I asked him* and *I asked a question.*

        Here are some additional examples:

I envy him his good luck.	She led me a merry chase.
He hit his opponent a sharp blow.	Forgive us our debts.

c. *PREPOSITIONAL PHRASE INDICATING THE AGENT IN A PASSIVE-VOICE SENTENCE*

    In a sentence with a passive-voice verb, a prepositional phrase based upon the preposition *by* is often used to indicate the agent (the performer of the action).

    Examples:

        He was hired *by the government.*
        She was struck *by a car.*

Pattern: **Subject—Passive Verb—**MODIFIER

                     | Prep.—Object |

    Note that when a sentence is changed from active to passive voice the *object* of the active verb becomes the *subject* of the passive verb and the *subject* of the active verb becomes the *object of the preposition.*

    Example:

        The *dog* licked the *child.* (Active)
        The *child* was licked by the *dog.* (Passive)

Note: When a sentence containing an indirect object is changed from the active to the passive, the normal procedure is to make the direct object the subject of the passive verb:

        He gave me a *gun.* (Active)
        A *gun* was given me by him. (Passive)

    However, the indirect object can also be shifted to become the subject of the passive verb:

        I was given the gun by him.

    In this sentence, the direct object *gun* is retained even though the passive verb cannot have an object. This unusual idiomatic construction is called a *retained object.*

d. *PHRASES WITHIN PHRASES*

    A prepositional phrase often performs a function within another prepositional phrase. The construction in which one prepositional phrase is the modifier of the object in another phrase is quite common.

    Examples:

    We threw the ball | over the top | of the house.

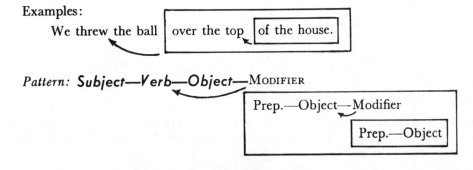

Pattern: **Subject—Verb—Object—**MODIFIER

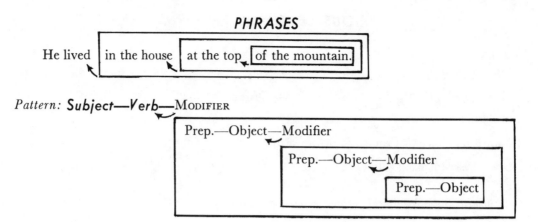

DO EXERCISES 29, 30, AND 31

C. GERUND PHRASES

1. FORM OF THE GERUND PHRASE

As has previously been pointed out, a verbal has some of the attributes of a verb. By virtue of its verb characteristics, a gerund can have an object, a complement, an adverbial modifier, or a combination of these elements.

Examples:

He denied having broken the *lamp*. (Object of gerund)
Being *rich* has advantages. (Complement of gerund)
Writing *well* requires much practice. (Adverbial modifier of gerund)

When a gerund has at least one of these elements, the word-group thus formed is called a *gerund phrase*.

A gerund phrase is a group of words consisting of a gerund, any element which completes its meaning (object or complement), and any adverbial elements which modify it.

$$\text{FORMULA: Gerund} + \begin{cases} \text{Object} \\ \text{Complement} \\ \text{Modifier} \end{cases}$$

Since various combinations of these elements can be made, there are five basic gerund phrase patterns:

1. Gerund—Object

   Raising pigeons is his only recreation.

2. Gerund—Complement

   Being healthy is very important.

3. Gerund—Adverbial Modifier

   He stressed the dangers of *driving rapidly*.

4. Gerund—Object—Adverbial Modifier

   Reading assignments carefully pays dividends.

5. Gerund—Complement—Adverbial Modifier

   Getting exhausted quickly may indicate lack of vitamins.

Note 1: Obviously, a gerund may have an adjective as a modifier of its substantive properties.

Example:

We desired *less* arguing.

However, such a modifier is not considered to be part of a gerund phrase. In other words, only those elements which are connected with the verb properties of the gerund are part of a gerund phrase.

Note 2: Only a verbal derived from a linking verb can have a complement. Of course, no verbal can have both a complement and an object.

In any of the above patterns, elements other than the gerund may have modifiers.

Examples:

Singing *old* songs is fun. (Modifier of object)
He admits having been a *poor* sport. (Modifier of complement)
Speaking *very* badly is a handicap. (Modifier of adverbial modifier)

In addition, the gerund phrase may contain practically any of the elements which we have considered previously—adjective-noun combinations, verb-adverb combinations (with the verb appearing as a gerund), infinitives, participles, gerunds (in addition to the gerund upon which the phrase is based), appositives, prepositional phrases, indirect objects. Furthermore, either the entire gerund phrase or any of the elements within it may be compound. Nevertheless, the framework of any gerund phrase will fit one of the basic gerund phrase patterns listed above.

2. FUNCTION OF THE GERUND PHRASE

Like the gerund, the gerund phrase is a substantive. It may perform practically any substantive function. (As with the prepositional phrase, it is helpful to draw a box around the gerund phrase to emphasize the fact that it functions as a unit.)

Examples:

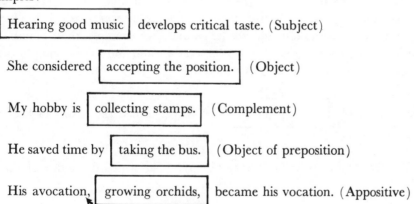

Hearing good music | develops critical taste. (Subject)

She considered | accepting the position. | (Object)

My hobby is | collecting stamps. | (Complement)

He saved time by | taking the bus. | (Object of preposition)

His avocation, | growing orchids, | became his vocation. (Appositive)

3. INDICATING THE PATTERN OF A SENTENCE CONTAINING A GERUND PHRASE

To indicate the pattern of a sentence containing a gerund phrase, we shall use the following method:

(1) **We shall show the function of the gerund phrase in the same way that we show the function of any other substantive.**

Example:

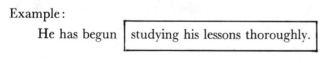

He has begun | studying his lessons thoroughly.

Partial pattern: **Subject—Verb—Object**

(2) **Then, in a box below the name of the function, we shall indicate the exact composition of the phrase, including all modifiers of elements making up the phrase.**

Example:

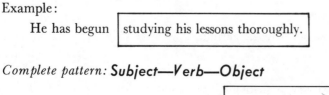

He has begun | studying his lessons thoroughly.

Complete pattern: **Subject—Verb—Object**

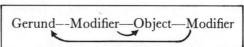

Gerund—Modifier—Object—Modifier

Some additional examples of this method of notation follow:

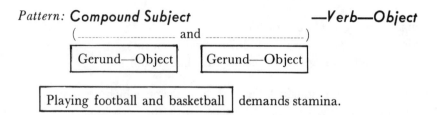

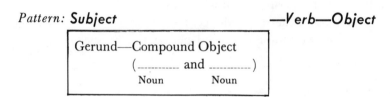

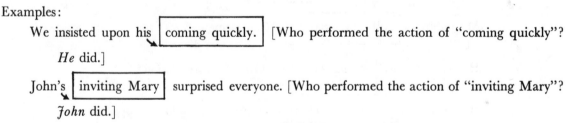

4. SOME SPECIAL NOTES ON THE GERUND PHRASE

a. *THE "SUBJECT IDEA" AND THE GERUND PHRASE*

We have seen that because of its verb characteristics the gerund can have an object, a complement, or an adverbial modifier. Can it have a subject? Strictly speaking, no. However, it is possible for there to be a person or thing which stands in a "subject relation" to the gerund. For example, there may be a person who performs the verb action indicated by the gerund. With both the gerund and the gerund phrase, such a "subject idea" can be expressed by a *possessive* serving as a modifier.

Examples:

We insisted upon his | coming quickly. | [Who performed the action of "coming quickly"?

He did.]

John's | inviting Mary | surprised everyone. [Who performed the action of "inviting Mary"?

John did.]

Note that in the last sentence *John* stands in a "subject relation" to *inviting* just as *Mary* stands in an "object relation." (Compare: *John invited Mary.*) *John* is the performer of the action; *Mary* is the receiver of the action.

In such a gerund phrase construction, the possessive modifies the entire gerund phrase and is not considered to be part of the phrase.

In writing sentences, the important thing to remember is that in many constructions the *possessive* is used to indicate the doer of the action expressed by a gerund:

Incorrect: She regretted *him* buying the house.
Correct: She regretted *his* buying the house.

If the possessive is not employed to indicate the doer of the action, the subject of the sentence often stands in a "subject relation" to the gerund.

Example:

She regretted buying the house.

Here, *she* is the performer of the action expressed by the gerund.

b. *PHRASES WITHIN PHRASES*

A gerund phrase may contain other phrases as elements functioning within it or may function as an element within another phrase.

Examples:

Prepositional Phrase Within a Gerund Phrase

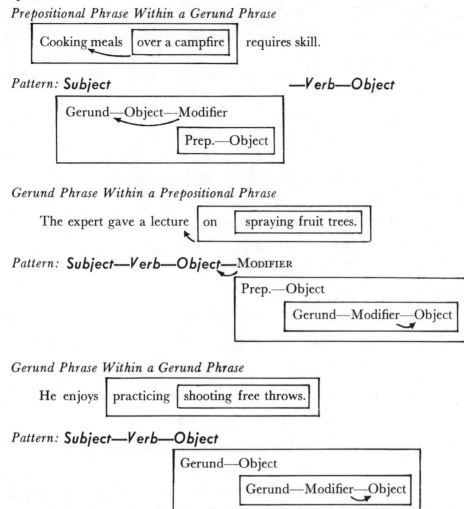

Gerund Phrase Within a Prepositional Phrase

The expert gave a lecture | on | spraying fruit trees.

Pattern: **Subject—Verb—Object**—Modifier

Gerund Phrase Within a Gerund Phrase

He enjoys | practicing | shooting free throws.

Pattern: **Subject—Verb—Object**

Note: In an adverbial prepositional phrase containing a gerund or gerund phrase as the object of the preposition, the gerund requires that the subject of the sentence be the performer of the action it expresses.

Example:

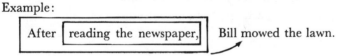

Note that *Bill* performed the action of *reading the newspaper.*

If a subject is used which does not logically serve as the "subject idea" of the gerund, the construction will be incorrect.

Incorrect: After eating breakfast, the sunrise was beautiful.

Note that the *sunrise* seems to have performed the action of *eating breakfast.* The sentence must be revised:

Correct: After eating breakfast, I watched a beautiful sunrise.

DO EXERCISE 32

D. PARTICIPIAL PHRASES

1. FORM OF THE PARTICIPIAL PHRASE

Like the gerund, a participle can have an object, a complement, an adverbial modifier, or a combination of these elements.

Examples:

Jack joined the boys playing *ball.* (Object of participle)

The teacher, feeling *ill,* left the room. (Complement of participle)
The girl standing *there* is my sister. (Modifier of participle)

When a participle has at least one of these elements, the word-group thus formed is called a *participial phrase.*

A participial phrase is a group of words consisting of a participle, any element which completes its meaning (object or complement), and any adverbial elements which modify it.

$$\text{FORMULA: Participle} + \begin{cases} \text{Object} \\ \text{Complement} \\ \text{Modifier} \end{cases}$$

Using these elements, we may form five basic participial phrase patterns:

1. Participle—Object

   The boy *waving the flag* is my nephew.

2. Participle—Complement

   His father, *becoming angry,* spanked him.

3. Participle—Modifier

   The plane *climbing vertically* is a jet fighter.

4. Modifier—Participle—Object

   The policeman, *quickly grasping the situation,* blocked the exit.

5. Modifier—Participle—Complement

   The titleholder, *suddenly growing careless,* lost the fight.

In a participial phrase, elements other than the participle may have modifiers.

Examples:

The crew digging the *irrigation* ditch is using a steam shovel. (Modifier of object)
The airplane, diving *very* low, dropped food. (Modifier of modifier)

Like the gerund phrase, the participial phrase may contain practically any of the elements we have studied, and either the entire participial phrase or any of its elements may be compound. Nevertheless, the framework of any participial phrase will fit one of the basic participial phrase patterns.

2. FUNCTION OF THE PARTICIPIAL PHRASE

Like the participle, the participial phrase functions as an adjective.

Examples:

The clown | juggling the hoops | amused the children.

A participial phrase may be either restrictive or non-restrictive.

Example:

Her cousin is the one | mowing the lawn. | (Restrictive)

Robert, | having delivered the package, | returned home. (Non-restrictive)

The same punctuation rules apply to participial phrases that apply to participles. (See p. 49.)

3. INDICATING THE PATTERN OF A SENTENCE CONTAINING A PARTICIPIAL PHRASE

To indicate the pattern of a sentence containing a participial phrase, we shall use the following method:

(1) **We shall show the function of the phrase by using the word "Modifier."**

    Example:

        Jane, | losing her temper, | smashed the mirror.

    Partial pattern: **Subject—**Modifier**—Verb—Object**

(2) **Next, if it is desired to show whether the participial phrase is restrictive or non-restrictive, we shall make a notation to this effect immediately below the word "Modifier." (This step may be omitted.)**

    Example:

        Jane, | losing her temper, | smashed the mirror.

    Partial pattern: **Subject—**Modifier   **—Verb—Object**
                  (Non-restrictive)

(3) **Finally, in a box below these notations, we shall indicate the exact composition of the phrase, including all modifiers of elements within the phrase.**

    Example:

        Jane, | losing her temper, | smashed the mirror.

    Complete pattern: **Subject—**Modifier   **—Verb—Object**
                (Non-restrictive)
                 | Participle—Modifier—Object |

Some additional examples of this method of notation follow:

    | Having blocked a punt, | the Wildcats recovered the ball.

    Pattern: Modifier   **—Subject—Verb—Object**
        (Non-restrictive)
        | Participle—Object |

    The player | shooting the ball | is the center.

    Pattern: **Subject—**Modifier   **—Linking Verb—Substantive Complement**
             (Restrictive)
          | Participle—Object |

    The band, | marching precisely and playing loudly, | entered the arena.

    Pattern: **Subject—**Compound Modifier   **—Verb—Object**
            (Non-restrictive)
         (_____ and _____)
        | Participle—Modifier | | Participle—Modifier |

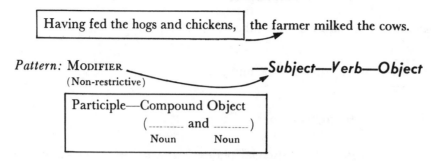

4. SOME SPECIAL NOTES ON THE PARTICIPIAL PHRASE

a. *THE "SUBJECT IDEA" AND THE PARTICIPIAL PHRASE*

We have seen that a "subject idea" may be expressed with a gerund. Similarly, a person or thing may stand in a "subject relation" to a participle. A person, for example, may perform the verb action indicated by the participle. In fact, such a "subject idea" is always present with a participle or participial phrase, for it is expressed by *the element modified by the participle or participial phrase.*

Examples:

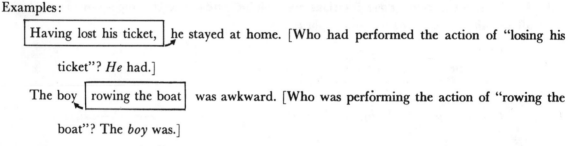

Note that in the last sentence *boy* stands in a "subject relation" to *rowing* just as *boat* stands in an "object relation." (Compare: *The boy rowed the boat.*) The *boy* is the performer of the action; the *boat* is the receiver of the action.

Note: At this point, it would be helpful to look back at the examples of participial phrases previously given and verify the fact that the element modified always stands in a "subject relation" to the participle.

Though the substantive modified by a participial phrase stands in a "subject relation" to the participle, it is *not* called the subject of the participle, and it is not considered to be part of the participial phrase.

Note: There is, however, one construction in which a substantive might with justification be considered to be the subject of a participial phrase since it has no other function in the sentence. This is the so-called "nominative absolute."

Example:

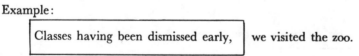

Here, *classes* has no function except that of expressing the "subject idea" of the participle. The entire construction, including the substantive *classes,* functions as a sentence modifier.

b. *"DANGLING" PARTICIPLES AND PARTICIPIAL PHRASES*

Since the participle or participial phrase should modify the substantive which performs the action indicated by it, in sentences containing these elements the performer of the action must be named and the participle or participial phrase must be near the substantive which it logically modifies. Otherwise the participle or participial phrase will be a "dangling" modifier:

"Dangling": Climbing the mountain, the town came into view.

Here, the performer of the action is not named. However, since every participle normally modifies a substantive which indicates the performer of the action, the participial phrase *climbing the mountain* attaches itself to the nearest substantive. Consequently, *the town* appears to be performing the action of *climbing the moun-*

tain. The obvious method of correction is to insert a word naming the performer of the action and to place the participial phrase near this word:

> *Correct:* Climbing the mountain, we saw the town come into view.

c. *SEQUENCE OF TENSES*

The principles governing sequence of tenses with participial phrases are the same as those which apply to participles alone. (See p. 49.)

d. *PHRASES WITHIN PHRASES*

A participial phrase may contain other phrases within it or may form part of another phrase.

Examples:

Prepositional Phrase Within a Participial Phrase

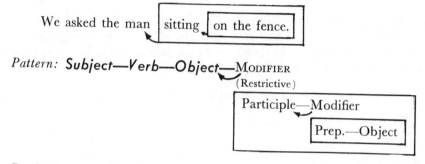

Participial Phrase Within a Prepositional Phrase

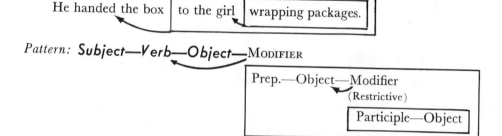

Participial Phrase Within a Gerund Phrase

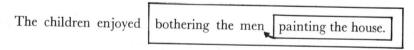

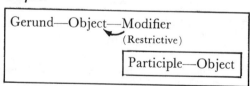

Note: For a further treatment of participles and participial phrases, see p. 289.

DO EXERCISE 33

E. INFINITIVE PHRASES

1. FORM OF THE INFINITIVE PHRASE

Like the other verbals, an infinitive can have an object, a complement, an adverbial modifier, or a combination of these elements.

Examples:

He expected to see *them*. (Object of infinitive)
The boy plans to be a *lawyer*. (Complement of infinitive)
To debate *well* was his goal. (Modifier of infinitive)

A word-group consisting of an infinitive and at least one of these elements is called an *infinitive phrase*.

An infinitive phrase is a group of words consisting of an infinitive, any element which completes its meaning (object or complement), and any adverbial elements which modify it.

$$\text{FORMULA: Infinitive} + \begin{cases} \text{Object} \\ \text{Complement} \\ \text{Modifier} \end{cases}$$

Note: As we shall see later, it is possible for an infinitive to have a subject of its own. An infinitive together with such a subject also constitutes an infinitive phrase, and any of the three other elements listed above may, of course, occur in a phrase of this sort in addition to the infinitive and its subject. For the time being, we shall confine our study to infinitive phrases which do not contain subjects.

These elements may be combined to form five basic infinitive phrase patterns:

1. Infinitive—Object

    She came *to see me*.

2. Infinitive—Complement

    He intends *to be rich*.

3. Infinitive—Modifier

    The child learned *to write plainly*.

4. Infinitive—Object—Modifier

    I was too sleepy *to study the essay carefully*.

5. Infinitive—Complement—Modifier

    The woman hopes *to become well soon*.

In any of these five patterns, elements other than the infinitive may have modifiers.

Examples:

I went to Kentucky to visit *my* parents. (Modifier of object)
She wanted to be a *good* driver. (Modifier of complement)
He liked to walk *rather* rapidly. (Modifier of modifier)

Like the other verbal phrases, the infinitive phrase may contain practically any of the elements we have studied, and either the entire infinitive phrase or any of its elements may be compound.

Note: In a compound infinitive phrase, "to" is often expressed only in the first phrase:
Example:
I plan *to* pull the weeds and water the flowers.

2. FUNCTIONS OF THE INFINITIVE PHRASE

Like the simple infinitive, the infinitive phrase may function as a substantive, an adjective, or an adverb.

Examples:

Substantive

To write the letter | required an entire hour. (Subject)

I want | to congratulate him. | (Object)

Nothing remained to do except | to wax the floor. | (Object of preposition)

The freshmen were told | to stand outside. | (Retained object)

His plan, | to attack at midnight, | seemed very unwise. (Appositive)

Adjective

That private has a good chance | to make corporal. |

Adverb

He wrote | to request a favor. | (Modifier of verb)

The pilot was afraid | to overload the plane. | (Modifier of adjective)

I was too busy | to attend the meeting. | (Modifier of adverb)

| To be frank, | you are very stupid. (Modifier of sentence)

3. INDICATING THE PATTERN OF A SENTENCE CONTAINING AN INFINITIVE PHRASE

To indicate the pattern of a sentence containing an infinitive phrase, we shall use the following method:

(1) **We shall first show the function of the infinitive phrase.**

Example:

I promised | to call him soon. |

Partial pattern: **Subject—Verb—Object**

(2) **Then, in a box below the name of the function, we shall indicate the exact composition of the phrase, including all modifiers of elements making up the phrase.**

Example:

I promised | to call him soon. |

Complete pattern: **Subject—Verb—Object**

Infinitive—Object—Modifier

Some additional examples of this method of notation follow:

He is the man | to write the article. |

Pattern: **Subject—Linking Verb—Substantive Complement**—MODIFIER

Infinitive—Object

She ran | to answer the telephone. |

Pattern: **Subject—Verb**—MODIFIER

Infinitive—Object

The landlord wanted | to repair the ceiling and the walls. |

Pattern: **Subject—Verb—Object**

> Infinitive—Compound Object
> (.......... and ....)
>   Noun   Noun

4. SOME SPECIAL NOTES ON THE INFINITIVE PHRASE

a. *THE "SUBJECT IDEA" AND THE INFINITIVE PHRASE*

The "subject idea" of an infinitive is usually expressed by some word standing outside the infinitive phrase—often by the subject of the sentence.

Examples:

We plan | to buy a house. | [Who will perform the action indicated by *to buy? We* **will.**]

They will run | to catch the bus. | [Who will perform the action indicated by *to catch? They* **will.**]

| To make good grades, | you must study. [Who will perform the action indicated by *to make? You* **will.**]

Note: In such a sentence as the last one, the subject of the sentence must constitute the "subject idea" of the infinitive. Otherwise, the construction will be incorrect. Compare the following sentences:

> *Incorrect:* To enjoy football, the rules must be known.
> *Correct:* To enjoy football, a person must know the rules.

Unlike the other verbals, the infinitive sometimes has its own subject contained within the verbal phrase.

Example:

I want | her to read the book. |

In this sentence *her* cannot be the object of *want*; the idea is not that "I want *her*." It is the subject of *to read,* since "she" is to perform the action indicated by *to read.* Consequently, we must consider it part of the infinitive phrase, which as a unit is the object of *want.*

Pattern: **Subject—Verb—Object**

> Subject—Infinitive—Object

Note that *her,* the subject of the infinitive, is the *objective-case* form of the personal pronoun *she.* The following rule is important:

> *The subject of an infinitive is always in the objective case.*

The construction in which the infinitive has a subject is a rather puzzling one because it is often difficult to determine whether a substantive preceding an infinitive is actually the subject of that infinitive. Let us examine some sentences:

> I consulted him to get advice.
> They wanted her to play the piano.
> She asked me to carry the basket.

At first glance, these sentences appear to have the same construction, but all are quite different. In the first sentence, *him* is definitely not the subject of *to get.* It is the object of *consulted,* and the infinitive phrase modifies *consulted:*

I consulted him | to get advice. |

In the second sentence the word *her* functions as the subject of the infinitive and performs no other function.

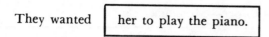

They wanted | her to play the piano. |

The following verbs are among those capable of having as an object an infinitive phrase containing such a subject: *want, desire, wish, expect; believe, think, know, suppose.*

Examples:

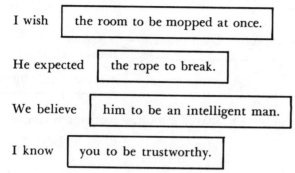

I wish | the room to be mopped at once. |

He expected | the rope to break. |

We believe | him to be an intelligent man. |

I know | you to be trustworthy. |

The last sentence is more difficult to analyze. It seems to mean that *she asked me* and what she asked was *that I carry the basket.* Thus, in the original sentence the word *me* apparently has a dual function: (1) as the direct object of the verb and (2) as the subject of an infinitive phrase which functions as a second object.

She asked [me] | me to carry the basket. |

      (Object)   (Second Object)

The word *me* indicates both the person to whom the request was directed and the person who is to perform the action. The same construction may occur with the following verbs: *request, order, tell,* and *teach.* Since the word preceding the infinitive does function as its subject, it is probably best to ignore its dual function and to consider this construction to be basically the same as that of the second sentence.

Often an infinitive phrase containing a subject comes immediately after the word *for.* In such instances, *for* may be either a preposition or an expletive.

In the following sentence, *for* is a preposition, and the infinitive phrase is the object of the preposition:

Preparations | for | us to arrive | were obviously incomplete.

However, the word *for* is often used as an expletive, or "filler-word," before an infinitive phrase containing a subject. In such a construction, *for* has no grammatical function in the sentence. An infinitive phrase introduced by the expletive *for* usually functions as a subject, a substantive complement, an object of a preposition, or a delayed subject.

Examples:

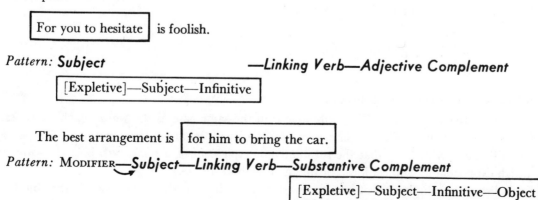

| For you to hesitate | is foolish.

Pattern: **Subject   —Linking Verb—Adjective Complement**
      [Expletive]—Subject—Infinitive

The best arrangement is | for him to bring the car. |
Pattern: Modifier—**Subject—Linking Verb—Substantive Complement**
                  [Expletive]—Subject—Infinitive—Object

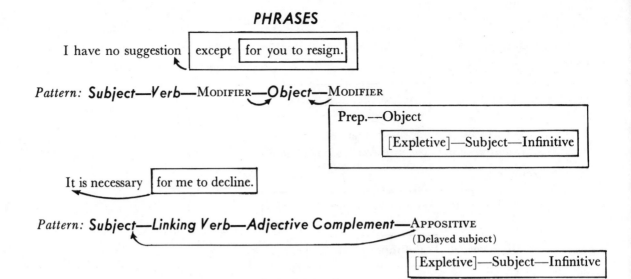

I have no suggestion   except   for you to resign.

Pattern: **Subject—Verb**—Modifier—**Object**—Modifier

Prep.——Object

[Expletive]—Subject—Infinitive

It is necessary   for me to decline.

Pattern: **Subject—Linking Verb—Adjective Complement**—Appositive
(Delayed subject)

[Expletive]—Subject—Infinitive

This last construction, with the infinitive phrase as a delayed subject, is particularly common in English.

b. *THE INFINITIVE WITHOUT "TO"*

After the verbs *let* and *make* and after verbs dealing with the senses (such as the verbs *see, hear,* and *feel*), the infinitive without *to* may be used in an infinitive phrase.

> Examples:
>
> > They let me *stay*. [*Compare:* They allowed me *to stay.*]
> > She made him *do* the work. [*Compare:* She forced him *to do* the work.]
> > I watched her *paint* the picture. [*Compare:* I wanted her *to paint* the picture.]

Note: Although this construction may be interpreted in other ways, we shall consider the substantive preceding the infinitive in the above sentences to be the subject of the infinitive:

I watched   her paint the picture.

Such an interpretation makes it clear that the objective case should be used for the substantives:

They saw   *him* and *me* break the window.

c. *USE OF CASE FORMS IN INFINITIVE PHRASES*

(1) **Subject of Infinitive**

The subject of an infinitive is in the objective case.

> Examples:
>
> > We expected *him* to notify us.
> > The club wanted *her* to be secretary.

(2) **Object of Infinitive**

The object of an infinitive is in the objective case.

> Examples:
>
> > She saw the bull charge *him*.
> > I planned to ask *them*.

(3) **Substantive Complement of Infinitive**

The substantive complement of an infinitive is in the same case as the word which expresses the "subject idea" of the infinitive. (This use of case is consistent with what we have previously learned about case forms with linking verbs. Note that the substantive complement of a finite verb is in the same case as the word which expresses the "subject idea" of the finite verb: *I am he.*)

The substantive complement of an infinitive which has its own subject is always in the objective case.

Example:

>She believed him to be *me*. [The "subject idea" of the infinitive is expressed by the subject of the infinitive, *him*, which is in the objective case. The substantive complement of the infinitive is therefore also in the objective case.]

The substantive complement of an infinitive which does not have its own subject may be in either the nominative case or the objective case, depending upon the case of the word which expresses the "subject idea" of the infinitive.

>Examples:

>>I would like to be *he*. [The "subject idea" of the infinitive is expressed by the word *I*, which is in the nominative case. The substantive complement of the infinitive is therefore also in the nominative case.]

>>We found a woman claiming to be *her*. [The "subject idea" of the infinitive is expressed by the word *woman*, which is in the objective case. The substantive complement of the infinitive is therefore also in the objective case.]

d. *USE OF INTERROGATIVE WORDS IN INFINITIVE PHRASES*

The interrogative pronouns *who, whom, which, what*, the interrogative adjectives *whose, which*, and *what*, and the interrogative adverbs *when, where, why*, and *how* can be used in infinitive phrases serving as substantives. They perform one of the usual functions within the phrase. However, the word-order of the infinitive phrase is shifted to allow these elements to come at the beginning of the phrase.

Examples:

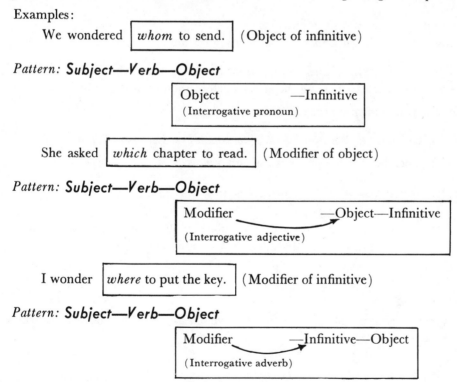

Note: Infinitive phrases of this sort are similar to noun clauses of indirect question and related clauses. Compare the following sentences:

>We wondered *whom to send*. (Infinitive phrase)
>We wondered *whom we should send*. (Noun clause)

>She asked *which chapter to read*. (Infinitive phrase)
>She asked *which chapter she should read*. (Noun clause)

>I wonder *where to put the key*. (Infinitive phrase)
>I wonder *where I should put the key*. (Noun clause)

The student should reconsider this similarity after studying the section on noun clauses in the next chapter.

When a phrase of this type is part of a question asked by the interrogative word within the phrase, the interrogative word is separated from the rest of the phrase to which it belongs.

Examples:

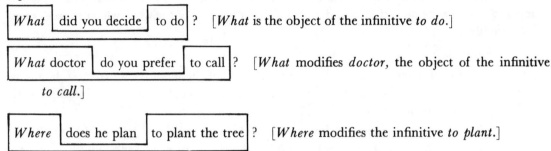

What did you decide to do ?   [*What* is the object of the infinitive *to do*.]

What doctor do you prefer to call ?   [*What* modifies *doctor*, the object of the infinitive *to call*.]

Where does he plan to plant the tree ?   [*Where* modifies the infinitive *to plant*.]

Note: This same separation of the interrogative word from the rest of its phrase takes place when the phrase is part of a noun clause of indirect question—*i.e.*, when such a direct question as those given above is turned into an indirect question. (See Note 3, p. 110.)

e. THE "SPLIT" INFINITIVE

A "split" infinitive is one which has an adverbial modifier between *to*, the "sign of the infinitive," and the infinitive itself.

Examples:

She resolved *to never split* an infinitive.
He promised *to always remember* the girl waiting for him.

Despite the traditional black-listing of this construction, there are times when it is acceptable. To illustrate, let us rearrange the last example by placing the adverb before the infinitive:

He promised *always* to remember the girl waiting for him.

Now it is uncertain whether *always* modifies *promised* or *to remember*. Let us try again:

He promised to remember the girl waiting for him *always*.

This sentence seems to mean that "the girl" was "always waiting for him." The "split" infinitive is preferable to such ambiguity.

However, the "split" infinitive is often awkward, particularly if the adverbial modifier consists of more than one word. On the whole, unless the only alternative is an ambiguous or stilted expression, it is advisable to avoid this construction.

f. SEQUENCE OF TENSES

The principles governing sequence of tenses with infinitive phrases are the same as those which apply to infinitives alone. (See p. 46.)

g. PUNCTUATION WITH INFINITIVE PHRASES

Infinitive phrases are punctuated in the same way as infinitives. (See p. 46.)

h. PHRASES WITHIN PHRASES

An infinitive phrase may contain other phrases within it or may function as a part of another phrase.

Examples:

Prepositional Phrase Within an Infinitive Phrase

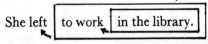

She left to work in the library.

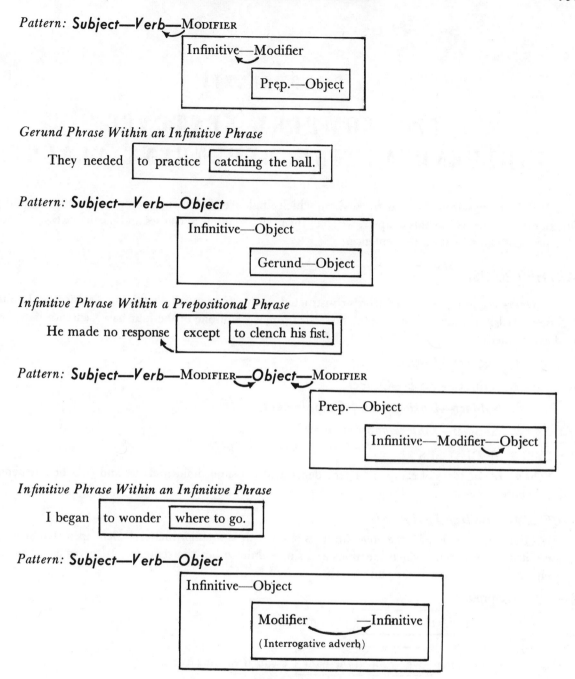

Pattern: **Subject—Verb—**MODIFIER

Infinitive—Modifier

Prep.—Object

Gerund Phrase Within an Infinitive Phrase

They needed | to practice | catching the ball.

Pattern: **Subject—Verb—Object**

Infinitive—Object

Gerund—Object

Infinitive Phrase Within a Prepositional Phrase

He made no response | except | to clench his fist.

Pattern: **Subject—Verb—**MODIFIER**—Object—**MODIFIER

Prep.—Object

Infinitive—Modifier—Object

Infinitive Phrase Within an Infinitive Phrase

I began | to wonder | where to go.

Pattern: **Subject—Verb—Object**

Infinitive—Object

Modifier —Infinitive

(Interrogative adverb)

DO EXERCISES 34 AND 35

CHAPTER XIV

THE COMPLEX SENTENCE:
INDEPENDENT AND DEPENDENT CLAUSES

WE have considered thus far the ways in which single-word elements, compound elements, and phrases function in a sentence. In this chapter, we shall turn our attention to clauses and particularly to the functions of dependent clauses within the sentence.

A. THE CLAUSE

A *clause* is a group of related words constructed upon a framework containing a subject and finite verb.[1] In other words, the clause is a unit built about the framework of one of the four basic sentence patterns which we have studied:

1. **Subject—Verb**
2. **Subject—Verb—Object**
3. **Subject—Linking Verb—Complement**
4. **Subject—Compound Predicate**

1. TYPES OF CLAUSES

There are two types of clauses: (a) the dependent (or subordinate) clause and (b) the independent (or main) clause.

a. THE DEPENDENT CLAUSE

As the name implies, a *dependent clause* is one which is a subordinate element in a sentence. Like the phrase, it is a word-group which functions as a single unit within the sentence. It serves as a single part of speech—a noun, an adjective, or an adverb.

Examples:

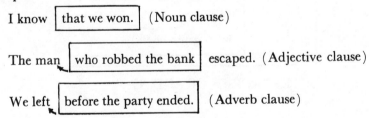

I know | that we won. | (Noun clause)

The man | who robbed the bank | escaped. (Adjective clause)

We left | before the party ended. | (Adverb clause)

b. THE INDEPENDENT CLAUSE

An *independent clause* is one which *does not* function as a subordinate element in a sentence. It does not serve as a single part of speech. All of the sentences which we have studied thus far may therefore be classified as independent clauses. Each of the following sentences consists of a single independent clause:

He was walking very slowly.
The movers lifted the packing crate carefully.
That man is guilty.
We bought tickets and attended the game.

[1] A *finite* verb is one which is capable of serving as a main verb in one of the basic sentence patterns. As we have already noted, verbals are not finite verbs.

Note: A sentence, as we shall see in the next chapter, may contain more than one independent clause, but no independent clause ever functions as a *subordinate* part of a sentence.

2. INDEPENDENT CLAUSES, DEPENDENT CLAUSES, AND PHRASES COMPARED

The independent clause and the dependent clause are alike in having a subject and a finite verb. The dependent clause and the phrase are alike in functioning as a single part of speech. The independent clause and the dependent clause differ in the fact that the independent clause does not function as a single part of speech. The dependent clause and the phrase differ in the fact that the phrase does not contain a subject and a finite verb. The following chart may help to make these various relationships clear:

Independent Clause	Has subject and finite verb	
Dependent Clause	Has subject and finite verb	Functions as a single part of speech
Phrase		Functions as a single part of speech

B. SIMPLE AND COMPLEX SENTENCES

Classified according to the number and the types of clauses which they contain, there are four kinds of sentences: (1) simple, (2) complex, (3) compound, and (4) compound-complex. In this section we shall deal with the first two kinds.

A *simple* sentence is one which consists of a single independent clause. It may contain any number of single-word elements, compound elements, and phrases, but it does not contain any dependent clauses. All of the sentences treated in the first thirteen chapters of this text were *simple* sentences.

A *complex* sentence is one which consists of one independent clause containing one or more dependent clauses. Since each dependent clause performs the function of a single part of speech within the independent clause, the complex sentence actually does not differ very much from the simple sentence in structure and does not offer anything new in over-all sentence pattern. Each complex sentence has a framework which matches one of the four basic sentence patterns; the dependent clause, acting as a unit, simply fits into the pattern in the same way that a single-word element, a compound element, or a phrase would do. The dependent clause does not have any new function; it is merely a word-group which performs one of the functions we have already studied—either a substantive function or a modifying function.

Examples:

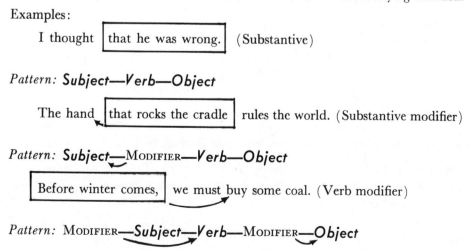

I thought | that he was wrong. | (Substantive)

Pattern: **Subject—Verb—Object**

The hand | that rocks the cradle | rules the world. (Substantive modifier)

Pattern: **Subject**—Modifier—**Verb—Object**

| Before winter comes, | we must buy some coal. (Verb modifier)

Pattern: Modifier—**Subject—Verb**—Modifier—**Object**

Note: As we study the various types of dependent clauses, we shall learn to indicate the patterns of complex sentences in complete detail.

C. THE SUBORDINATING CONJUNCTION

Since a large number of dependent clauses contain subordinating conjunctions, it is desirable to consider this element before we go further.

Like the preposition and the coordinating conjunction, the subordinating conjunction performs a *connecting* function. A subordinating conjunction connects its dependent clause with another element and shows at the same time the relationship between them.

Examples:

The boy whistled *because* he was afraid. [The subordinating conjunction *because* connects the dependent clause *he was afraid* with the verb *whistled* and shows the causal relationship which exists between them.]

The dog will come *if* you call him. [The subordinating conjunction *if* connects the dependent clause *you call him* with the verb *will come* and shows the conditional relationship which exists between them.]

The subordinating conjunction is considered to be a part of the dependent clause although a pure subordinating conjunction does not perform any grammatical function *within* the dependent clause. In dealing with the function of the entire dependent clause as a unit, we shall always include the subordinating conjunction if one is present.

Examples:

The boy whistled │ because he was afraid. │ [The entire dependent clause, including *because*, functions as an adverb.]

The dog will come │ if you call him. │ [The entire dependent clause, including *if*, functions as an adverb.]

Note:　There is a very close similarity between prepositions and subordinating conjunctions. A preposition performs a connecting and relating function for the substantive which is its object. (See p. 79.) A subordinating conjunction performs the same sort of function for a dependent clause. Examine the following sentences:

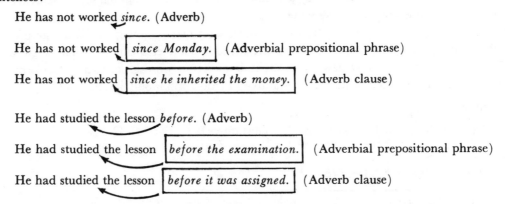

He has not worked *since*. (Adverb)

He has not worked │ *since Monday.* │ (Adverbial prepositional phrase)

He has not worked │ *since he inherited the money.* │ (Adverb clause)

He had studied the lesson *before*. (Adverb)

He had studied the lesson │ *before the examination.* │ (Adverbial prepositional phrase)

He had studied the lesson │ *before it was assigned.* │ (Adverb clause)

Note that *since* and *before* may function either as prepositions or as subordinating conjunctions. Note also the similarity of the various adverbial modifiers. (See Note. 3, p. 82.)

The subordinating conjunction is a final addition to the list of parts of speech which we have gradually accumulated. The basic grammatical functions performed within the sentence and the parts of speech which perform them may be summarized as follows:

Functions	*Parts of Speech*
1. The substantive function	{ 1. Noun { 2. Pronoun
2. The verb function	3. Verb

Functions		*Parts of Speech*
3. The modifying function	{	4. Adjective
		5. Adverb
4. The connecting function	{	6. Preposition
		7. Conjunction { Coordinating / Subordinating

It will be noted that the *interjection,* the eighth part of speech, is not included in this list; it is an independent element and hence does not perform a grammatical function within the sentence.

D. TYPES OF DEPENDENT CLAUSES

Dependent clauses may be divided according to function into three types: (1) the noun clause, (2) the adjective clause, and (3) the adverb clause.

1. THE NOUN CLAUSE

A *noun clause* is a dependent clause which functions as a substantive.

a. FORM OF THE NOUN CLAUSE

A noun clause is usually either a direct quotation or a clause introduced by a subordinating conjunction, an interrogative word, or an indefinite relative.

Examples:

The farmer said, *"We need rain."* (Direct quotation)

She promised *that she would tell him.* (Clause introduced by subordinating conjunction *that*)

I wonder *how he fixed the car.* (Clause introduced by interrogative word *how.*)

He will take *whoever wishes to go.* (Clause introduced by indefinite relative pronoun *whoever.*)

b. FUNCTION OF THE NOUN CLAUSE

The noun clause performs a substantive function.

Examples:

That he would be elected was obvious. (Subject)

I know *that you will be happy.* (Object)

My reason for going is *that my mother is ill.* (Complement)

The fact *that he is very old* must be considered. (Appositive)

I learned nothing except *what he told me.* (Object of preposition)

They will give *whoever wins the contest* a medal. (Indirect object)

He was told *that you dislike him.* (Retained object)

Determining *what he believes* is difficult. (Object of gerund)

My father, knowing *when I would arrive,* met me at the station. (Object of participle)

I want you to remember *how I worked the problem.* (Object of infinitive)

c. TYPES OF NOUN CLAUSES

(1) Noun Clauses of Direct Quotation

Probably the simplest noun clause is that which consists of the direct quotation of a sentence. There is, of course, no introductory word with such a noun clause.

(a) Types of Direct Quotations

The direct quotation may be declarative, imperative, exclamatory, or interrogative.

i. *Declarative*

A direct quotation of a declarative statement is usually the object of a verb of *saying, thinking, replying, observing, etc.*

Examples:

>He said, "The parade has begun."
>"He will come," she thought.

ii. Imperative

A direct quotation of an imperative statement is usually the object of a verb of *saying, requesting, ordering, commanding, etc.*

Examples:

>John demanded, "Give me the book."
>"Tell me a story," she requested.

iii. Exclamatory

A direct quotation of an exclamatory statement is usually the object of a verb of *exclaiming, crying, shouting, etc.*

Examples:

>He exclaimed, "The dam has broken!"
>"I've been hit!" he cried.

iv. Interrogative

A direct quotation of a question is usually the object of a verb of *asking, inquiring, etc.*

Examples:

>She asked, "Why did he go?"
>"Did you read the paper?" George inquired.

Note: It is only when a direct quotation consists of a single complete sentence and functions as a substantive in a clause that it can properly be considered a noun clause.

>Example:
>
>She said, "I am afraid of mice."

If a direct quotation used with a verb of *saying, etc.,* consists of more than one sentence, the entire quotation serves as the object of the verb. However, it cannot be considered a noun clause, though it functions in much the same way.

>Example:
>
>She said, "I am afraid of mice. They give me the creeps."

If the direct quotation in such a construction is not a complete sentence, it also serves as the object of the verb but is not a noun clause.

>Example:
>
>She replied, "No."

If the direct quotation stands by itself (as it often does in dialogue), it is an independent clause—not a noun clause.

>Examples:
>
>"I hate bugs."
>"I am afraid of mice."

(b) Punctuation of Noun Clauses of Direct Quotation

Noun clauses of direct quotation are punctuated as indicated by the following examples:

Direct quotation of declarative or imperative statement

>He said, "The first game of the season will show our strength."
>"The first game of the season will show our strength," he said.
>"The first game of the season," he said, "will show our strength."

Punctuation patterns:

He said, "_____."
"_____," he said.
"_____," he said, "_____."

Direct quotation of exclamatory statement

He cried, "The time for revenge has finally come!"
"The time for revenge has finally come!" he cried.
"The time for revenge," he cried, "has finally come!"

Punctuation patterns:

He cried, "_____!"
"_____!" he cried.
"_____," he cried, "_____!"

Direct quotation of question

He asked, "Why did you do that?"
"Why did you do that?" he asked.
"Why," he asked, "did you do that?"

Punctuation patterns:

He asked, "_____?"
"_____?" he asked.
"_____," he asked, "_____?"

Note: See p. 281 for rules applying to punctuation of direct quotations.

(2) Noun Clauses of Indirect Statement and Related "That"-Clauses

(a) Clauses of Indirect Statement

A noun clause which *indirectly* quotes a declarative, imperative, or exclamatory statement is usually introduced by the subordinating conjunction *that*. Such a clause usually does not give the exact words of the original statement, and it is not set off by quotation marks or comma punctuation.

Examples:

She thought *that he would come.* [*Compare:* She thought, "He will come."]
He cried *that he had been hit.* [*Compare:* He cried, "I've been hit!"]
She requested *that he tell her a story.* [*Compare:* She requested, "Tell me a story."]

(b) Related *That*-Clauses

Some *that*-clauses cannot be classified as clauses of indirect statement, although they are identical with these clauses in form.

Examples:

That he would come seemed probable.
I saw *that he had been hit.*
It was necessary *that he tell her a story.*

Note that in these sentences a restatement of the clause as a direct quotation cannot be substituted for the *that*-clause.

(c) The Subordinating Conjunction *that*

In such sentences as those given above, the subordinating conjunction *that* serves as an introductory connective linking the noun clause with the rest of the sentence. It also serves as a sort of signpost indicating the subordinate nature of the noun clause which it introduces.

Note: The connecting and subordinating functions of the subordinating conjunction *that* introducing a noun clause are neither as distinct nor as important as those of subordinating conjunctions introducing adverb clauses. (See p. 134.) In fact, *that* is often omitted in such constructions.

Examples:
He said (that) he had written a letter.
I realized (that) he was mistaken.

(3) Noun Clauses of Indirect Question and Related Clauses

(a) Clauses of Indirect Question

A noun clause may indirectly quote a question. Such a clause usually does not give the exact words of the original question. It is not set off by quotation marks or comma punctuation, nor is a question mark used after it. Note the following sentences:

I asked, *"Has John finished his work?"* (Direct question)
I asked *whether John had finished his work.* (Indirect question)

He wondered, *"How will I do it?"* (Direct question)
He wondered *how he would do it.* (Indirect question)

In order to understand the types of indirect questions, we must first review the types of direct questions from which they are derived. There are, as we have previously seen, two types of direct questions:

(1) **Those which ask questions by means of tone of voice or inverted word-order. (Such questions may be answered with "yes" or "no.")**

Examples:
He painted the table?
Has she swept the floor?

(2) **Those which ask questions by means of an interrogative word—an interrogative pronoun, adjective, or adverb. (These questions cannot be answered by "yes" or "no.")**

Examples:
Who trimmed the hedge? (Interrogative pronoun)
Which player won the trophy? (Interrogative adjective)
When did you see him? (Interrogative adverb)

These two types of direct questions produce two different types of indirect questions: (1) indirect questions introduced by *whether* or *if*, and (2) indirect questions introduced by interrogative words.

i. Indirect Questions Introduced by "whether" or "if"

A direct question which is asked by means of tone of voice or inverted word-order becomes an indirect question introduced by the subordinating conjunction *whether* or *if*.

Examples:
"You know the answer?" he asked. (Direct question)
He asked whether I knew the answer. (Indirect question)

She wondered, "Will he come?" (Direct question)
She wondered whether he would come. (Indirect question)

I asked, "Has he returned the book?" (Direct question)
I asked if he had returned the book. (Indirect question)

Note: Some grammarians object to the use of *if* to introduce an indirect question and insist upon the substitution of *whether* for *if*.

In such indirect questions the subordinating conjunction *whether* or *if* is an introductory connective linking the noun clause with the rest of the sentence. It also serves as a signpost indicating that a noun clause of indirect question follows.

Note 1: Since the subordinating conjunction in this construction is a distinctive sign of this type of indirect question, it is never omitted.

Note 2: Do not use *where* instead of *whether* to introduce an indirect question of the type just studied. This error is particularly common in speaking.

ii. Indirect Questions Introduced by Interrogative Words

A direct question which is asked by means of an interrogative word becomes an indirect question introduced by the same interrogative word.

All of the interrogative words used in direct questions are also used in indirect questions:

1. The interrogative pronouns *who* (*whom*), *which*, *what*
2. The interrogative adjectives *whose*, *which*, *what*
3. The interrogative adverbs *when*, *where*, *why*, *how*

Examples:

Interrogative pronouns

She asked, "*Who* has read the lesson?" (Direct question)
She asked *who* had read the lesson. (Indirect question)

I wondered, "For *whom* is she looking?" (Direct question)
I wondered for *whom* she was looking. (Indirect question)

He asked, "*Which* is correct?" (Direct question)
He asked *which* was correct. (Indirect question)

They wondered, "*What* will be done?" (Direct question)
They wondered *what* would be done. (Indirect question)

Interrogative adjectives

We asked, "*Whose* baby is crying?" (Direct question)
We asked *whose* baby was crying. (Indirect question)

The student wondered, "*Which* questions will the teacher ask?" (Direct question)
The student wondered *which* questions the teacher would ask. (Indirect question)

He asked, "*What* clothing should I take?" (Direct question)
He asked *what* clothing he should take. (Indirect question)

Interrogative adverbs

She wondered, "*When* will the concert start?" (Direct question)
She wondered *when* the concert would start. (Indirect question)

The lawyer asked, "*Where* is the agreement?" (Direct question)
The lawyer asked *where* the agreement was. (Indirect question)

They wondered, "*Why* has he returned?" (Direct question)
They wondered *why* he had returned. (Indirect question)

I asked, "*How* will I do it?" (Direct question)
I asked *how* I would do it. (Indirect question)

Note 1: In all of these sentences, the noun clause is the object of the verb of *asking* or *wondering*. It may be helpful to draw a box around the dependent clause to emphasize the fact that it functions as a unit.

Examples:

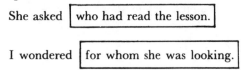

She asked | who had read the lesson.

I wondered | for whom she was looking.

Note 2: In the indirect question as in the direct question, the case of the interrogative pronoun depends upon its function. It is *not* the function of the noun clause but the function of the interrogative pronoun *within* the noun clause that determines the case form.

Examples:

I asked *who* saw him. (Subject of noun clause)
I asked *whom* he saw. (Object of noun clause)

In both of these examples the noun clause is the object of *asked*. Note that the function of the noun clause has nothing to do with the case of the interrogative pronoun.

Note 3: The interrogative word may be part of an infinitive phrase within the indirect question. Note the following sentences:

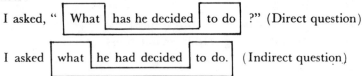

I asked, " | What | has he decided | to do | ?" (Direct question)

I asked | what | he had decided | to do. | (Indirect question)

The interrogative pronoun *what* is the object of the infinitive *to do* in both sentences. Note that it is separated from the rest of the phrase to which it belongs. (See p. 100.)

In an indirect question introduced by an interrogative word, the interrogative word has a dual function: (1) it is an introductory connective linking the noun clause with the rest of the sentence, and (2) it performs a grammatical function within its own clause. The interrogative pronoun functions within its own clause as a substantive; the interrogative adjective, as a modifier of a substantive; and the interrogative adverb, as a modifier of a verb or another modifier.

(b) Related Clauses

We have already seen that there are *that*-clauses which are not clauses of indirect statement. Similarly, there are certain noun clauses which are closely related to clauses of indirect question but which do not actually constitute indirect statements of questions.

These clauses may be introduced by the following words:

1. The subordinating conjunction *whether* (not *if*)
2. The indefinite relative pronouns *who* (*whom*), *which, what, whoever* (*whomever*), *whichever, whatever*
3. The indefinite relative adjectives *whose, which, what, whichever, whatever*
4. The indefinite relative adverbs *when, where, why, how*

The terminology of the last three groups should give no difficulty. Since the clauses introduced by these words are not questions, the introductory words are called *indefinite relatives* instead of *interrogative words*. In form and function the indefinite relatives are practically identical with the interrogative words.

Examples:

Whether I could go | was doubtful. (Subordinating conjunction)

I know | *who* borrowed the book. | (Indefinite relative pronoun)

| *Whoever* broke the window | should pay for it. (Indefinite relative pronoun)

It is uncertain | *which* car he will buy. | (Indefinite relative adjective)

| *Why* she changed her mind | is a mystery. (Indefinite relative adverb)

Note that a restatement of the clause as a direct question cannot be substituted for the noun clause in any of these sentences. It is this fact that distinguishes these noun clauses from noun clauses of indirect question and that makes it necessary to call the introductory word an "indefinite relative" instead of an "interrogative" word.

Note: The student should note that *because* is not among the words which may introduce a noun clause. A clause beginning with *because* should function as an adverb.

Incorrect: The reason was *because* he was sick.
Correct: The reason was *that* he was sick.

d. *INDICATING THE PATTERN OF A SENTENCE CONTAINING A NOUN CLAUSE*

To indicate the pattern of a sentence containing a noun clause, we shall use the following method:

(1) **We shall show the function of the noun clause in the same way that we show the function of any other substantive.**

Example:

We thought | that he had the key. |

Partial pattern: **Subject—Verb—Object**

(2) **Then, in a box below the name of the function, we shall indicate the exact composition of the noun clause. We shall use the abbreviation "Sub. Conj." as a notation for the subordinating conjunction.**

Example:

We thought | that he had the key. |

Complete pattern: **Subject—Verb—Object**

Sub. Conj.—*Subject—Verb—Object*

Note: In indicating the pattern of a noun clause of direct quotation, it may be desirable to use the notation "Direct quotation" beneath the word indicating the function of the noun clause. See the examples below.

Some additional examples of this method of notation follow:

She said, | "I need a new hat." |

Pattern: **Subject—Verb—Object**
(Direct quotation)

*Subject—Verb—*Modifier—*Object*

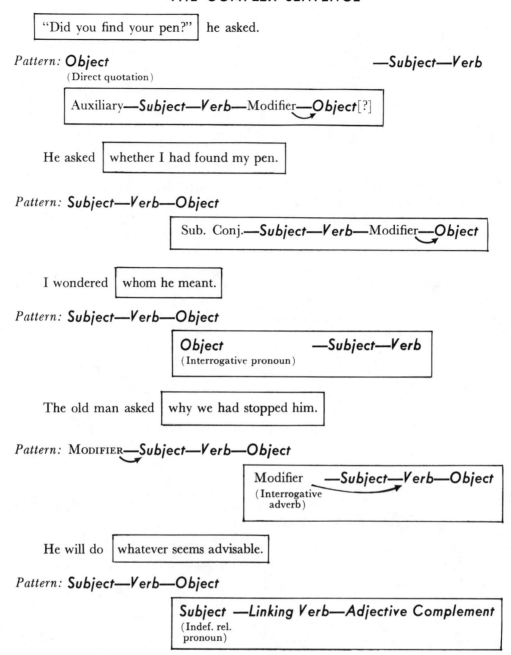

"Did you find your pen?" | he asked.

Pattern: **Object**   —*Subject*—*Verb*
(Direct quotation)

Auxiliary—*Subject*—*Verb*—Modifier—*Object*[?]

He asked | whether I had found my pen.

Pattern: **Subject—Verb—Object**

Sub. Conj.—*Subject*—*Verb*—Modifier—*Object*

I wondered | whom he meant.

Pattern: **Subject—Verb—Object**

Object   —*Subject*—*Verb*
(Interrogative pronoun)

The old man asked | why we had stopped him.

Pattern: MODIFIER—*Subject*—*Verb*—*Object*

Modifier   —*Subject*—*Verb*—*Object*
(Interrogative adverb)

He will do | whatever seems advisable.

Pattern: **Subject—Verb—Object**

Subject —*Linking Verb*—*Adjective Complement*
(Indef. rel. pronoun)

Note: It may be profitable to review the method of notation used with questions and exclamatory sentences, since many of the points touched upon there apply to noun clauses as well. (See pp. 76–77.)

e. *SOME SPECIAL NOTES ON THE NOUN CLAUSE*

(1) Use of the Subjunctive in Noun Clauses

We have already noted that the *subjunctive mode* is used when the speaker looks upon a statement as expressing unreality, doubt, uncertainty, desire, possibility, or probability rather than fact. (See p. 19.) We shall now consider the forms of the subjunctive and its use in noun clauses.

(a) The Forms of the Subjunctive

The forms of the indicative have gradually replaced the distinctive forms of the subjunctive. Consequently, there are now relatively few subjunctive forms which differ from the corresponding indicative forms. In the conjugations which follow, the distinctive forms of the subjunctive are italicized. (Note that the subjunctive does not have future or future perfect tenses.)

i. The Verb "to be"

The verb *to be* retains a larger number of distinctive subjunctive forms than any other verb. Since these forms are carried over into the conjugation of other verbs when *to be* is used as an auxiliary, *to be* is by far the most important verb to be considered in connection with the subjunctive mode.

Subjunctive Mode
Active Voice

Singular   Plural

Present Tense

[that] I *be*	[that] we *be*
[that] you *be*	[that] you *be*
[that] he *be*	[that] they *be*

Past Tense

[that] I *were*	[that] we were
[that] you were	[that] you were
[that] he *were*	[that] they were

Present Perfect Tense

[that] I have been	[that] we have been
[that] you have been	[that] you have been
[that] he has been	[that] they have been

Past Perfect Tense

[that] I had been	[that] we had been
[that] you had been	[that] you had been
[that] he had been	[that] they had been

Note: The word *that* is inserted in brackets throughout the conjugation in order to give each form a subjunctive flavor.

ii. The Verb "to have"

The only important distinctive subjunctive form of the verb *to have* is the third person singular of the present tense.

Subjunctive Mode
Active Voice

Singular   Plural

Present Tense

[that] I have	[that] we have
[that] you have	[that] you have
[that] he *have*	[that] they have

Past Tense

[that] I had	[that] we had
[that] you had	[that] you had
[that] he had	[that] they had

Present Perfect Tense

[that] I have had	[that] we have had
[that] you have had	[that] you have had
[that] he has had	[that] they have had

Past Perfect Tense

[that]	I	had had
[that]	you	had had
[that]	he	had had

[that]	we	had had
[that]	you	had had
[that]	they	had had

iii. Other Verbs

Verbs other than *to be* and *to have* have a distinctive subjunctive form in the third person singular of the present tense. Otherwise, their only distinctive subjunctive forms are those involving use of *to be* and *to have* as auxiliaries. The verb *to love* may serve as a typical example:

Subjunctive Mode
Active Voice

Singular   Plural

Present Tense

[that]	I	love
[that]	you	love
[that]	he	*love*

[that]	we	love
[that]	you	love
[that]	they	love

Past Tense

[that]	I	loved
[that]	you	loved
[that]	he	loved

[that]	we	loved
[that]	you	loved
[that]	they	loved

Present Perfect Tense

[that]	I	have loved
[that]	you	have loved
[that]	he	has loved

[that]	we	have loved
[that]	you	have loved
[that]	they	have loved

Past Perfect Tense

[that]	I	had loved
[that]	you	had loved
[that]	he	had loved

[that]	we	had loved
[that]	you	had loved
[that]	they	had loved

Passive Voice

Singular   Plural

Present Tense

[that]	I	*be loved*
[that]	you	*be loved*
[that]	he	*be loved*

[that]	we	*be loved*
[that]	you	*be loved*
[that]	they	*be loved*

Past Tense

[that]	I	*were loved*
[that]	you	were loved
[that]	he	*were loved*

[that]	we	were loved
[that]	you	were loved
[that]	they	were loved

Present Perfect Tense

[that]	I	have been loved
[that]	you	have been loved
[that]	he	has been loved

[that]	we	have been loved
[that]	you	have been loved
[that]	they	have been loved

Past Perfect Tense

[that]	I	had been loved
[that]	you	had been loved
[that]	he	had been loved

[that]	we	had been loved
[that]	you	had been loved
[that]	they	had been loved

(b) The Subjunctive in Indirect Imperative Statements and Related Noun Clauses

The present subjunctive is used in the indirect statement of an imperative sentence. Often the indirect statement is in the passive voice.

Examples:

"Face the wall," the robber demanded.
The robber demanded that he *face* the wall. (Present active subjunctive)

The captain ordered, "Destroy the maps."
The captain ordered that the maps *be destroyed*. (Present passive subjunctive)

The present subjunctive is also used in *that*-clauses closely related to the indirect imperative. Note that in the following sentences the noun clause cannot be changed to a direct quotation:

It is desirable that he *be* present.
That he *be notified* is of the utmost importance.
I moved that the president *appoint* the committee.

(c) The Subjunctive in Noun Clauses Expressing Wishes

The past subjunctive and the past perfect subjunctive are used in noun clauses expressing wishes which are contrary to fact.

Examples:

I wish that she *were* here. (Past subjunctive)
He wishes that he *had been* more industrious. (Past perfect subjunctive)

(d) An Additional Note on the Subjunctive

Other methods of expression are often substituted for the subjunctive. For instance, an infinitive phrase, a potential verb phrase, or a future verb showing determination may be used instead of the subjunctive construction which we have been considering. Compare the following examples:

I requested that he *give* a speech. (Subjunctive)
I requested *him to give a speech*. (Infinitive phrase)

He intended that the committee *be consulted*. (Subjunctive)
He intended that the committee *should be consulted*. (Potential verb phrase)

We insist that she *be invited*. (Subjunctive)
We insist that she *shall be invited*. (Future verb showing determination)

(2) **Sequence of Tenses in Sentences Containing Noun Clauses**

In a sentence containing a dependent clause, the tense of the verb in the dependent clause is determined by the relationship of two or all three of the following factors: (a) the time of the speaking or writing of the sentence, (b) the time of the action of the verb in the dependent clause, and (c) the time of the action of the verb in the independent clause. The relationship between the tense of the verb in the dependent clause and the tense of the verb in the independent clause is called *sequence of tenses*. In this section, we shall consider the proper *sequence of tenses* in sentences containing noun clauses of indirect statement and related clauses and noun clauses of indirect question and related clauses.

Note: Noun clauses of direct quotation need no special treatment here, since the tense of the verb in such a noun clause depends entirely upon the relationship of the time of the action of the verb to the time that the quoted sentence comes into being. In other words, one merely employs the tense that would naturally be used at the time of speaking or writing the quoted sentence.

(a) Sequence of Tenses When Verb of Noun Clause Is in the Indicative Mode

The tense of an indicative mode verb in a noun clause depends upon all three of the time factors mentioned above. We shall consider in detail the sequence of tenses when the verb of the main clause is in one of the simple tenses: present, future, or past.

The following diagram shows the use of the simple tenses in noun clauses when the verb of the main clause is in the present tense:

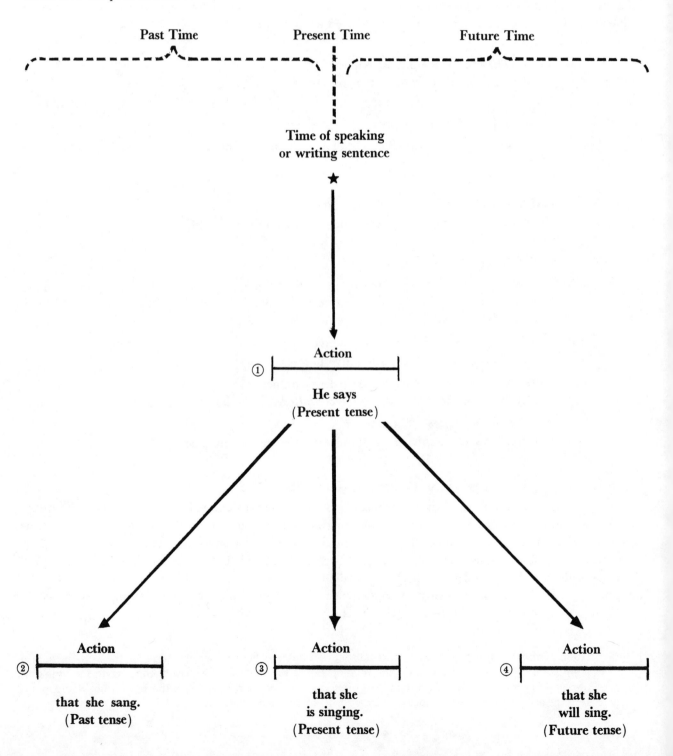

EXPLANATION OF DIAGRAM

① The action of the verb of the independent clause is taking place at the time of the speaking or writing of the sentence, and the verb (*says*) is therefore in the present tense.

② If the action of the verb of the noun clause took place prior to the time of the action of the main verb, the verb of the noun clause is in the *past tense*:

He says that she *sang*.

③ If the action of the verb of the noun clause is taking place at the same time as the action of the main verb, the verb of the noun clause is in the *present tense*:

He says that she *is singing*.

Usually the *progressive* form is used to indicate actual contemporaneous action. The *simple* form is used to indicate a customary or habitual action:

He says that she *sings*.

④ If the action of the verb of the noun clause is in the future with reference to the time of the action of the main verb, the verb of the noun clause is in the *future tense*:

He says that she *will sing*.

Note that the tense of the verb in each of these indirect quotations is the same that it would be in a corresponding direct quotation:

He says that she *sang*.
He says, "She *sang*."

He says that she *is singing*.
He says, "She *is singing*."

He says that she *sings*.
He says, "She *sings*."

He says that she *will sing*.
He says, "She *will sing*."

———————————

The following diagram shows the use of the simple tenses in noun clauses when the verb of the main clause is in the future tense:

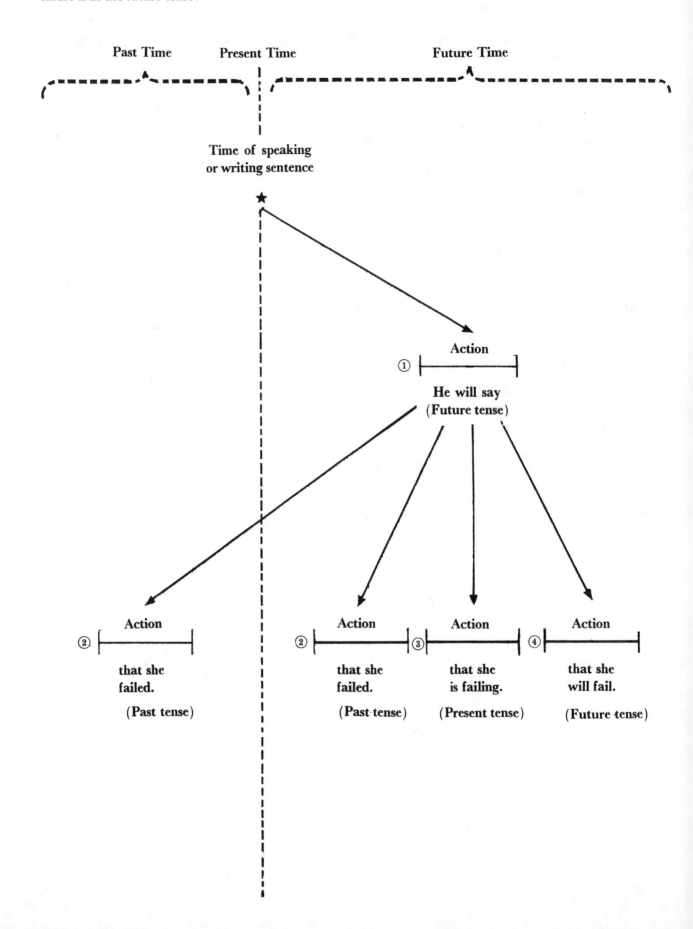

EXPLANATION OF DIAGRAM

① The action of the verb of the independent clause is in the future with reference to the time of the speaking or writing of the sentence, and the verb (*will say*) is therefore in the future tense.

② If the action of the verb of the noun clause took place prior to the time of the action of the main verb, the verb of the noun clause is in the *past tense*:

He will say that she *failed*.

As indicated in the diagram, the action of the verb of the noun clause may be in the future with reference to the time of the speaking or writing of the sentence.

③ If the action of the verb of the noun clause is taking place at the same time as the action of the main verb, the verb of the noun clause is in the *present tense*:

He will say that she *is failing*.

Usually the *progressive* form of the present tense is used to indicate actual contemporaneous action.

④ If the action of the verb of the noun clause is in the future with reference to the time of the action of the main verb, the verb of the noun clause is in the *future tense*:

He will say that she *will fail*.

Note that the tense of the verb in each of these indirect quotations is the same that it would be in a corresponding direct quotation:

He will say that she *failed*.
He will say, "She *failed*."

He will say that she *is failing*.
He will say, "She *is failing*."

He will say that she *will fail*.
He will say, "She *will fail*."

———————————

The following diagram shows the use of the most common tenses when the verb of the main clause is in the past tense:

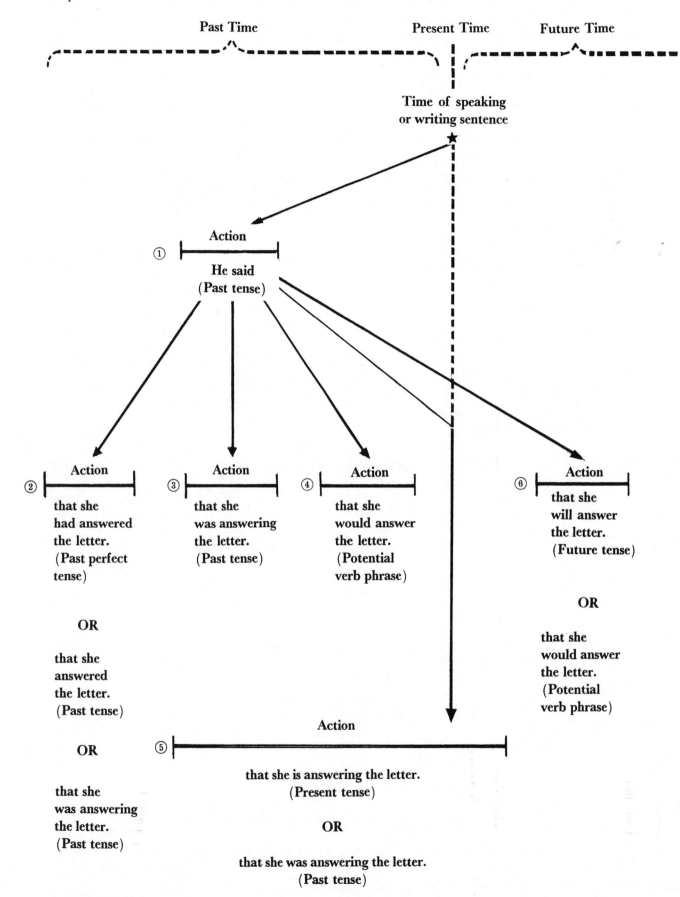

EXPLANATION OF DIAGRAM

① The action of the verb of the independent clause took place prior to the time of the speaking or writing of the sentence, and the verb (*said*) is therefore in the past tense.

② If the action of the verb of the noun clause took place prior to the time of the action of the main verb, the verb of the noun clause is in the *past perfect tense* or the *past tense*:

> He said that she *had answered* the letter.
> He said that she *answered* the letter.
> He said that she *was answering* the letter.

The use of the *past perfect tense* places particular emphasis upon the priority of the action of the verb of the noun clause. The use of the *simple past tense* places less emphasis upon the time of the verb action. The *past tense progressive* is used to show the continuing nature of the action with reference to a time prior to the action of the main verb. Note the following sentence:

> He said that she *was answering* the letter when he arrived.

③ If the action of the verb of the noun clause took place at the same time as the action of the main verb, the verb of the noun clause is in the *past tense*:

> He said that she *was answering* the letter.

Usually the *progressive* form of the past tense is used to indicate actual contemporaneous action. (Note that this form is identical with that just discussed in section 2.)

④ If the action of the verb of the noun clause is in the future with reference to the time of the action of the main verb but is in the past with reference to the time of the speaking or writing of the sentence, the verb of the noun clause is a *potential verb phrase* using *should* or *would* as an auxiliary:

> He said that she *would answer* the letter.

Note the following sentence, in which the time of the action of *answering* is clearly indicated:

> He said that she *would answer* the letter, and she *did answer* it.

⑤ If the action of the verb of the noun clause was taking place at the time of the action of the main verb and is still taking place at the time of the speaking or writing of the sentence, the verb of the noun clause is usually in the *present tense,* particularly if it is desired to emphasize the fact that the action is still in progress:

> He said that she *is answering* the letter.

Note the following sentence:

> He said a few minutes ago that she *is answering* the letter now.

This same sequence of tenses is used for actions which are customary, habitual, or universally true:

> He said that she *plays* the piano.
> He said that mice *like* cheese.

If no emphasis is to be placed upon the fact that the action is still continuing, the *past tense* (usually the *past progressive*) may be used to indicate an action in progress at the time of the action of the main verb and still in progress:

> He said that she *was answering* the letter.

The listener or reader, of course, cannot determine from this sentence whether or not the action is still continuing.

⑥ If the action of the verb of the noun clause is in the future with reference to both the time of the action of the main verb and the time of the speaking or writing of the sentence, the verb of the noun clause is in the *future tense* if it is desired to emphasize the fact that the action is still to take place:

He said that she *will answer* the letter.

Note the following sentence:

He said this morning that she *will answer* the letter tomorrow.

If there is no desire to place emphasis upon the fact that the action is still in the future, the verb of the noun clause may be a *potential verb phrase* using *should* or *would* as an auxiliary, even though the action has not taken place at the time of speaking or writing:

He said that she *would answer* the letter.

Note the following sentence:

He said that she *would answer* the letter, and I believe that she *will answer* it.

Examine the relationship between the tense of the verb in each of these indirect quotations and the tense of the verb in a corresponding direct quotation:

He said that she *had answered* (or *answered*) the letter.
He said, "She *answered* the letter."

He said that she *was answering* the letter.
He said, "She *was answering* the letter."

He said that she *was answering* the letter.
He said, "She *is answering* the letter."

He said that she *would answer* the letter.
He said, "She *will answer* the letter."

He said that she *is answering* (or *was answering*) the letter.
He said, "She *is answering* the letter."

He said that she *will answer* the letter.
He said, "She *will answer* the letter."

In the preceding diagrams, we have dealt primarily with the use of the simple tenses in both the independent clause and the noun clause. It is not necessary to give a similar detailed treatment of the perfect tenses. After mastering the three diagrams just presented and the two diagrams explaining the simple and perfect tenses (see pp. 9–12), the student should have no difficulty in determining the proper sequence of tenses with the perfect tenses. Generally speaking, the *present perfect* reacts like the *present*; the *past perfect*, like the *past*; and the *future perfect*, like the *future*.

The examples given above have all been noun clauses of indirect declarative statement. However, the same rules for sequence of tenses apply to noun clauses of indirect question and to noun clauses related to either of these types. Note the sequence of tenses in the following examples:

She *said* that she *would go* home. (Noun clause of indirect statement)
That she *would go* home *seemed* unlikely. (Related clause)

I *wondered* whether he *would win* the contest. (Noun clause of indirect question)
It *was* doubtful whether he *would win* the contest. (Related clause)

(b) Sequence of Tenses When Verb of Noun Clause Is in the Subjunctive Mode

The tense of a subjunctive mode verb in a noun clause depends upon the relationship between the time of the action of the verb of the noun clause and the time of the action of the main verb.

If the time of the action of the subjunctive mode verb of a noun clause is in the future with reference to the time of the action of the main verb, the verb of the noun clause is in the *present tense*, no matter what the tense of the main verb may be:

She demanded that he *leave* the room.
She demands that he *leave* the room.
She will demand that he *leave* the room.

If the time of the action (or supposed action) of the subjunctive mode verb of a noun clause is the same as the time of the action of the main verb, the verb of the noun clause is in the *past tense,* no matter what the tense of the main verb may be:

He wished that he *were* rich.
He wishes that he *were* rich.
He will wish that he *were* rich.

If the time of the action (or supposed action) of the subjunctive mode verb of a noun clause is prior to the time of the action of the main verb, the verb of the noun clause is in the *past perfect tense,* no matter what the tense of the main verb may be:

He wished that he *had studied.*
He wishes that he *had studied.*
He will wish that he *had studied.*

Note that these rules for sequence of tenses apply to noun clauses of indirect imperative statement and related noun clauses and to noun clauses expressing wishes contrary to fact. (See p. 115.)

(3) Noun Clauses in Apposition

A noun clause is often used in apposition with another substantive.

Examples:

I heard a rumor *that he would retire soon.*

Pattern: **Subject—Verb—Object—**Appositive
Sub. Conj.—**Subject—Verb—**Modifier

The fact *that she has gone* may be significant.

Pattern: **Subject—**Appositive   **—Linking Verb—Adjective Complement**
Sub. Conj.—**Subject—Verb**

Note that the appositive can be substituted for its antecedent in both of these sentences:

I heard *that he would retire soon.*
That she has gone may be significant.

In such a sentence as the last one, the anticipatory *it* with the noun clause as delayed subject is often used.

Examples:

It may be significant *that she has gone.*
It is obvious *that they were wrong.*
It is necessary *that you go at once.*

(4) The Noun Clause Following an Adjective Complement

The following sentences contain a peculiar construction involving a noun clause following an adjective complement:

He is sure *that he will win.*
We are sorry *that you lost.*
She is uncertain *whether she will go.*

The clause in this construction is sometimes explained as an adverb clause modifying the adjective complement. However, this interpretation is rather unsatisfactory, particularly in view of the fact that the clause has the typical form of the noun clause.

A more acceptable explanation is that which interprets the clause as a noun clause functioning as the object of an understood preposition:

> He is sure (of) *that he will win.* [*Compare:* He is sure of winning.]
> We are sorry (concerning) *that you lost.* [*Compare:* We are sorry concerning your losing.]
> She is uncertain (about) *whether she will go.* [*Compare:* She is uncertain about going.]

The clause may also be interpreted as a noun clause functioning as the object of a "combination" verb made up of the linking verb and the adjective complement. Note that a single verb can be substituted for the linking verb and its adjective complement without changing the meaning of the sentence:

> He *is sure* that he will win.
> He *knows* that he will win.

> We *are sorry* that you lost.
> We *regret* that you lost.

> She *is uncertain* whether she will go.
> She *doubts* whether she will go.

This last explanation has the advantage of interpreting the construction as it stands without assuming an "understood" element.

(5) Compounds

Noun clauses may be linked together to form compounds. Such compounds are punctuated like the other compounds we have studied.

Example:

I knew | that John would propose and that Mary would accept him.

Often, in this type of construction, the subordinating conjunction *that* is expressed before the first noun clause only.

Example:

He hoped | that the rain would stop and the skies would clear.

Pattern: **Subject—Verb—Compound Object**

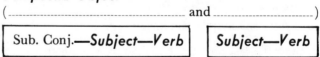

Note: A clause *cannot* be linked with a single-word element or a phrase to form a compound.

(6) Phrases Within Clauses

A noun clause may contain any kind of phrase.

Examples:

Prepositional Phrase Within a Noun Clause

She said | that he would wait | at the corner.

Pattern: **Subject—Verb—Object**

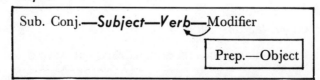

Gerund Phrase Within a Noun Clause

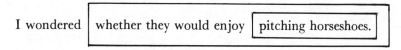

Pattern: **Subject—Verb—Object**

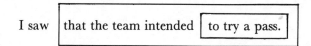

Infinitive Phrase Within a Noun Clause

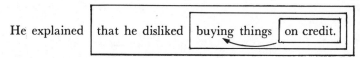

Pattern: **Subject—Verb—Object**

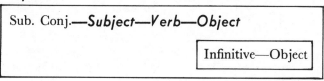

Note: Of course, any phrases contained within noun clauses can have other phrases within them.

Example:

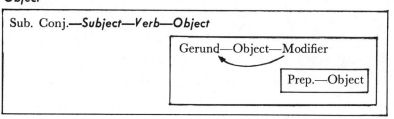

Pattern: **Subject—Verb—Object**

(7) **Clauses Within Phrases**

A noun clause may be contained within a phrase. The clause in this type of construction performs a substantive function within the phrase.

Examples:

Noun Clause Within a Prepositional Phrase

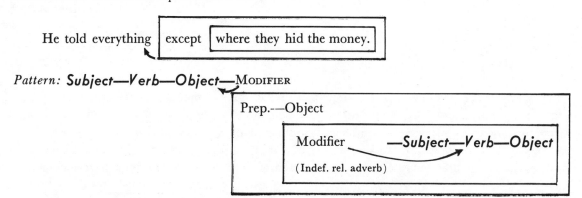

Pattern: **Subject—Verb—Object—**MODIFIER

Noun Clause Within a Gerund Phrase

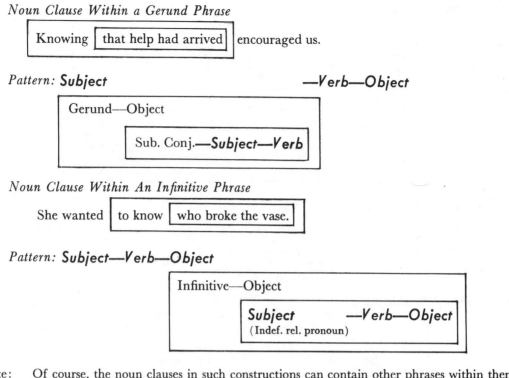

Knowing | that help had arrived | encouraged us.

Pattern: **Subject**   **—Verb—Object**

Gerund—Object

Sub. Conj.—**Subject—Verb**

Noun Clause Within An Infinitive Phrase

She wanted | to know | who broke the vase.

Pattern: **Subject—Verb—Object**

Infinitive—Object

Subject   **—Verb—Object**
(Indef. rel. pronoun)

Note: Of course, the noun clauses in such constructions can contain other phrases within them.

      Example:

      He tried | to remember | whether he had left the key | in the lock. |

      Pattern: **Subject—Verb—Object**

Infinitive—Object

Sub. Conj.—**Subject—Verb—Object**—Modifier

Prep.—Object

(8) Clauses Within Clauses

A noun clause may contain another noun clause within it.

Example:

He said | that he knew | why the experiment had failed. |

Pattern: **Subject—Verb—Object**

Sub. Conj.—**Subject—Verb—Object**

Modifier   **—Subject—Verb**
(Indef. rel. adverb)

(9) A Final Note

Phrases and dependent clauses are grammatical units which contain grammatical units within them. Therefore, since phrases and dependent clauses may be contained within other phrases and clauses (as the last three sections have demonstrated), the number of possible combinations is practically unlimited.

However, the important thing to keep in mind is that, no matter how many phrases and dependent clauses may be within other phrases and clauses, each of these grammatical units performs one of a very limited number of functions. Consequently, many sentences which appear somewhat complicated at first glance prove to be quite simple in structure after one isolates every phrase and every clause unit and determines the function of each.

DO EXERCISES 36, 37, AND 38

2. THE ADJECTIVE CLAUSE

An adjective clause is a dependent clause which functions as a modifier of a substantive.

a. *FORM OF THE ADJECTIVE CLAUSE*

An adjective clause is usually introduced by a relative pronoun, a relative adjective, or a relative adverb.

Examples:

The man *who bought the house* is wealthy. (Introduced by relative pronoun *who*)
I am hunting the man *whose radio awakened me.* (Introduced by relative adjective *whose*)
We visited the town *where he was born.* (Introduced by relative adverb *where*)

b. *FUNCTION OF THE ADJECTIVE CLAUSE*

An adjective clause always modifies a substantive. It follows the substantive which it modifies. (Usually it comes immediately after the substantive.)

An adjective clause may be either restrictive or non-restrictive.

(1) Restrictive Adjective Clauses

A restrictive adjective clause *limits* or *restricts* the substantive which it modifies in such a way that the modifier is necessary for the proper *identification* of the substantive. It thus forms such a close union with the substantive that no punctuation is necessary or desirable.

Examples:

The repairman found the tube *which was bad.*
The girl *whom you saw in the yard* is my sister.

(2) Non-Restrictive Adjective Clauses

A non-restrictive adjective clause gives added information about a substantive which is presumed to be sufficiently identified without the modifying adjective clause. A non-restrictive clause is set off by comma punctuation.

Examples:

My father, *who recently retired,* sold his business.
Our team, *which was previously undefeated,* lost to Centerville.

c. *TYPES OF ADJECTIVE CLAUSES*

Adjective clauses may be divided into three types. The classification is based upon the kind of element which introduces the clause.

(1) The Adjective Clause Introduced by a Relative Pronoun

Most adjective clauses are introduced by one of the relative pronouns: *who (whom), which, that.* This type of adjective clause always modifies the antecedent of the relative pronoun.[6]

Examples:

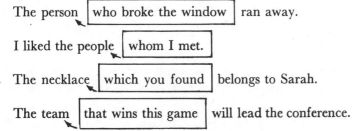

The person |who broke the window| ran away.

I liked the people |whom I met.|

The necklace |which you found| belongs to Sarah.

The team |that wins this game| will lead the conference.

[6] The antecedent of a pronoun is the substantive to which it refers.

(a) Functions of the Relative Pronoun

The relative pronoun in an adjective clause performs two functions: (1) it relates back to its antecedent and thus connects the adjective clause with this antecedent, and (2) it performs a substantive function in the adjective clause.

Note 1: *What* (= that which), *whoever* (= anyone who), *whichever* (= either one which), and *whatever* (= anything which) are sometimes considered to be introducers of adjective clauses. Such an interpretation requires that each of these words be explained as containing both an antecedent and a relative pronoun. It seems simpler to call the clauses introduced by these words noun clauses. (See pp. 110–11.)

Note 2: Let us examine the functions of the relative pronouns in the examples given above:

> The person who broke the window ran away.

Who relates back to its antecedent *person* and thus connects the adjective clause with *person*. At the same time, *who* functions in the adjective clause as the subject of the verb *broke*.

> I liked the people whom I met.

Whom relates back to its antecedent *people* and thus connects the adjective clause with *people*. At the same time, *whom* functions in the adjective clause as the object of the verb *met*.

> The necklace which you found belongs to Sarah.

Which relates back to its antecedent *necklace* and thus connects the adjective clause with *necklace*. At the same time, *which* functions in the adjective clause as the object of the verb *found*.

> The team that wins this game will lead the conference.

That relates back to its antecedent *team* and thus connects the adjective clause with *team*. At the same time, *that* functions in the adjective clause as the subject of the verb *wins*.

i. *The Relative Pronoun and Its Antecedent: Reference and Agreement*

a. REFERENCE

The relative pronoun refers to a substantive which is its antecedent.

1. *Who* and *whom* are used to refer to substantives denoting persons.
2. *Which* is used to refer to substantives denoting animals and things.
3. *That* may be used to refer to any substantive but cannot be used in a non-restrictive adjective clause.

A relative pronoun should not be used to refer to a clause or to an unexpressed substantive.

> *Vague:* He found his hat, which pleased him.

In this sentence, *which* has no substantive antecedent. Consequently, it seems to refer to *hat*. The meaning intended, however, is that the *finding* of the hat pleased him. The sentence should be revised:

> He found his hat, a fact which pleased him.

It may be necessary to recast such a faulty sentence:

> Since he had found his hat, he was pleased.

b. AGREEMENT

The relative pronouns do not have varying forms to show person and number, but each relative pronoun nevertheless agrees with its antecedent in both person and number. In turn, then, if a relative pronoun is the subject of a verb, its verb must agree with the relative pronoun in person and number.

> Examples:
> A man who tries hard will succeed. [*Who* is singular because it agrees with its antecedent *man*. The singular verb form *tries* is therefore used to agree with the singular subject *who*.]
> Men who try hard will succeed. [*Who* is plural because it agrees with its antecedent *men*. The plural verb form *try* is therefore used to agree with the plural subject *who*.]

ii. The Substantive Function of the Relative Pronoun

The relative pronoun may perform any substantive function in the adjective clause. *The case of the relative pronoun depends entirely upon its function within the clause.* The function and case of its antecedent do *not* affect the case of the relative pronoun.

Examples:

I saw the man *who* wrote you. (Subject; nominative case)

I saw the man *whom* you invited. (Object; objective case)

I saw the man to *whom* you sent the book. (Object of preposition; objective case)

I saw the man *whom* you wanted me to visit. (Object of infinitive; objective case)

I saw the man *whom* you insisted upon my meeting. (Object of gerund; objective case)

Note: If you have difficulty in determining the function (and hence the case) of the pronoun in the adjective clause, the following procedure may be helpful:
1. Isolate the adjective clause.
2. Change it to a sentence by
   a. Substituting the antecedent for the relative pronoun, and
   b. Changing the word order if necessary.
3. Determine the function of the substituted antecedent in the resulting sentence. This function will be identical with that of the relative pronoun in the original clause.

Example:

The girl *who/whom* he recommended was accepted.

1. The adjective clause is "*who/whom* he recommended."
2. Substituting *the girl* for the relative pronoun and changing the word-order, we have:

   He recommended the girl.
3. *The girl* is the object of *recommended*. Therefore, the relative pronoun in the original clause is the object of *recommended* and should be in the objective case. Thus, the correct sentence is the following:

   The girl *whom* he recommended was accepted.

(b) Omission of the Relative Pronoun

If a relative pronoun in a restrictive adjective clause is not the subject of the clause, it is often omitted.

Examples:

The story (which) she wrote had a surprising ending.

He is the person (whom) I talked with yesterday.

(2) The Adjective Clause Introduced by a Relative Adjective

Adjective clauses are sometimes introduced by one of the relative adjectives: *whose, which.* This type of adjective clause always modifies the antecedent of the relative adjective.[7]

Example:

He is the boy | whose book I borrowed. |

The relative adjective in an adjective clause performs two functions: (1) it relates back to its antecedent and thus connects the adjective clause with this antecedent, and (2) it performs an adjective function in the adjective clause.

Note: Let us examine the functions of the relative adjective in the example given above:

He is the boy | whose book I borrowed. |

Whose relates back to its antecedent *boy* and thus connects the adjective clause with *boy.* At the same time, *whose* functions in the adjective clause as a modifier of the substantive *book.*

(3) The Adjective Clause Introduced by a Relative Adverb

Adjective clauses are often introduced by one of the relative adverbs: *where, when, why.* Since each of

[7] The antecedent of the relative adjective is the substantive to which it refers.

these relative adverbs is equivalent to a prepositional phrase containing a relative pronoun, the construction is very closely related to the adjective clause introduced by a relative pronoun.

Examples:

I visited the house | where (= in which) he lived. |

He selected a time | when (= during which) I was absent. |

I know the reason | why (= because of which) he left. |

(a) Functions of the Relative Adverb

The relative adverb, like the relative pronoun and the relative adjective, performs two functions: (1) it relates back to its antecedent and thus connects the adjective clause with this antecedent, and (2) it performs an adverbial function in the adjective clause.

Note 1: The functions of a relative adverb may best be understood by comparing it with the prepositional phrase to which it is equivalent. Let us examine our first example:

I visited the house | where he lived. |

This is equivalent to the following sentence:

I visited the house | in which he lived. |

Which in the second sentence obviously relates back to its antecedent *house*; therefore, *where* in the first sentence (which includes a relative pronoun meaning within it) must also relate back to *house*. The phrase *in which* in the second sentence functions as an adverb in the adjective clause, modifying the verb *lived*; therefore, *where* in the first sentence must also function as an adverb in the adjective clause.

Note 2: The subordinating conjunction *that* is sometimes used instead of a relative adverb.

Examples:

I saw the place *that* (= where) he fell.
I remember the time *that* (= when) I met her.
He told me the reason *that* (= why) he resigned.

(b) Omission of the Relative Adverb

Like the relative pronoun, the relative adverb is often omitted in restrictive adjective clauses.

Examples:

I noted the time (when) John arrived.
The reason (why) she cried is obvious.

d. *INDICATING THE PATTERN OF A SENTENCE CONTAINING AN ADJECTIVE CLAUSE*

To indicate the pattern of a sentence containing an adjective clause, we shall use the following method:

(1) We shall show the function of the adjective clause by using the word "Modifier" and drawing an arrow to the substantive modified.

Example:

Students | who work diligently | make good grades.

Partial pattern: **Subject**—Modifier—**Verb**—Modifier—**Object**

(2) Next, if it is desired to show whether the adjective clause is restrictive or non-restrictive, we shall make a notation to this effect immediately below the word "Modifier."

Example:

Students | who work diligently | make good grades.

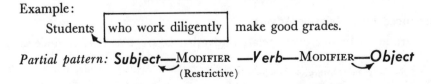

Partial pattern: **Subject**—Modifier —**Verb**—Modifier—**Object**
(Restrictive)

(3) Then, in a box below these notations we shall indicate the composition of the adjective clause, show-ing beneath the function of each relative its exact nature—i.e., "relative pronoun," "relative adjec-tive," or "relative adverb."

Example:

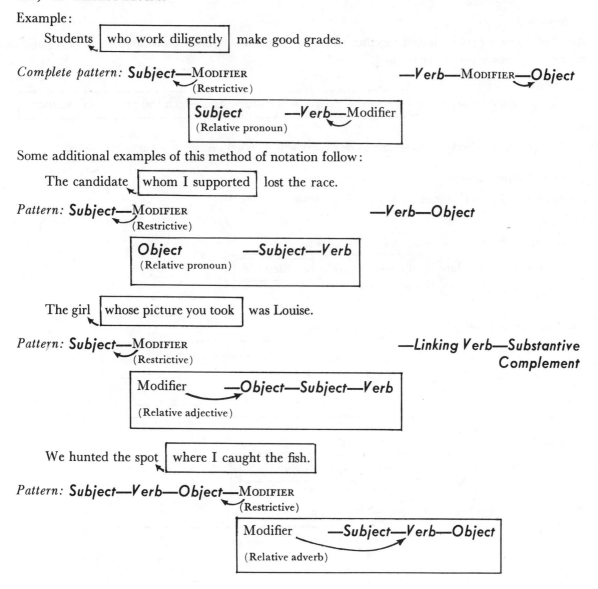

Some additional examples of this method of notation follow:

e. *SOME SPECIAL NOTES ON THE ADJECTIVE CLAUSE*

(1) **Sequence of Tenses**

The tense of the verb in an adjective clause is determined solely by the relationship between the time of the action indicated by the verb of the adjective clause and the time of the speaking or writing of the sentence. The tense of the verb of the adjective clause is therefore independent of the tense of the main verb.

(2) **The Appositive and the Adjective Clause**

An appositive is equivalent to an elliptical adjective clause of the third basic pattern—*i.e.*, a clause with a linking verb. Compare the following sentences:

He enjoyed his hobby, *which was photography.* (Adjective clause)

He enjoyed his hobby, *photography.* (Appositive)

Note that in the first sentence *photography* performs a substantive function and the entire clause *which was photography* performs a modifying function. Omission of the words *which was* leaves only the word *photog-*

raphy to perform both substantive and modifying functions. This dual function, as we have noted, is characteristic of the appositive. (See pp. 63–64.)

(3) Compounds

Adjective clauses may be linked together to form compounds. Compounds of this type are punctuated like the other compounds we have studied.

Example:

He presented a program | which the mayor will endorse and which the people will support.

Note: Of course, an adjective clause *cannot* be linked with a noun clause to form a compound.

(4) Phrases Within Clauses

An adjective clause may contain any kind of phrase.

Examples:

Prepositional Phrase Within an Adjective Clause

We watched the boys | who were playing | in the yard.

Pattern: **Subject—Verb—Object—**Modifier

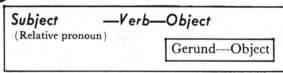

Gerund Phrase Within an Adjective Clause

I invited George, | who enjoys | hearing symphonies.

Pattern: **Subject—Verb—Object—**Modifier

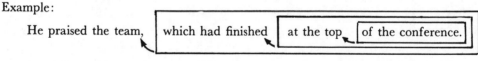

Note: Of course, any phrases contained within adjective clauses can have other phrases within them.
Example:

He praised the team, | which had finished | at the top | of the conference.

Pattern: **Subject—Verb—Object—**Modifier

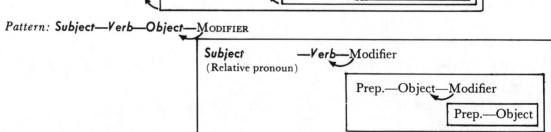

(5) Clauses Within Phrases

An adjective clause may be contained within a phrase. The clause in such a construction performs a modifying function within the phrase.

Examples:

Adjective Clause Within a Prepositional Phrase

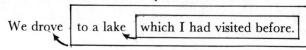

Pattern: **Subject—Verb—**Modifier

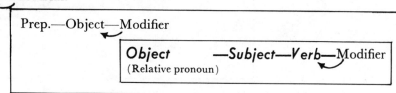

Adjective Clause Within an Infinitive Phrase

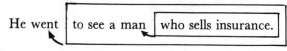

Pattern: **Subject—Verb—**Modifier

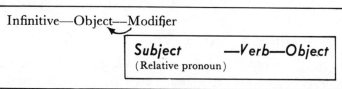

Note: Of course, the adjective clauses in such constructions can contain other phrases within them.

Example:

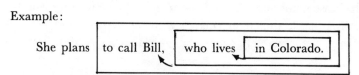

Pattern: **Subject—Verb—Object**

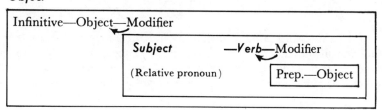

(6) **Clauses Within Clauses**

An adjective clause may contain a noun clause or another adjective clause. An adjective clause may, of course, be contained within a noun clause.

Examples:

Noun Clause Within an Adjective Clause

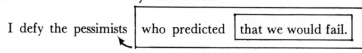

Pattern: **Subject—Verb—Object—**Modifier

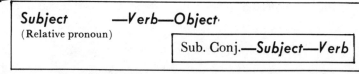

Adjective Clause Within a Noun Clause

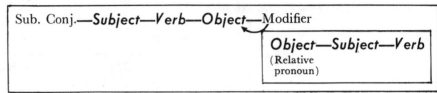

I know | that you will enjoy the book | which you are reading. |

Pattern: **Subject—Verb—Object**

> Sub. Conj.—*Subject—Verb—Object*—Modifier
>
> > *Object—Subject—Verb*
> > (Relative
> > pronoun)

Note: At this point, it would be well to re-read the final section on noun clauses, pp. 126–27.

DO EXERCISES 39 AND 40

3. THE ADVERB CLAUSE

An adverb clause is a dependent clause which functions as a modifier of a verb, an adjective, or an adverb.

a. *FORM OF THE ADVERB CLAUSE*

An adverb clause is introduced by a subordinating conjunction which connects the adverb clause with the element modified and shows the relationship between the clause and the element modified.

Note the following example:

She returned | after I left. |

In this sentence, *after I left* is an adverb clause modifying the verb *returned*. The word *after* is a subordinating conjunction introducing the clause. It connects the adverb clause with the verb *returned* and shows the relationship between the clause and the verb. Note that a change in the subordinating conjunction would indicate a different relationship:

> She returned *before* I left.
> She returned *as* I left.

Note: A few of the words which introduce adverb clauses—especially *when* and *where*—have an adverbial function in the adverb clause in addition to their connective function. However, since this adverbial function is of little significance, we shall make no distinction between these words and other words which introduce adverb clauses. We shall call all such words "subordinating conjunctions."

Some of the common subordinating conjunctions used to introduce adverb clauses are the following: *when, before, after, until, while, since, as, where, as if, because, so that, though, although, if, unless, than, that.*

b. *FUNCTION OF THE ADVERB CLAUSE*

An adverb clause modifies a verb, an adjective, or an adverb.

Note: Sometimes an adverb clause seems to modify an entire predicate or an entire clause instead of the verb alone. However, for the sake of simplicity, we shall consider such a clause to be a verb modifier.

An adverb clause may be either restrictive or non-restrictive.

(1) **Restrictive Adverb Clauses**

Most adverb clauses are restrictive. Such clauses are punctuated as follows:

(a) If the adverb clause follows the independent clause, no punctuation is used.

Examples:

We shouted *when the team scored.*

> I go *wherever I am sent.*
> He does *as he pleases.*
> She is smarter *than I thought.*
> They fought *because they were attacked.*

(b) If the adverb clause precedes the independent clause, it is set off from the independent clause by comma punctuation.

> Examples:
>
> *Before he arrived at the front,* defeat seemed certain.
> *Wherever I looked,* I saw dust.
>
> *Since he had bought a ticket,* he was determined to attend.
> *If our candidate wins,* we will celebrate.

Note 1: If the introductory adverb clause is *very* short, the comma *may* be omitted.

> Example:
>
> *When I arrived* they had gone.

However, since the use of the comma in such instances is also quite correct, it is best for the student to acquire the habit of inserting the comma in all constructions of this sort. In the exercises in this text, a comma will be required after every introductory adverb clause.

Note 2: The punctuation used for the adverb clause preceding the independent clause is actually enclosure within commas though, of course, only one comma is used when the adverb clause begins the sentence. Note the following sentences:

> But Nero played the fiddle *while Rome burned.*
> But, *while Rome burned,* Nero played the fiddle.

(c) If the adverb clause falls within the independent clause, it is set off from the independent clause by comma punctuation.

> Examples:
>
> The president, *after he had delivered the speech,* left the convention hall.
> My sister, *before I could stop her,* called the fire department.

(2) Non-Restrictive Adverb Clauses

A few adverb clauses are non-restrictive. Such a clause is set off by comma punctuation even when it follows the independent clause. Particular attention to the punctuation of non-restrictive adverb clauses will be given later in the treatment of clauses of cause and clauses of concession.

c. *TYPES OF ADVERB CLAUSES*

Adverb clauses are classified according to meaning as clauses of time, place, manner, cause, purpose, concession, condition, and degree.

Note: All of the clauses listed except the clause of degree modify verbs. Degree clauses modify adjectives and adverbs.

(1) Adverb Clause of Time

An adverb clause of time is usually introduced by one of the following subordinating conjunctions: *when, before, after, until, while, since, as, as soon as, as often as, whenever.*[8]

> Examples:
>
> *When the teacher entered,* the students became quiet.
> The rain began *before the game ended.*
> *After you finish the exam,* you may leave.
> We waited *until the bell rang.*
> *While I was studying the lesson,* he was reading the comics.
> The letter arrived *since you inquired yesterday.*

[8] Though a subordinating conjunction is usually a single word, it may consist of a group of words, such as *as soon as* and *as long as.* A conjunction of this type may be termed a "group" subordinating conjunction.

> *As you read the theme,* check the punctuation.
> I came *as soon as I heard the news.*
> *As long as he is coach,* the team will win.
> He writes *as often as he can.*
> *Whenever she has time,* she makes cookies.

The adverb clause of time modifies a verb and functions like a single-word adverb expressing time. Compare the following sentences:

> He mowed the grass *yesterday.*
>
> He mowed the grass │ *while I slept.* │

(2) Adverb Clause of Place

An adverb clause of place is usually introduced by one of the following subordinating conjunctions: *where, wherever, everywhere.*

> Examples:
>
> I live *where tornadoes are common.*
> *Wherever she goes,* he will follow.
> He found poverty *everywhere he went.*

The adverb clause of place modifies a verb and functions like a single-word adverb expressing place. Compare the following sentences:

> I found the book *there.*
>
> I found the book │ *where I left it.* │

Note: The word *where* may introduce noun clauses and adjective clauses as well as adverb clauses.

> Examples:
>
> I know *where he put the saw.* (Noun clause)
> We saw the house *where he died.* (Adjective clause)

Any clause introduced by *where* should be carefully examined to determine its function in the sentence.

(3) Adverb Clause of Manner

An adverb clause of manner is usually introduced by one of the following subordinating conjunctions: *as, as if, as though.*

> Examples:
>
> The boy swims *as he was taught.*
> She ran *as if she were frightened.*
> He talked *as though he might come.*

Note: *Like* is not accepted as a subordinating conjunction. It is used colloquially to introduce adverb clauses of manner, but formal usage requires *as, as if,* or *as though.*

> Examples:
>
> Do *as* [not *like*] I say.
> It looks *as if* [not *like*] it may rain.

The adverb clause of manner modifies a verb and functions like a single-word adverb expressing manner. Compare the following sentences:

> She walked *slowly.*
>
> She walked │ *as if she were discouraged.* │

In an adverb clause introduced by *as if* or *as though,* the verb is usually a future tense verb, a subjunctive verb, or a potential verb phrase.

Examples:

He talks as if he *will resign.* (Future tense verb)
She smiled as if she *were* pleased. (Subjunctive verb)
He acted as if he *might reconsider.* (Potential verb phrase)

(4) Adverb Clause of Cause

An adverb clause of cause is usually introduced by one of the following subordinating conjunctions: *because, since, inasmuch as.*

Examples:

He ate rapidly *because he was late.*
Since tomorrow is a holiday, I shall sleep until noon.
Inasmuch as he owes me, he must pay me.

Note: Since *as* is used to introduce adverb clauses of time and manner, it is best not to use it to introduce clauses of cause. Note the possible interpretations of the following sentence:

We hurried as the bus was approaching.

This may mean: *We hurried at the time the bus was approaching.* If a causal relationship is intended, the use of *because* or *since* will make the meaning clear:

We hurried because the bus was approaching.

The adverb clause of cause modifies a verb.

Example:

We left early | because we were tired.

Some adverb clauses of cause are non-restrictive. Such a non-restrictive clause is set off by comma punctuation even if it follows the independent clause.

Example:

He is certain to pass, *since he studies hard.*

Here the adverb clause is non-restrictive; it is not essential to the independent clause but merely gives an added explanation of it.

Of course, many adverb clauses of cause are restrictive or necessary to the meaning of the sentence. Restrictive clauses are not set off by comma punctuation.

Example:

I worked *because I needed the money.*

Note: The student can often determine whether an adverb clause of cause is restrictive or non-restrictive by reading the sentence aloud and noting whether he pauses before the adverb clause. If a pause seems natural, the adverb clause is probably non-restrictive and should be set off by a comma.

(5) Adverb Clause of Purpose

An adverb clause of purpose is usually introduced by one of the following subordinating conjunctions: *that, in order that, so that.*[9]

Examples:

He sacrificed his life *that others might live.*
He ran *in order that he might catch his train.*
Mary studied *so that she would know the lesson.*

The adverb clause of purpose modifies a verb.

Example:

We hurried | so that we would not be late.

[9] In colloquial usage, *so* is sometimes substituted for *so that* in adverb clauses of purpose.

(6) Adverb Clause of Concession

An adverb clause of concession is usually introduced by one of the following subordinating conjunctions: *though, although, even if, even though.*

Examples:

Though she is beautiful, she is dumb.
He attended classes, *although he was ill.*
Even if I warn him, he will not change his ways.
They stayed, *even though they were uncomfortable.*

The adverb clause of concession modifies a verb.

Example:

| Although the train was late, | I missed it.

Adverb clauses of concession are usually, but not always, non-restrictive. Hence, even when following an independent clause, such an adverb clause is usually set off by comma punctuation:

He left the room, *although I begged him to stay.*

If the adverb clause of concession deals with a supposed fact rather than an actual fact, the subjunctive or a potential verb phrase is used.

Examples:

Even if he *were* rich, he would still live like a beggar. (Subjunctive)
Even if he *should be* rich, he would still live like a beggar. (Potential verb phrase)

Note: Such adverb clauses of "supposed concession" may have inverted word-order and contain no subordinating conjunction.

Examples:

Were he rich, he would still live like a beggar.
Should he be rich, he would still live like a beggar.

(7) Adverb Clause of Condition

An adverb clause of condition is usually introduced by one of the following subordinating conjunctions: *if, unless, in case.*

Examples:

If the letter comes, I shall call you.
He will not come *unless you invite him.*
In case you need help, notify the police.

The adverb clause of condition modifies a verb.

Example:

| If you will wash the car, | he will polish it.

If the adverb clause of condition deals with a past or present condition which is either doubtful or contrary to fact, the subjunctive is used.

Examples:

If I *had been* there, it would not have happened.
If she *were* certain, she would tell you.

If the clause deals with a future condition, the subjunctive may be used if it is desired to emphasize doubt that the condition will exist.

Example:

If he *be elected,* it will be unfortunate for the country.

Note: Adverb clauses of contrary-to-fact condition may have inverted word-order and contain no subordinating conjunction.

> Examples:
>
> *Had I been there,* it would not have happened.
> *Were she certain,* she would tell you.

(8) Adverb Clause of Degree

An adverb clause of degree is usually introduced by one of the following subordinating conjunctions: *than, as, that.*

> Examples:
>
> The play was longer *than I anticipated.*
> The rent is as high *as you feared.*
> The game was so rough *that many were hurt.*

Unlike the other adverb clauses we have studied, the adverb clause of degree modifies an adjective or an adverb. It therefore functions like those single-word adverbs which modify adjectives and adverbs, for such single-word adverbial modifiers usually indicate degree.

(a) Degree Clauses Introduced by *than*

Perhaps the easiest degree clause to understand is the *than*-clause which follows and modifies a comparative degree adjective or adverb ending in *-er.*

> Examples:

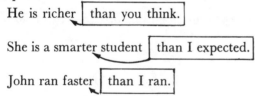

In the first of these sentences, the clause *than you think* modifies the comparative degree adjective *richer.* In the second sentence, the clause *than I expected* modifies the comparative degree adjective *smarter.* In the third sentence, the clause *than I ran* modifies the comparative degree adverb *faster.*

Actually, though, what seems to be modified by the adverb clause in each of these sentences is the comparative aspect of the adjective or adverb. To make this clearer, we shall examine some sentences in which the *than*-clause follows a comparative degree adjective or adverb formed with *more* or *less.* Here the comparative aspect of the adjective or the adverb is contained in a separate word instead of in a suffix.

> Examples:

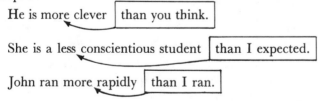

In each of these sentences, the adverb clause modifies the word which indicates the comparative degree; it modifies the adverb *more* or *less.*

Note: It may be difficult to see that the adverb clause modifies *more* or *less* in these sentences. Let us examine the first sentence in detail. The basic sentence is *He is clever.* If we add *more,* we have the sentence: *He is more clever.* However, this is incomplete, for the word *more* lacks meaning except with reference to something else. Adding a clause gives meaning to the word *more*; and, since the clause gives meaning to *more,* it modifies *more.* The completed sentence then becomes the following:

> He is more clever | than you think.

A similar analysis can be given for the second and third sentences.

(b) Degree Clauses Introduced by *as*

The construction which shows equivalent degree is quite similar to the patterns just examined. In this construction the adverb clause is introduced by the subordinating conjunction *as* and modifies the adverb *as*.

Examples:

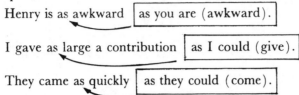

Henry is as awkward | as you are (awkward).

I gave as large a contribution | as I could (give).

They came as quickly | as they could (come).

Note 1: In the first example the basic sentence is *Henry is awkward*. When we add the adverb *as*, we have the sentence: *Henry is as awkward*. The word *as* needs a modifier to give it meaning. With the addition of the adverb clause, we have:

Henry is as awkward | as you are (awkward).

Note 2: Many grammarians insist on the use of the adverb *so* instead of *as* in negative statements.

Examples:

This game was not *so* exciting as the crowd expected.
I am not *so* tired as you think.

However, at present *so* and *as* seem to be used interchangeably in such negative statements.

(c) Degree Clauses Introduced by *that*

Still another adverb clause of degree is introduced by *that* and modifies the adverb *so* or the adjective *such*. This clause shows result as well as degree.

Examples:

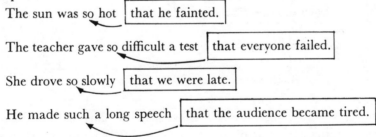

The sun was so hot | that he fainted.

The teacher gave so difficult a test | that everyone failed.

She drove so slowly | that we were late.

He made such a long speech | that the audience became tired.

Note 1: In the first example the basic sentence is *The sun was hot*. When we add the adverb *so*, we have the sentence: *The sun was so hot*. The word *so* needs a modifier to give it meaning. The addition of the adverb clause gives us the completed sentence:

The sun was so hot | that he fainted.

Note 2: It should be obvious that failure to state a degree clause produces an incomplete construction.

Incomplete: He is a much better player.
Complete: He is a much better player than Bill (is).

Of course, a construction which is incomplete by itself may be proper in its context.

Correct: I believe that John will defeat Bill. He is a much better player.

Constructions involving *so* and *such,* however, should always have the degree clause expressed.

Incomplete: The lesson is so difficult.
Complete: The lesson is so difficult that I do not understand it.

d. *ELLIPTICAL ADVERB CLAUSES*

An elliptical clause is one in which some of the words are understood rather than expressed. Note the following elliptical adverb clauses of time, manner, concession, condition, and degree. The portions which are understood are inserted in parentheses.

Time

> While (he is) working, he wastes no time.
> When (she was) notified, she accepted graciously.

Manner

> She raved as if (she were) mad.
> He did the work as (he was) directed.

Concession

> Though (she is) beautiful, she is dumb.
> He attended classes, although (he was) ill.

Condition

> If (it is) possible, you must take a vacation.
> If (it is) necessary, I can stay here.

Degree

> He is taller than I (am tall).
> I like him better than (I like) her.

Note: There are two main rules to remember with reference to elliptical degree clauses:

a. The things which are compared must be sufficiently similar to be capable of comparison.

> *Incorrect: College courses* are more difficult than *high school.*
> *Correct: College courses* are more difficult than *high school courses.*
> *Correct: College* is more difficult than *high school.*

b. The case of a pronoun in an elliptical clause is the same that it would be if the understood words were expressed.

Example:

> He is taller than *I.* [The pronoun *I* is in the nominative case because it is the subject of the complete adverb clause *than I am tall.*]
> I like him better than *her.* [The pronoun *her* is in the objective case because it is the object of the complete adverb clause *than I like her.*]

Such elliptical clauses are entirely correct if the meaning is clear. However, dangling elliptical clauses must be avoided:

> *Dangling:* While studying my algebra, any noise disturbs me.
> *Correct:* While I am studying my algebra, any noise disturbs me.
> *Correct:* While studying my algebra, I am disturbed by any noise.

e. *INDICATING THE PATTERN OF A SENTENCE CONTAINING AN ADVERB CLAUSE*

To indicate the pattern of a sentence containing an adverb clause, we shall use the following method:

(1) **We shall show the function of the adverb clause by using the word "Modifier" and drawing an arrow from this word to the element modified.**

Example:

> If I have time, I shall write a letter.

Partial pattern: MODIFIER—*Subject—Verb—Object*

(2) **Then, in a box below the word "Modifier," we shall indicate the composition of the adverb clause. We shall use the abbreviation "Sub. Conj." as a notation for the subordinating conjunction.**

Example:

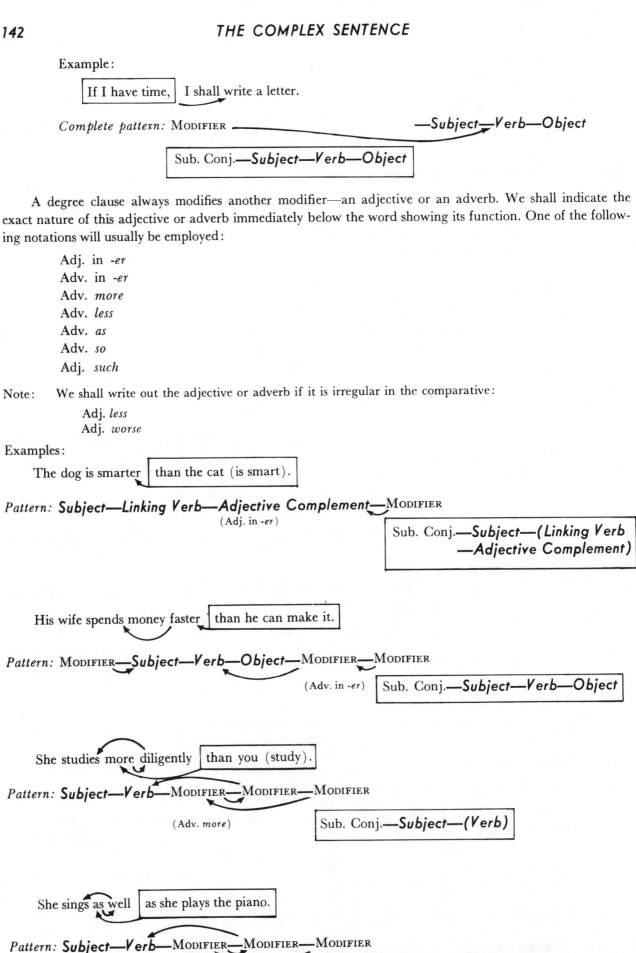

If I have time, | I shall write a letter.

Complete pattern: MODIFIER ——————————————— —*Subject—Verb—Object*

Sub. Conj.—*Subject—Verb—Object*

A degree clause always modifies another modifier—an adjective or an adverb. We shall indicate the exact nature of this adjective or adverb immediately below the word showing its function. One of the following notations will usually be employed:

Adj. in *-er*
Adv. in *-er*
Adv. *more*
Adv. *less*
Adv. *as*
Adv. *so*
Adj. *such*

Note: We shall write out the adjective or adverb if it is irregular in the comparative:

Adj. *less*
Adj. *worse*

Examples:

The dog is smarter | than the cat (is smart).

Pattern: **Subject—Linking Verb—Adjective Complement—**MODIFIER
(Adj. in *-er*)
Sub. Conj.—*Subject—(Linking Verb
—Adjective Complement)*

His wife spends money faster | than he can make it.

Pattern: MODIFIER—*Subject—Verb—Object—*MODIFIER—MODIFIER
(Adv. in *-er*) Sub. Conj.—*Subject—Verb—Object*

She studies more diligently | than you (study).

Pattern: **Subject—Verb—**MODIFIER—MODIFIER—MODIFIER
(Adv. *more*)   Sub. Conj.—*Subject—(Verb)*

She sings as well | as she plays the piano.

Pattern: **Subject—Verb—**MODIFIER—MODIFIER—MODIFIER
(Adv. *as*)   Sub. Conj.—*Subject—Verb—Object*

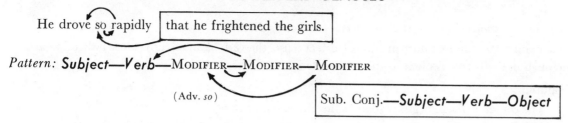

He drove so rapidly | that he frightened the girls.

Pattern: **Subject—Verb**—MODIFIER—MODIFIER—MODIFIER

(Adv. *so*) Sub. Conj.—**Subject—Verb—Object**

Note: In analyzing the structure of a sentence containing an elliptical clause, the student should first insert the words which are understood.

f. SOME SPECIAL NOTES ON THE ADVERB CLAUSE

(1) Sequence of Tenses

(a) When Tense of Verb of Adverb Clause Is Independent of Tense of Main Verb

The tense of the verb in an adverb clause is usually determined simply by the relationship between the time of the action of the verb of the adverb clause and the time of the speaking or writing of the sentence. In sentences in which this is true, the tense of the verb of the adverb clause is independent of the tense of the main verb.

Note: By its meaning, the subordinating conjunction of an adverb clause often imposes restrictions upon the time (and hence the tense) of the verb of the adverb clause. For example, the subordinating conjunction *after* restricts the verb of its clause to a time *prior to* the time of the main verb:

> She *came* after I *called* her.

Here it is impossible to change the verb *to call* to the present or future tense because the meaning of the subordinating conjunction will not allow it. This is, of course, a matter of logic rather than of grammar or syntax.

(b) When Tense of Verb of Adverb Clause Is Dependent upon Tense of Main Verb

In some adverb clause constructions the tense of the verb of the adverb clause is determined by the relationship of all three of the time factors which are present: (1) the time of the speaking or writing of the sentence, (2) the time of the action of the verb of the dependent clause, and (3) the time of the action of the verb of the independent clause.

We shall examine three constructions of this sort.

i. Adverb Clause of Purpose

The tense of the verb of an adverb clause of purpose depends upon the relationship of the time of the action it indicates to the time of the action of the main verb and the time of speaking or writing the sentence.

Generally speaking, if the time of the action of the verb of the adverb clause is *prior to* the time of the speaking or writing of the sentence, the verb will be a potential verb phrase with *might, could,* or *would* as an auxiliary:

> I worked so that he *might rest.* [The *resting* has already taken place.]
> She stayed at home so that her mother *could go.* [The *going* has already taken place.]

If the time of the action of the verb of the adverb clause is *the same as* the time of the speaking or writing of the sentence or is *in the future,* the verb will usually be a future tense verb or a potential verb phrase with *may* or *can* as an auxiliary—particularly if the main verb is in the present, future, present perfect, or future perfect:

> She studied so that she *will pass* the course. [The *passing* is still in the future.]
> I will watch the baby so that you *may attend* the movie. [The *attending* is still in the future.]

Note: If the main verb is in the past or past perfect, the verb of the adverb clause may be a potential verb phrase with *might, could,* or *would* as an auxiliary, even though the action is still in the future with reference to the time of the speaking or writing of the sentence:

> She studied so that she *would pass* the course.

In this sentence, the act of *passing* may still be in the future.

ii. Adverb Clause Containing a Present Tense Verb Indicating Future Action

When the main verb is in the future or future perfect tense, the verb of an adverb clause indicating action which will happen in the future is often in the present tense.

Examples:

The conference will begin as soon as the chairman *arrives.*

I shall have finished my work before you *leave.*

Note: The future action indicated by the verb of the adverb clause may occur *prior to, at the same time as,* or *after* the time of the action of the main verb.

iii. Adverb Clause Containing a Subjunctive Mode Verb

When the verb of an adverb clause is in the subjunctive mode, the sequence of tenses is determined in the same way that it is with a noun clause containing a subjunctive mode verb. (See pp. 122–23.)

Examples:

He walked as if he *were* tired. [The past subjunctive indicates a time which is identical with the time of the action of the main verb, *walked.*]

He walked as if he *had been hurt.* [The past perfect subjunctive indicates a time prior to the time of the action of the main verb, *walked.*]

(2) Adverb Clauses Modifying Verbals

An adverb clause may modify a verbal—an infinitive, a participle, or a gerund. The adverb clause in such a construction is part of a verbal phrase.

Examples:

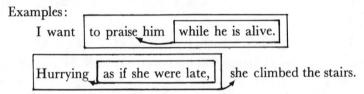

(3) Subordinating Conjunctions Modified by Adverbs

A subordinating conjunction may be modified by an adverb.

Examples:

The train arrived *just after* I left the station.

You are tired *merely because* you are hungry.

Note: Compare this construction with that in which an adverb modifies a preposition. (See p. 79.)

(4) Compounds

Adverb clauses may be linked together to form compounds. Such compounds are punctuated like the other compounds we have studied. Usually one subordinating conjunction serves for all units of the compound.

Example:

Although you worked and he helped, | the job is unfinished.

Note: Of course, an adverb clause *cannot* be linked with a noun clause or an adjective clause to form a compound.

(5) Phrases Within Clauses

An adverb clause may contain any kind of phrase.

Examples:

Prepositional Phrase Within an Adverb Clause

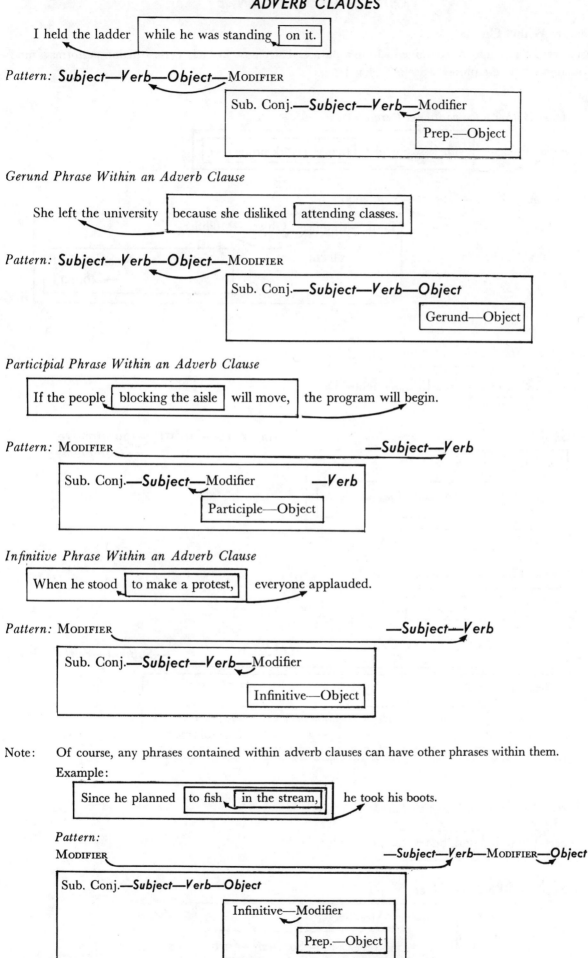

I held the ladder | while he was standing | on it.

Pattern: **Subject—Verb—Object—**MODIFIER

Sub. Conj.—**Subject—Verb**—Modifier

Prep.—Object

Gerund Phrase Within an Adverb Clause

She left the university | because she disliked | attending classes.

Pattern: **Subject—Verb—Object—**MODIFIER

Sub. Conj.—**Subject—Verb—Object**

Gerund—Object

Participial Phrase Within an Adverb Clause

If the people | blocking the aisle | will move, | the program will begin.

Pattern: MODIFIER **—Subject—Verb**

Sub. Conj.—**Subject—**Modifier **—Verb**

Participle—Object

Infinitive Phrase Within an Adverb Clause

When he stood | to make a protest, | everyone applauded.

Pattern: MODIFIER **—Subject—Verb**

Sub. Conj.—**Subject—Verb—**Modifier

Infinitive—Object

Note: Of course, any phrases contained within adverb clauses can have other phrases within them.

Example:

Since he planned | to fish | in the stream, | he took his boots.

Pattern:

MODIFIER **—Subject—Verb—**MODIFIER**—Object**

Sub. Conj.—**Subject—Verb—Object**

Infinitive—Modifier

Prep.—Object

(6) **Clauses Within Phrases**

An adverb clause may be contained within a phrase. The clause in such a construction performs a modifying function within the phrase. (See p. 144.)

Examples:

Adverb Clause Within a Prepositional Phrase

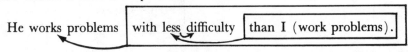

He works problems │ with less difficulty │ than I (work problems) .

Pattern: **Subject—Verb—Object**—Modifier

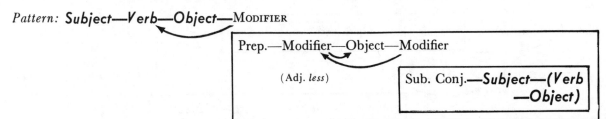

Prep.—Modifier—Object—Modifier

(Adj. *less*)

Sub. Conj.—***Subject—(Verb —Object)***

Adverb Clause Within a Gerund Phrase

Loafing │ while others work │ is my hobby.

Pattern: **Subject**   **—Linking Verb**—Modifier—***Substantive Complement***

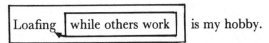

Gerund—Modifier

Sub. Conj.—***Subject—Verb***

Adverb Clause Within a Participial Phrase

Frowning │ as if he were angry, │ John closed the door.

Pattern: Modifier   **—Subject—Verb—Object**

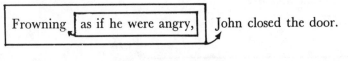

Participle—Modifier

Sub. Conj.—***Subject—Linking Verb—Adjective Complement***

Adverb Clause Within an Infinitive Phrase

I expect │ to wait │ until he returns.

Pattern: **Subject—Verb—Object**

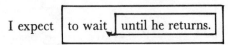

Infinitive—Modifier

Sub. Conj.—***Subject—Verb***

Note: Of course, the adverb clauses in such constructions can contain other phrases within them.

Example:

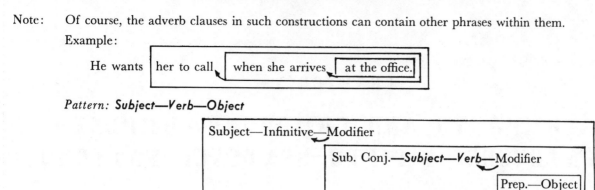

Pattern: **Subject—Verb—Object**

(7) Clauses Within Clauses

An adverb clause may contain a noun clause, an adjective clause, or another adverb clause. An adverb clause may, in turn, be contained within a noun clause or an adjective clause.

Examples:

Noun Clause Within an Adverb Clause

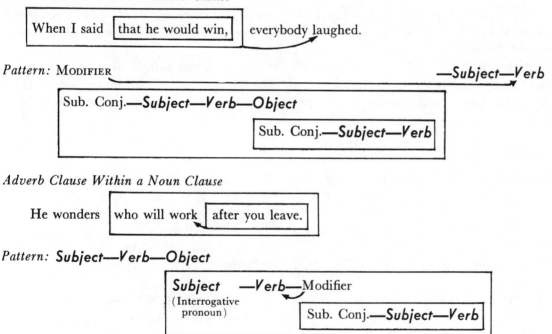

Note: It is advisable to re-read, once again, the final section on noun clauses, pp. 126–27.

DO EXERCISES 41, 42, AND 43

CHAPTER XV

COMPOUND AND COMPOUND-COMPLEX SENTENCES: A FIFTH SENTENCE PATTERN

UP to this point, we have studied four basic sentence patterns:

1. *Subject—Verb*
2. *Subject—Verb—Object*
3. *Subject—Linking Verb—Complement*
4. *Subject—Compound Predicate*

The fourth pattern, we noted, consists of a subject and a compound predicate made up of two or more simple predicates of the types found in the first three patterns. In other words, the fourth sentence pattern is produced by combining elements used in the first three basic patterns.

We now come to a fifth and final basic sentence pattern: the *compound pattern*. It consists of two or more *independent units* which fit any of the first four basic sentence patterns. It is, therefore, derived from the first four patterns in somewhat the same way that the fourth pattern is derived from the first three.

Examples:

Independent Unit	*Independent Unit*	
The cat retreated,	and the dog followed	it.
Subject *Verb*	*Subject* *Verb*	*Object*

Independent Unit	*Independent Unit*	*Independent Unit*
He worked,	she supervised,	and I watched them.
Subject *Verb*	*Subject* *Verb*	*Subject* *Verb* *Object*

Independent Unit	*Independent Unit*
We were exhausted,	but we pitched the tent and built a fire.
Subject *Linking Verb* *Adjective Complement*	*Subject* *Compound Predicate*

Independent Unit	*Independent Unit*
They found the hotel which you suggested,	but no rooms were available.
Subject *Verb* *Object* *Adjective Clause*	*Subject* *Linking Verb* *Adjective Complement*

As shown by the last example, any independent unit in a sentence fitting the *compound pattern* may contain a dependent clause. In other words, an independent unit may be equivalent to either a simple sentence or a complex sentence.

Note: The units which form a sentence fitting the compound pattern must, of course, be *logically* connected; they may or may not be joined by words which serve as *grammatical* connectives.

We have, then, only five basic sentence patterns:

1. *Subject—Verb*
2. *Subject—Verb—Object*

3. *Subject—Linking Verb—Complement*
4. *Subject—Compound Predicate*
5. *Compound Pattern*

The framework of any normal English sentence will fit one of these patterns.

A. STRUCTURE OF COMPOUND AND COMPOUND-COMPLEX SENTENCES

Sentences fitting the compound pattern are divided into two types, the distinction being made according to whether or not there is a dependent or subordinate clause in the sentence. A *compound sentence* is made up of two or more independent units which contain no dependent clauses. A *compound-complex sentence* is made up of two or more independent units, at least one of which is *complex—i.e.,* contains one or more dependent clauses.

Altogether, as we have seen, there are four types of sentences as far as clause structure is concerned: (1) simple, (2) complex, (3) compound, and (4) compound-complex. The following chart will clarify the differences between these types:

Type of Sentence	Independent Clauses	Dependent Clauses
Simple	One	None
Complex	One	One or more
Compound	Two or more	None
Compound-Complex	Two or more	One or more

In the remainder of this section we shall study in detail both compound and compound-complex sentences, giving particular attention to the ways in which the independent units are connected with each other and to the proper punctuation of the various sentences.

1. SENTENCES HAVING UNITS CONNECTED BY COORDINATING CONJUNCTIONS

The independent units which compose a compound or compound-complex sentence may be connected by coordinating conjunctions—either single conjunctions or pairs of conjunctions.

a. *UNITS CONNECTED BY SINGLE COORDINATING CONJUNCTIONS*

The independent units of a compound or compound-complex sentence may be connected by the single coordinating conjunctions *and, but, or, for, nor.* The conjunctions *and* and *or* are used in both two-unit and multiple-unit compounds; the other conjunctions connect only two-unit compounds.

(1) **Conjunctions Used**

(a) The Conjunction *and*

The conjunction *and* is used to connect the parts of compounds consisting of *added* units.

> Examples:
>
> She smiled sweetly, *and* he grinned shyly.
> George is swimming, Bill is playing tennis, *and* Jack is sleeping.

(b) The Conjunction *nor*

The conjunction *nor* is used to connect the parts of compounds consisting of *added negative* units.

> Example:
>
> He would not apologize, *nor* would he promise to change his ways.

This construction is primarily a rhetorical or literary device. (Note the inverted word-order of the second clause.)

(c) The Conjunction *but*

The conjunction *but* is used to connect the parts of compounds consisting of *contrasted* units.

Examples:

> Henry studied the lesson, *but* he didn't understand it.
> We had planned a picnic, *but* we had to postpone it.

(d) The Conjunction *or*

The conjunction *or* is used to connect the parts of compounds consisting of *alternative* units.

Examples:

> The burglar used a skeleton key, *or* I forgot to lock the door.
> Take a taxi, *or* catch the Englewood bus.

(e) The Conjunction *for*

The conjunction *for* is used to connect the parts of two-unit compounds in which the second unit expresses the *cause* of the action indicated in the first unit or gives *evidence* for the statement made in the first unit.

Examples:

> He was tired, *for* he had worked all day. (Cause)
> The old man heard me, *for* he lifted his head. (Evidence)

Note 1: All of the examples given above are compound sentences; however, all statements made in this section apply to both compound and compound-complex sentences.

Note 2: A coordinating conjunction may be used to connect two separate sentences.

Example:

> He was quick. But the snake was quicker.

This sort of construction is practically the same as that in a compound or compound-complex sentence. The only significant difference is that the independent units are placed in separate sentences for effect.

(2) Punctuation Used

As indicated by previous examples, a sentence containing independent units connected by single coordinating conjunctions normally follows one of the following punctuation patterns:

(a) Two-unit compound

$$\textit{Punctuation pattern:} \ \underline{\hspace{5cm}}, \left\{ \begin{array}{l} \text{and} \\ \text{but} \\ \text{or} \\ \text{for} \\ \text{nor} \end{array} \right\} \underline{\hspace{4cm}}.$$

(b) Multiple-unit compound

$$\textit{Punctuation pattern:} \ \underline{\hspace{3cm}}, \ \underline{\hspace{3cm}}, \left\{ \begin{array}{l} \text{and} \\ \text{or} \end{array} \right\} \underline{\hspace{3cm}}.$$

There are two situations in which these patterns are not followed:

(a) If both independent units are very short, the comma may be omitted in a two-unit compound sentence.

Example:

> The sky darkened and lightning flashed.

(b) If any of the independent units contains internal comma punctuation near a break between independent units, a semicolon is used instead of a comma to separate the units.

Example:

> We fed him steak, peas, and potatoes; but he was still hungry.

A compound-complex sentence often requires such a use of the semicolon because of comma punctuation used to enclose a subordinate clause.

Example:

> The old prospector was discouraged; but, when I suggested giving up, he was indignant.

b. *UNITS CONNECTED BY PAIRS OF CONJUNCTIONS (CORRELATIVES)*

The independent units of a compound or compound-complex sentence may also be connected by pairs of conjunctions. The correlatives usually employed in this construction are the following: *not only . . . but also* (or *but*) and *either . . . or.*

> Examples:
>> *Not only* did he say it, *but* he actually believed it.
>> *Either* do your work, *or* take the consequences.

Note the inverted word-order in the first example.

Note: In compound sentences as well as in compound elements, the construction following one correlative must be equivalent to that following the other. Note that in the examples given above a complete independent clause follows each correlative.

The punctuation of sentences containing independent units connected by pairs of conjunctions is normally that used in the examples given above.

> *Punctuation patterns:* Not only _____, but (also) _____.
> Either _____, or _____.

A semicolon is substituted for the comma if either unit contains internal comma punctuation near the break between the independent units.

2. SENTENCES HAVING UNITS JOINED WITHOUT COORDINATING CONJUNCTIONS

The independent units of a compound or compound-complex sentence may be joined without the use of coordinating conjunctions. Such sentences may either have no connectives whatsoever or contain conjunctive adverbs serving as connectives.

a. *UNITS JOINED WITHOUT CONNECTIVES*

Independent units of compound or compound-complex sentences may be joined without connectives. In such sentences, a semicolon is normally used to separate the independent units.

> Examples:
>> He wanted to hear the news; his wife wanted to listen to a soap opera.
>> The lightning flashed; the thunder boomed; the rain poured down.

As indicated by these examples, in this type of sentence the independent units are usually parallel in structure.

The punctuation patterns for this sort of sentence are the following:

(1) Two-unit compound

Punctuation pattern: _____; _____.

(2) Multiple-unit compound

Punctuation pattern: _____; _____; _____.

b. *UNITS CONNECTED BY CONJUNCTIVE ADVERBS*

Conjunctive adverbs may be used to connect the independent units of compound or compound-complex sentences. A conjunctive adverb in this construction performs a dual function: (1) it serves as an adverbial modifier of its own independent clause, and (2) it serves as a transitional connective linking its clause with the independent clause which precedes it.

> Example:
>> I need a vacation; however, I do not expect to get one.

In this example, the conjunctive adverb *however* qualifies or modifies the entire second clause in the same way that a sentence adverb modifies an entire sentence. At the same time, it serves to indicate the logical connection between the two contrasted clauses.

A conjunctive adverb may be placed in the middle of its own clause instead of at the beginning. In fact, it is often preferable to place it in this position.

Example:

> George plans to attend; his father, however, cannot be present.

Some of the most common single-word conjunctive adverbs are the following: *accordingly, also, besides, consequently, furthermore, hence, however, likewise, meanwhile, moreover, nevertheless, next, otherwise, so, still, then, therefore, thus, though, too, whereas, yet.*[1] In performing their connecting function, these words may show a wide variety of relationships between the two clauses they connect.

Examples:

> His statement was not tactful; *moreover,* it was not true. (Addition)
> Jack wants to succeed; *yet* he is not willing to work for success. (Contrast)
> She will arrive eventually; *meanwhile,* we shall wait patiently. (Time relation)
> Our food stocks are low; we must *therefore* conserve them. (Cause-effect relation)

In addition to these single-word elements, there are also a number of phrases which function as conjunctive adverbs. Some of these are the following: *as a result, at the same time, for this reason, on the contrary, on the other hand.*

Examples:

> My brother never reads; *as a result,* his knowledge of world affairs is quite limited. (Cause-effect relation)
> The landlord was not indifferent; *on the contrary,* he seemed very sympathetic. (Contrast)

(1) Punctuation Used with Conjunctive Adverbs

In a compound or compound-complex sentence in which the only element connecting the units is a conjunctive adverb, the same semicolon punctuation is employed that is used when there is no connective whatsoever.

Examples:

> She is lazy; yet she does her work.
> The store was closed; so we returned home.[2]
> The situation seemed hopeless; nevertheless, he continued to fight.

Note: There is a growing tendency to use a comma before *yet* and *so*; however, until this practice becomes firmly established, it is advisable to use the semicolon in all constructions of this sort.

The conjunctive adverb itself may or may not be set off by commas. If the conjunctive adverb is closely connected with its clause, no comma punctuation is used; if it is loosely connected with its clause, it is enclosed within commas. Generally speaking, conjunctive adverbs consisting of phrases are set off, and those consisting of one-syllable words (such as *hence, so, still, thus, yet*) are not set off. Of the other conjunctive adverbs, those most likely to be enclosed in commas are the following: *consequently, furthermore, however,* and *moreover.*

Examples:

> Checkers is a fairly simple game; chess, *on the other hand,* is exceedingly complex. (Phrase)
> I had exposed him; *hence* he hated me. (One-syllable word)
> I favor the plan; the decision, *however,* will be made by the committee.
> We must cooperate; *otherwise* we shall fail.

Note: In setting off a conjunctive adverb, place a comma before as well as after it unless the semicolon serves as the preceding mark of enclosure. The patterns of punctuation are the following:

> _____; _____, however, _____.
> _____; however, _____.

[1] Of course, many of these same words can perform other functions in a sentence. Several of them, such as *so, then,* and *too,* may be used as pure adverbs with no connective function.

[2] Use the conjunctive adverb *so* very sparingly. Sentences strung together by use of *so* or *and so* are extremely ineffective.

(2) Some Special Notes on the Conjunctive Adverb

(a) Conjunctive Adverbs Used in Addition to Coordinating Conjunctions

A conjunctive adverb may be used in a compound or compound-complex sentence in which the independent units are joined by a coordinating conjunction.

Examples:

The children received improper training; *and, as a result,* they became unmanageable.

The organization made little progress, *but* it *nevertheless* continued its efforts.

Note that the punctuation used between the independent units in such sentences depends upon whether there is internal comma punctuation near the break between units.

Note: The fact that a coordinating conjunction can be used with a conjunctive adverb provides us with a simple method of distinguishing between *so* functioning as a subordinating conjunction and *so* functioning as a conjunctive adverb.

So used as a conjunctive adverb introducing an independent unit may be preceded by the conjunction *and*. If no such conjunction is present, a semicolon is used before *so*.

Example:

The teacher dismissed the class; so I went to the library.

Note that the conjunction *and* can be inserted:

The teacher dismissed the class, and so I went to the library.

So used as a subordinating conjunction is a colloquial substitute for *so that*. No punctuation separates the adverb clause of purpose introduced by *so* from the main clause.

Example:

We ran so (= *so that*) we would not be late.

Note that the conjunction *and* cannot be inserted:

We ran [and] so we would not be late.

As we have previously noted, both *so* and *and so* should be used very infrequently. Some grammarians insist that the *only* proper use of *so* as a connective is its use in the subordinating conjunction *so that*.

(b) Conjunctive Adverbs Used to Connect Separate Sentences

A conjunctive adverb may be used to connect two separate sentences. A construction of this sort is quite similar to the compound and compound-complex sentences we have been studying. However, the conjunctive adverb in this construction performs its connective function across a period and a break between sentences instead of across a semicolon.

Example:

We oppose some of his policies. However, we shall vote for him.

Note that this could be written as follows:

We oppose some of his policies; however, we shall vote for him.

Note: The use of conjunctive adverbs to connect separate sentences is a means of achieving smooth transitions between sentences. Such a linkage not only ties sentences together but also indicates the logical relationship they bear to each other. Consequently, the reader is able to grasp and relate the various ideas quickly and easily.

3. SENTENCES HAVING UNITS JOINED BY A COMBINATION OF METHODS

In a compound or compound-complex sentence containing more than two independent units a combination of methods may be used to join the various units.

Examples:

They invited John; he accepted the invitation; however, he did not come.

Punctuation pattern: _____; _____; however, _____.

(No connective)   (Conjunctive adverb)

I don't like him; moreover, he does not like me; but we were very polite to each other when we met.

Punctuation pattern: _____; moreover, _____; but _____.
          (Conjunctive adverb)   (Conjunction)

She wrote to me, and I answered the letter; but she has not written since.

Punctuation pattern: _____, and _____; but _____.
              (Comma + Conjunction)   (Semicolon + Conjunction)

Note: The use of the semicolon in the last example has the effect of dividing the sentence into two major parts. The first part consists of two independent clauses joined by *and*; the second part consists of a single independent clause which is contrasted with the first two clauses by use of the conjunction *but*.

B. INDICATING THE PATTERN OF A COMPOUND OR COMPOUND-COMPLEX SENTENCE

To indicate the pattern of a compound or compound-complex sentence, we shall use the following method:

(1) **We shall use the words "*Compound Pattern*" as the top line of the notations.**

Example:

I had a poor background, and the subject was quite difficult; the teacher, however, explained things very clearly.

Partial pattern: **Compound Pattern**

(2) **Beneath this notation, using the method employed in treating other compounds, we shall show the over-all pattern of the sentence—including conjunctions and conjunctive adverbs used to connect the units, and punctuation used between units, around conjunctive adverbs, and at the end of the sentence.**

Example:

I had a poor background, and the subject was quite difficult; the teacher, however, explained things very clearly.

Partial pattern: **Compound Pattern**

(_____, and _____; _____, however, _____.)

(3) **Then, after numbering each of the independent units, we shall indicate the exact structure of each independent unit on a separate line. (A conjunction is not part of either of the units it connects; a conjunctive adverb is a clause modifier within its clause.)**

Example:

I had a poor background, and the subject was quite difficult; the teacher, however, explained things very clearly.

Complete pattern: **Compound Pattern**

(_____, and _____; _____, however, _____.)
         1   2   3

1. *Subject—Verb*—Modifier—*Object*
2. *Subject—Linking Verb*—Modifier—*Adjective Complement*
3. *Subject—*Modifier   —*Verb—Object*—Modifier—Modifier
       (Conjunctive adverb)

This method of analysis emphasizes the fact that compound and compound-complex sentences are for the most part composed of elements which we have already studied. Some additional examples of this method of analysis follow:

The temperature is high, but the humidity is low.

Pattern: **Compound Pattern**

(_____, but _____.)
      1   2

1. *Subject—Linking Verb—Adjective Complement*
2. *Subject—Linking Verb—Adjective Complement*

She waxed the floors; he beat the rugs.

Pattern: **Compound Pattern**

(_____; _____.)
      1   2

1. *Subject—Verb—Object*
2. *Subject—Verb—Object*

Not only is the price exorbitant, but the workmanship is poor.

Pattern: **Compound Pattern**

(Not only _____, but _____.)
          1   2

1. *Linking Verb—Subject—Adjective Complement*
2. *Subject—Linking Verb—Adjective Complement*

I polished the car, but it rained as soon as I finished working.

Pattern: **Compound Pattern**

(_____, but _____.)
     1   2

1. *Subject—Verb—Object*
2. *Subject—Verb—*Modifier

Sub. Conj.—*Subject—Verb—Object*

C. A SPECIAL NOTE ON THE COMPOUND-COMPLEX SENTENCE

From the standpoint of structure, the compound-complex sentence is capable of more complication than any other type of English sentence. It contains two or more independent clauses. At least one of these independent clauses must contain a dependent clause, and it is possible for *all* of the independent clauses to contain one or more dependent clauses. Furthermore, each dependent clause may contain dependent clauses within it. In addition to the various clauses, a compound-complex sentence may contain practically any construction involving single-word elements, compounds, and phrases.

The compound-complex sentence, then, comes as the climax of the study of sentence structure which we started with simple sentences consisting of only a subject and a verb. Perhaps more striking than its complexity, though, is its inherent simplicity. The functions performed in such a sentence are actually quite limited in number; and, though a sentence may contain numerous elements, if the functions of these elements are correctly understood, every part of the sentence falls into place without difficulty.

DO EXERCISES 44 AND 45

CHAPTER XVI

GRAMMAR AND LOGIC: UNITY, COORDINATION, AND SUBORDINATION

IF sentences are to communicate a person's thoughts accurately, the *grammatical* relationships of the elements which compose each sentence must correspond with the *logical* relationships of the ideas which make up the thought or thoughts expressed by that sentence. The most important aspects of this correspondence between grammar and logic are unity, coordination, and subordination.

Just as *sentence elements* must be linked together to form a *grammatical unit,* the *thought elements underlying the sentence* must be connected in such a way that they form a *logical unit.* As we noted in the first chapter, a sentence is a group of words which conveys at least one complete thought. In a simple or complex sentence, one complete thought is expressed. In a compound or compound-complex sentence, two or more closely related thoughts are expressed—one by each independent unit. Every sentence, though, whether it expresses one complete thought or more than one, must communicate a *single logical unit.* The following sentence lacks the necessary logical unity:

Disconnected: Our coach was born in 1901, and he enjoys fishing.

Since there is no apparent logical connection between the thoughts expressed in the two clauses, they should not be placed in the same sentence. The grammatical unity of a sentence must be matched by logical unity of the thought or thoughts conveyed.

In addition to the matter of unity, there is a further way in which the logic and grammar of a sentence must correspond. In each sentence, through proper use of coordination and subordination in constructing the sentence, the writer [1] must indicate the relative importance of the ideas expressed.

Ideas which are of equal importance are usually expressed by coordinate constructions connected by coordinating conjunctions. Such constructions will, of course, constitute compounds of various sorts. Note the coordinate constructions in the following sentences:

The boy was *tall* and *skinny.* (Coordinate words)
She liked *making cookies* and *baking cakes.* (Coordinate phrases)
We wondered *why he had gone* and *when he would return.* (Coordinate dependent clauses)
I wanted to deposit the check, but *the bank was closed.* (Coordinate independent clauses)

By his use of such coordinate constructions, a writer indicates that he considers the ideas involved to have an equivalence of importance which matches their equivalence of expression.

If one idea in a sentence is less important than another, this difference should be indicated by grammatical subordination. An important idea should be expressed by a grammatically important sentence element; a less important idea should be expressed by a grammatically subordinate sentence element. Note the following sentence:

Poor: The man was walking across the street and was hit by a truck.

Obviously, the fact that the man "was walking across the street" is much less important than the fact that he "was hit by a truck." This difference in importance should be made obvious in the structure of the sentence:

Improved: While walking across the street, the man was hit by a truck.

In the revised sentence, the less important idea has been subordinated by being expressed in an elliptical adverb clause.

[1] Or speaker.

Often the relative importance of two ideas is not inherent within the ideas themselves but depends entirely upon the intention of the writer. Let us consider the following sentences:

My brother is a doctor.
My brother lives in Illinois.

These sentences may be combined to form a single sentence which emphasizes the fact that "my brother lives in Illinois":

My brother, who is a doctor, lives in Illinois.

If, however, it is desired to emphasize the fact that "my brother is a doctor," the sentence may be written as follows:

My brother, who lives in Illinois, is a doctor.

Either of these sentences may be correct, depending upon which idea the writer desires to emphasize.

To summarize, the principle underlying unity, coordination, and subordination in a sentence is simply this: *The grammar and the logic of a sentence must coincide exactly.* If they do, the sentence will be unified and will consist of parts which are properly coordinated and subordinated.

DO EXERCISE 46

CHAPTER XVII

EFFECTIVE SENTENCES

IN the preceding chapters, we have been primarily concerned with the writing of correct sentences. We need to go one step further. A person composing a sentence usually finds that it would be possible to express the thought involved in a number of different sentence forms, all of them grammatically correct. Yet the varying sentences which he might compose would not be equally effective. In this concluding chapter, we shall consider the principles underlying the writing of *effective* correct sentences.

What determines the effectiveness of a sentence? Generally speaking, it is determined by the nature of the reader.[1] More specifically, the effectiveness of a sentence depends upon the extent to which the sentence meets certain fundamental requirements originating in the natural preferences of the reader.

The most important of these reader requirements is **ease of comprehension.** The reader is basically lazy. He is willing to expend only a minimum amount of mental energy in acquiring the thought contained in a sentence. Yet he wants maximum returns from this minimum effort. And the *effect* of a sentence upon him varies accordingly.[2]

Other things being equal, the fewer the words used to communicate a thought to the reader, the more effective the communication of it will be. A short sentence is therefore more effective than a long one if they both convey the same meaning. It does not follow, however, that all sentences should be short. Indeed, many thoughts are of such complexity that they can be communicated only through the use of long sentences. But no sentence should be wordy. No sentence should contain more words than are necessary to communicate the desired thought. The more condensed the expression of a thought, the more forceful it will be.[3]

In addition to *condensation, repetition* is a means of increasing ease of comprehension. When a sentence contains repetition (or *parallelism*) of structure, the reader finds it extremely easy to follow the structural pattern and can, in fact, often anticipate the thought as well as the structure. Note the effect gained by use of parallel construction in the following sentences:

> You can lead a horse to water, but you can't make him drink.
> More people are interested in making money than in earning it.
> A participle functions as an adjective; a gerund functions as a substantive.[4]

As is indicated by these examples, repetition of structure often involves repetition of words as well. Such verbal repetition, when skillfully employed, is also an aid to comprehension.

Normal word-order, like *condensation* and *repetition,* usually makes for ease of comprehension, and thus for effectiveness. There is, however, an important exception to this rule. When a sentence contains an element which qualifies the main thought, it is often easier to comprehend *the thought as qualified* if the qualifying element comes first, for the main thought is withheld until after the mind has been properly prepared to qualify the thought when it is presented. A sentence thus constructed so that the main thought is not completed until the sentence is ended is called a *periodic sentence.*[5]

---

[1] Throughout this chapter, reference is made to the "reader" and the "writer," but what is said applies equally well to the "hearer" and the "speaker" in oral communication.

[2] Obviously, the level of comprehension is not the same with all readers, and one's style of writing must be adjusted to suit one's audience. A sentence which a college student easily comprehends may be entirely too difficult for a sixth-grader.

[3] The effectiveness of most figures of speech results from the condensation of expression which they make possible. A simile or a metaphor, for example, compares something relatively unfamiliar to something familiar. Through thus drawing upon the reader's previous experience, it conveys a wealth of meaning with great economy of words.

[4] Sentences in which entire clauses are parallel in form are called *balanced sentences.* They are often useful for emphasizing a contrast or a comparison.

[5] A sentence in which the main thought is completed before the end of the sentence is called a *loose sentence.* Most sentences fall within this classification.

Examples:

> If a miracle happens, we shall win.
> Although he had replaced the faulty tubes, the radio would not work.
> Unless I am badly mistaken, she enjoyed the party very much.

The effectiveness of the periodic sentence depends not only upon its **ease of comprehension** but also upon its **climactic arrangement of ideas**—another reader requirement.

The reader has a natural desire to find a gradual increase in significance as he reads a sentence. If more ideas than one are presented, he wishes them to build up to a climax. He does not want to begin with the essential and proceed to the non-essential. The periodic sentence, with the main idea placed at the end of the sentence, meets the reader's unconscious demand for climactic arrangement of ideas. Another construction involving climactic arrangement is the series of coordinate elements. To avoid anticlimax, one should arrange such elements in order of importance or significance.

Examples:

> He was *cynical, deceitful,* and *traitorous.*
> I escaped with *a torn coat, a bruised arm,* and *a broken jaw.*

A final reader requirement is **variety**—both in sentence length and sentence structure. The writer should make a conscious effort to vary the length of his sentences. The use of too many short sentences produces a choppy effect; the use of too many long sentences produces monotony. Furthermore, the writer should consciously vary the structure of his sentences. The reader soon tires of a constant diet of sentences which are similar in structure, even though each sentence taken by itself is effective. To write effectively, one must make judicious use of all of the types of sentence structure which we have studied during the course of this book.

EXERCISES

IMPORTANT NOTE

In most of the exercises in this workbook, you are required to write sentences. Any of these sentences will be counted *entirely wrong* if it contains an error of *any* kind—in spelling, capitalization, grammar, sentence structure, punctuation, idiom, meaning. A sentence is either *correct* or *incorrect*; there is no middle ground. Be sure that each sentence makes sense and is correct in every way. Read the preliminary instructions carefully before doing each exercise. Failure to follow these instructions will make your exercises incorrect.

You are expected to revise or rewrite all incorrect sentences when the exercises are returned by the instructor. You will then either (1) resubmit the corrected exercises to the instructor or (2) preserve them in your notebook for examination and discussion at individual conferences. (Your instructor will tell you which of these procedures you are to follow.)

EXERCISE 1

SUBJECTS AND VERBS

Make a complete sentence of each of the following by inserting a verb.

Special Instructions:

.... 1. Do not insert any word which is not part of the verb.

.... 2. Do not use any verb more than once in these sentences. (After you have used one form of a verb, do not use another form of the same verb. You may repeat *auxiliaries* but not *primary verbs.* Be particularly careful not to repeat forms of the primary verb *to be.*) Any sentence in which a verb previously used is repeated will be considered incorrect.

.... 3. Do not use the verb contained in the example.

.... 4. Do not capitalize any word which you insert in a blank.

.... 5. Be sure that the completed sentence makes good sense and is correct in every way.

Example:

The boy ___*had dropped*___ the watch.

---

1. The secretary ___typed___.

2. The girl ___loved___ the doll.

3. The quarterback ___is___ good.

4. The teacher ___dismissed___ the class.

5. She ___likes___ the speaker.

6. The superintendent ___resigned___.

7. The horse ___threw___ the child.

8. The farmer ___fixed___ the tractor.

9. A reporter ___covered___ the story.

10. The mechanic ___dismantled___ the engine.

Make a complete sentence of each of the following by inserting a subject.

Special Instructions:

.... 1. Use a subject which consists of only one word.

.... 2. Place *a, an,* or *the* before the subject if one of these articles is needed to avoid primer or telegraphic style; otherwise insert only one word in each blank. (Particularly guard against inserting such words as *his, her, your, their.*)

163

.... 3. Do not use any subject more than once in these sentences. Any sentence in which a subject previously used is repeated will be considered incorrect.

.... 4. Do not use names of people in these sentences.

.... 5. Capitalize only the first word in each sentence.

.... 6. Be sure that the completed sentence makes good sense.

.... 7. Do not use the subject contained in the example.

Example: *The pitcher* .... threw the ball.

---

11. .... The teacher .... prepared a lecture.

12. .... The hostess .... was indignant.

13. .... The president .... resigned.

14. .... A farmer .... has harvested the wheat.

15. .... The comittee .... should consider the petition.

16. .... A pollster .... had completed the survey.

17. .... The secretary .... has notified the president.

18. .... The mayor .... will be a candidate.

19. .... An engineer .... is examining the report.

20. .... The patient .... had been watching television.

A FINAL WORD TO THE STUDENT

Use the following procedure to check your exercise before you hand it in:

1. Re-read the special instructions one at a time.

2. After you re-read each separate instruction, examine your completed exercise to make certain that you have followed that particular instruction exactly.

3. Revise your work wherever necessary.

4. When you are certain that the special instruction you are considering has been observed throughout your exercise, place a check (√) to the left of that special instruction and go on to the next one until you have completed the entire list.

This process will take several minutes of your time, but failure to recheck your exercises in this manner may mean that you have wasted all of the time and effort you have spent in doing the exercise.

EXERCISE 2

SUBSTANTIVES

Supply a subject for the verb by placing in each blank a *single-word* substantive of the type specified below the blank.

Special Instructions:

1. Use a subject which consists of only one word.
2. Place *a, an,* or *the* before the subject if one of these articles is needed to avoid primer or telegraphic style; otherwise insert only one word in each blank. (Particularly guard against inserting such words as *his, her, your, their.*)
3. Do not use any subject more than once in this exercise. Any sentence in which a subject previously used is repeated will be considered incorrect.
4. Capitalize the first word in each sentence.
5. Be sure that the complete sentence makes good sense and is correct in every way. (Be especially careful in inserting collective nouns and indefinite pronouns. The subject must fit the verb.)
6. Do not use the subject contained in the example.

Example:

The automobile had scraped the curb.
        Common noun

---

1. The paper has disappeared.
   Common noun

2. The policeman is a detective.
   Common noun

3. The men have organized a club.
   Common noun

4. The children were eating doughnuts.
   Common noun

5. John answered the doorbell.
   Proper noun

X 6. Abraham Lincoln has become a hero.
   Proper noun

7. The class was unruly.
   Collective noun

8. The team have disagreed.
   Collective noun

Using "Snoopy" would make this correct. Abraham Lincoln is a proper noun. Isn't that the point.

9. _____You_____ should demand a refund.
   Personal pronoun
   2nd person, singular

10. _____We_____ have rented an apartment.
    Personal pronoun
    1st person, plural

11. _____He_____ gave a speech.
    Personal pronoun
    3rd person, singular

12. _____She_____ will enjoy the movie.
    Personal pronoun
    3rd person, singular

13. _____I_____ knew the answer.
    Personal pronoun
    1st person, singular

14. _____They_____ painted the house.
    Personal pronoun
    3rd person, plural

15. _____This_____ is the one.
    Demonstrative pronoun

16. _____These_____ are the pictures.
    Demonstrative pronoun

17. _____Someone_____ has borrowed the magazine.
    Indefinite pronoun

18. _____Many_____ are incorrect.
    Indefinite pronoun

19. _____Nobody_____ is ready.
    Indefinite pronoun

20. _____Few_____ have received promotions.
    Indefinite pronoun

A FINAL WORD TO THE STUDENT

Use the following procedure to check your exercise before you hand it in:

1. Re-read the special instructions one at a time.
2. After you re-read each separate instruction, examine your completed exercise to make certain that you have followed that particular instruction exactly.
3. Revise your work wherever necessary.
4. When you are certain that the special instruction you are considering has been observed throughout your exercise, place a check (√) to the left of that special instruction and go on to the next one until you have completed the entire list.

This process will take several minutes of your time, but failure to recheck your exercises in this manner may mean that you have wasted all of the time and effort you have spent in doing the exercise.

EXERCISE 3

VERBS

Fill in each blank with the specified tense form of the verb indicated. Every verb will be in the *active* voice and the *indicative* mode.

Special Instructions:

——— 1. Be sure that the verb agrees with its subject in person and number.

——— 2. If in doubt about the principal parts of any verb, refer to your dictionary or to p. 284 of this text.

——— 3. Do not use *progressive* or *emphatic* forms unless they are specifically called for.

——— 4. For the future and future perfect tenses, use *shall* in the first person and *will* in the second and third persons.

Example:

She ____*swept*____ the rug.
to sweep—past tense

1. The train ____did arrive____ late.
   to arrive—past tense, emphatic

X 2. The orchestra ____has been finishing____ the selection.
   to finish—present perfect tense

3. I ____am reading____ the magazine.
   to read—present tense, progressive

4. Before the war Jack ____had been____ a clerk.
   to be—past perfect tense

5. The girl ____has broken____ her ankle.
   to break—present perfect tense

6. We ____do study____ the assignments.
   to study—present tense, emphatic

7. The mayor ____has been reading____ his mail.
   to read—present perfect tense, progressive

8. George ____had brought____ his car.
   to bring—past perfect tense

9. The janitor ____was leaving____ the building.
   to leave—past tense, progressive

10. The editor ____has rejected____ the story.
    to reject—past perfect tense

11. It ____does seem____ peculiar.
    to seem—present tense, emphatic

12. Next month they ____will have worked____ for ten years.
    to work—future perfect tense

167

13. They _____have seen_____ the play.
    to see—present perfect tense

14. Everybody _____was_____ present.
    to be—past tense

15. He _____will be expecting_____ you.
    to expect—future tense, progressive

16. The police _____had made_____ an investigation.
    to make—past perfect tense

17. The firecrackers _____disturb_____ me.
    to disturb—present tense

18. The soprano _____will sing_____ five numbers.
    to sing—future tense

19. Our team _____did win_____ the tournament.
    to win—past tense, emphatic

20. By next year I _____shall have fulfilled_____ the requirements.
    to fulfill—future perfect tense

21. He _____had eaten_____ before he left.
    to eat—past perfect tense

22. The flowers _____will bloom_____ soon.
    to bloom—future tense

23. They _____had been living_____ in Chicago.
    to live—past perfect tense, progressive

24. A turtle _____bit_____ the swimmer.
    to bite—past tense

25. She _____has written_____ three novels.
    to write—present perfect tense

A FINAL WORD TO THE STUDENT

Use the following procedure to check your exercise before you hand it in:

1. Re-read the special instructions one at a time.
2. After you re-read each separate instruction, examine your completed exercise to make certain that you have followed that particular instruction exactly.
3. Revise your work wherever necessary.
4. When you are certain that the special instruction you are considering has been observed throughout your exercise, place a check (√) to the left of that special instruction and go on to the next one until you have completed the entire list.

This process will take several minutes of your time, but failure to recheck your exercises in this manner may mean that you have wasted all of the time and effort you have spent in doing the exercise.

Name_____   Section_____

Date_____   Score___*100*___

EXERCISE 4

FIRST BASIC SENTENCE PATTERN

Subject—Verb

Each sentence written in this exercise will consist of a subject and a verb and will therefore fit the first basic sentence pattern.

Special Instructions:

_____ 1. Use a subject which consists of only one word. (The verb may consist of more than one word.)

_____ 2. Place *a, an,* or *the* before the subject if one of these articles is needed to avoid primer or telegraphic style, but do not use any other words in addition to the subject and the verb. (Particularly guard against inserting such words as *his, her, your, their.*)

_____ 3. Do not use a possessive (such as *mine, his, hers, theirs, yours, men's*) as the subject of any sentence.

_____ 4. Do not use any subject more than once in this exercise.

_____ 5. Do not use any verb more than once in this exercise. (After you have used one form of a verb, do not use another form of the same verb. You may repeat auxiliaries but not primary verbs.)

_____ 6. Do not use the passive voice.

_____ 7. Use only the indicative mode.

_____ 8. Capitalize the first word in each sentence, and place a period at the end of each sentence.

_____ 9. Be sure that each sentence is a statement, not a question.

_____10. Be sure that each sentence makes good sense. (Each verb must be complete without an object or complement—*i.e.,* must be *intransitive.* If you are not sure that any given verb can be intransitive, consult your dictionary.)

_____11. Do not use the subjects or verbs contained in the examples.

Write five sentences to fit the first pattern, using a *common noun* as the subject.

Pattern: **Subject**   **—Verb**
(Common noun)

Example: The boy   sang.

Subject (Common noun)	—	**Verb**
1. The deer		ran.
2. The girl		laughed
3. A dog		barked
4. The ship		sank.
5. The wind		blew

Write five sentences to fit the first pattern, using a *pronoun* as the subject.

Pattern: **Subject—Verb**
(Pronoun)

Example: She   has gone.

Subject —	Verb
(Pronoun)	

6. It   was destroyed.

7. He   yelled.

8. We   rejoiced.

9. I   returned.

10. They   arrived.

A FINAL WORD TO THE STUDENT

Use the following procedure to check your exercise before you hand it in:

1. Re-read the special instructions one at a time.
2. After you re-read each separate instruction, examine your completed exercise to make certain that you have followed that particular instruction exactly.
3. Revise your work wherever necessary.
4. When you are certain that the special instruction you are considering has been observed throughout your exercise, place a check (√) to the left of that special instruction and go on to the next one until you have completed the entire list.

This process will take several minutes of your time, but failure to recheck your exercises in this manner may mean that you have wasted all of the time and effort you have spent in doing the exercise.

EXERCISE 5

SECOND BASIC SENTENCE PATTERN

Subject—Verb—Object

Each sentence written in this exercise will consist of a subject, a verb, and an object and will therefore fit the second basic sentence pattern.

Special Instructions:

_____ 1. Use a single-word subject and a single-word object. (The verb may consist of more than one word.)

_____ 2. Place *a, an,* or *the* before a noun if one of these articles is needed to avoid primer or telegraphic style, but do not use any other words in addition to the subject, the verb, and the object. (Particularly guard against inserting such words as *his, her, your, their.*)

_____ 3. Do not use a possessive (such as *mine, his, hers, theirs, yours, men's*) as the subject or object in any sentence.

_____ 4. Do not use any noun more than once in this exercise.

_____ 5. In sentences calling for pronouns, do not use the same pronoun word-form twice. However, you may use *different case forms* of the *same* personal pronoun—*I, me; he, him; she, her; we, us; they, them.*

_____ 6. Do not use any verb more than once in this exercise. (After you have used one form of a verb, do not use another form of the same verb. You may repeat auxiliaries but not primary verbs.)

_____ 7. Use only the indicative mode.

_____ 8. Capitalize the first word in each sentence, and place a period at the end of each sentence.

_____ 9. Be sure that each sentence is a statement, not a question.

_____10. Be sure that each sentence makes good sense.

_____11. Do not use any of the nouns, pronouns, or verbs contained in the examples.

_____12. Be sure that each of your sentences fits the second sentence pattern. The object must receive the action of the verb. The following sentence does *not* fit the pattern because the verb is intransitive:
   The boy came home.

Write four sentences to fit the second pattern, using a *common noun* as the subject and a *common noun* as the object.

Pattern: **Subject   —Verb—Object**
   (Common noun)   (Common noun)

Example: The truck   smashed   the wagon.

Subject	—	**Verb**	—	**Object**
(Common noun)				(Common noun)
1. The boy		caught		the ball.
2. The captain		sees		the ship.

171

3. The soldiers attacked the village.

4. A monkey climbed a tree.

Write three sentences to fit the second pattern, using a *common noun* as the subject and a *pronoun* as the object. Be sure that the case form of every pronoun is correct.

Pattern: **Subject —Verb—Object**
  (Common noun)   (Pronoun)

Example: The cat scratched her.

Subject	—	Verb	—	Object
(Common noun)				(Pronoun)
5. The car		passed		me .
6. The party		surprized		us .
7. The rain		soaked		him .

Write three sentences to fit the second pattern, using a *pronoun* as the subject and a *pronoun* as the object. Be sure that the case form of every pronoun is correct.

Pattern: **Subject—Verb—Object**
  (Pronoun)   (Pronoun)

Example: Nobody likes that.

Subject	—	Verb	—	Object
(Pronoun)				(Pronoun)
8. Everybody		saw		her.
9. Few		recognized		him.
10. We		confronted		them.

A FINAL WORD TO THE STUDENT

Use the following procedure to check your exercise before you hand it in:

1. Re-read the special instructions one at a time.
2. After you re-read each separate instruction, examine your completed exercise to make certain that you have followed that particular instruction exactly.
3. Revise your work wherever necessary.
4. When you are certain that the special instruction you are considering has been observed throughout your exercise, place a check (√) to the left of that special instruction and go on to the next one until you have completed the entire list.

This process will take several minutes of your time, but failure to recheck your exercises in this manner may mean that you have wasted all of the time and effort you have spent in doing the exercise.

EXERCISE 6

THIRD BASIC SENTENCE PATTERN

Subject—Linking Verb—Complement

Each sentence written in this exercise will consist of a subject, a linking verb, and a complement and will therefore fit the third basic sentence pattern.

Special Instructions:

----- 1. Use a single-word subject and a single-word complement. (The verb may consist of more than one word.)

----- 2. Place *a, an,* or *the* before a noun if one of these articles is needed to avoid primer or telegraphic style, but do not use any other words in addition to the subject, the linking verb, and the complement. (Particularly guard against inserting such words as *his, her, your, their.*)

----- 3. Do not use a possessive (such as *mine, his, hers, theirs, yours, men's*) as the subject or complement in any sentence.

----- 4. Do not use any noun or pronoun more than once in this exercise.

----- 5. Do not use any adjective complement more than once in this exercise.

----- 6. Use the verb *to be* as the linking verb in all sentences, but strive for variety in the form of the verb. (Use *is, are, was, were, shall be, will be, has been, have been, had been, etc.*)

----- 7. Use only the indicative mode.

----- 8. Capitalize the first word in each sentence, and place a period at the end of each sentence.

----- 9. Be sure that each sentence is a statement, not a question.

-----10. Be sure that each sentence makes good sense.

-----11. Do not use any subject or complement contained in the examples.

Write three sentences to fit the third pattern, using a *common noun* as the subject and a *common noun* as the complement.

Pattern: **Subject   —Linking Verb—Substantive Complement**
(Common noun)   (Common noun)

Example: The judge   had been   a lawyer.

	Subject —	Linking Verb	— Substantive Complement
	(Common noun)		(Common noun)
1.	The man	is	a father.
2.	The minister	has been	a lawyer.
3.	The girls	will be	cheerleaders.

Write three sentences to fit the third pattern, using a *common noun* as the subject and an *adjective* as the complement.

Pattern: **Subject** —*Linking Verb—Adjective Complement*
(Common noun)

Example: The examination   was   difficult.

Subject (Common noun)	—	Linking Verb	—	Adjective Complement
4. The dog		is		sick.
5. The reporter		was		frustrated.
✱ 6. A woman		will be		~~injured~~

Write two sentences to fit the third pattern, using a *common noun* as the subject and a *personal pronoun* as the complement. Be sure that the personal pronoun is in the *nominative case*.

Pattern: **Subject** —*Linking Verb—Substantive Complement*
(Common noun)   (Personal pronoun)

Example: The winner   will be   you.

Subject (Common noun)	—	Linking Verb	—	Substantive Complement (Personal pronoun)
7. The contestant		was		she.
8. The winner		is		he.

Write two sentences to fit the third pattern, using either a *demonstrative pronoun* or an *indefinite pronoun* as the subject and a *personal pronoun* as the complement. Be sure that the personal pronoun is in the *nominative case*.

Pattern: **Subject** —*Linking Verb—Substantive Complement*
(Demonstrative or indefinite pronoun)   (Personal pronoun)

Example: This   is   it.

Subject (Demonstrative or indefinite pronoun)	—	Linking Verb	—	Substantive Complement (Personal pronoun)
9. These		are		they.
10. That		was		he.

A FINAL WORD TO THE STUDENT

Use the following procedure to check your exercise before you hand it in:

1. Re-read the special instructions one at a time.
2. After you re-read each separate instruction, examine your completed exercise to make certain that you have followed that particular instruction exactly.
3. Revise your work wherever necessary.
4. When you are certain that the special instruction you are considering has been observed throughout your exercise, place a check (√) to the left of that special instruction and go on to the next one until you have completed the entire list.

This process will take several minutes of your time, but failure to recheck your exercises in this manner may mean that you have wasted all of the time and effort you have spent in doing the exercise.

EXERCISE 7

REFLEXIVE AND RECIPROCAL PRONOUNS

Use each of the indicated pronouns as the object in a sentence which fits the specified pattern.

Special Instructions:

------- 1. Use a substantive consisting of one word as the subject.

------- 2. Place *a, an,* or *the* before a noun if one of these articles is needed to avoid primer or telegraphic style, but do not use any other words in addition to the subject, the verb, and the object. (Particularly guard against inserting such words as *his, her, your, their.*)

------- 3. Do not use a possessive (such as *mine, his, hers, theirs, yours, men's*) as the subject of any sentence.

------- 4. Do not use any noun or pronoun more than once in this exercise. (You will use the singular pronoun *you* in sentence 2 and the plural pronoun *you* in sentence 7, but these are considered to be different pronouns.)

------- 5. Do not use any verb more than once in this exercise. (After you have used one form of a verb, do not use another form of the same verb. You may repeat auxiliaries but not primary verbs.)

------- 6. Use only the indicative mode.

------- 7. Be sure that the pronoun is the *object* of the verb. The verb must be a *transitive* verb. The following sentence *would not* fit the pattern:

      I came myself.

The verb *came* is not a transitive verb.

------- 8. Capitalize the first word in each sentence, and place a period at the end of each sentence.

------- 9. Be sure that each sentence is a statement, not a question.

------10. Be sure that each sentence makes good sense.

		Subject	—	Verb	—	Object
						(Pronoun indicated in left-hand column)
myself	1.	I		hurt		myself.
yourself	2.	You		called		yourself.
himself	3.	The president		drives		himself.
herself	4.	The girl		loves		herself.

175

itself   5. The satellite   destroyed   itself.

This is misspelled. Should the entire sentence be wrong?

ourselves ✗ 6. We   (defened)   ourselves.

yourselves   7. You   respect   yourselves.

themselves   8. The ecologists   protested   themselves.

each other   9. The women   admire   each other.

one another   10. ~~They~~   love   one another.

A FINAL WORD TO THE STUDENT

Use the following procedure to check your exercise before you hand it in:

1. Re-read the special instructions one at a time.
2. After you re-read each separate instruction, examine your completed exercise to make certain that you have followed that particular instruction exactly.
3. Revise your work wherever necessary.
4. When you are certain that the special instruction you are considering has been observed throughout your exercise, place a check (√) to the left of that special instruction and go on to the next one until you have completed the entire list.

This process will take several minutes of your time, but failure to recheck your exercises in this manner may mean that you have wasted all of the time and effort you have spent in doing the exercise.

EXERCISE 8

LINKING VERBS USED IN THE THIRD PATTERN

Use each of the indicated linking verbs in a sentence which fits the specified pattern.

Special Instructions:

1. Use a single-word subject and a single-word complement. (The verb may consist of more than one word.)
2. Use either a substantive or an adjective as the complement.
3. Place *a, an,* or *the* before a noun if one of these articles is needed to avoid primer or telegraphic style, but do not use any other words in addition to the subject, the linking verb, and the complement. (Particularly guard against inserting such words as *his, her, your, their.*)
4. Do not use a possessive (such as *mine, his, hers, theirs, yours, men's*) as the subject or complement in any sentence.
5. Do not use any noun or pronoun more than once in this exercise.
6. Do not use any adjective complement more than once in this exercise.
7. Use only the indicative mode.
8. Capitalize the first word in each sentence, and place a period at the end of each sentence.
9. Be sure that each sentence is a statement, not a question.
10. Be sure that each sentence makes good sense.
11. Do not use any subject or complement contained in the examples given for these linking verbs in the text.

		Subject	—	Linking Verb (Verb indicated in left-hand column)	—	Complement
to be	1.	The vice-president		is		A candidate.
to appear	2.	The sea		appears		calm.
to become	3.	The baby		became		restless.
to feel	4.	The patient		felt		sick.
to grow	5.	The oak		grew		tall.
to look	6.	The lawn		looks		dry.
to remain	7.	The horse		remains		a winner.
to seem	8.	The woman		seems		nervous.
to smell	9.	The fish		smell		awful.
to taste	10.	The steak		tastes		delicious.

A FINAL WORD TO THE STUDENT

Use the following procedure to check your exercise before you hand it in:

1. Re-read the special instructions one at a time.
2. After you re-read each separate instruction, examine your completed exercise to make certain that you have followed that particular instruction exactly.
3. Revise your work wherever necessary.
4. When you are certain that the special instruction you are considering has been observed throughout your exercise, place a check (√) to the left of that special instruction and go on to the next one until you have completed the entire list.

This process will take several minutes of your time, but failure to recheck your exercises in this manner may mean that you have wasted all of the time and effort you have spent in doing the exercise.

EXERCISE 9

REVIEW OF BASIC SENTENCE PATTERNS

This exercise is a review of the three basic sentence patterns. Write one sentence to fit each of the indicated patterns.

Special Instructions:

_____ 1. Use subjects, objects, and complements consisting of single words.

_____ 2. Use *a, an,* or *the* before a noun if one of these articles is needed to avoid primer or telegraphic style, but do not use any other words which are not called for by the pattern. (Particularly guard against inserting such words as *his, her, your, their.*)

_____ 3. Do not use a possessive (such as *mine, his, hers, theirs, yours, men's*) as a subject, object, or complement in any sentence.

_____ 4. Do not use any noun or pronoun more than once in this exercise.

_____ 5. Do not use any adjective complement more than once in this exercise.

_____ 6. Do not use any verb more than once in this exercise. (After you have used one form of a verb, do not use another form of the same verb. You may repeat auxiliaries but not primary verbs.)

_____ 7. Do not use the passive voice.

_____ 8. Use only the indicative mode.

_____ 9. Capitalize the first word in each sentence, and place a period at the end of each sentence.

_____10. Be sure that each sentence is a statement, not a question.

_____11. Be sure that each sentence makes good sense.

_____12. Be certain that you follow the specified pattern. (Note whether a noun or pronoun is called for.)

Subject — **Verb**
(Noun)

1. __The dee_____ __run_____

Subject — **Verb**
(Pronoun)

2. __He_____ __laughed_____

Subject — **Verb** — **Object**
(Noun) (Noun)

3. __The girl_____ __threw_____ __the ball._____

Subject — **Verb** — **Object**
(Pronoun) (Noun)

4. __She_____ __bought_____ __the present._____

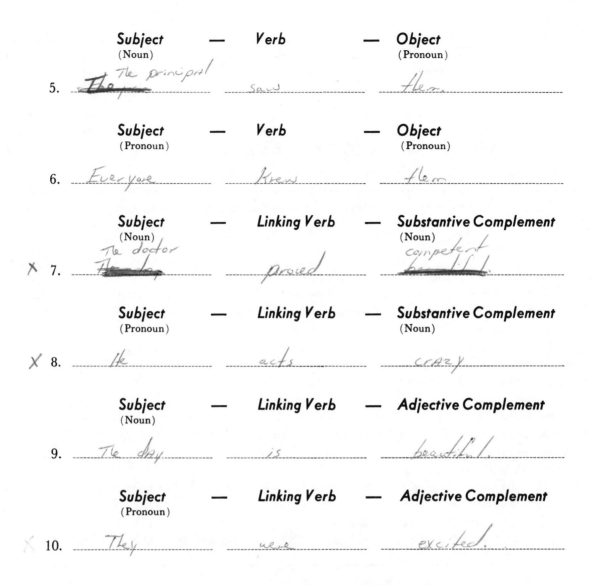

	Subject (Noun)	—	Verb	—	Object (Pronoun)
5.	~~They~~ The principal		saw		them

	Subject (Pronoun)	—	Verb	—	Object (Pronoun)
6.	Everyone		knew		them

	Subject (Noun)	—	Linking Verb	—	Substantive Complement (Noun)
X 7.	~~They~~ The doctor		proved		~~beautiful~~ competent

	Subject (Pronoun)	—	Linking Verb	—	Substantive Complement (Noun)
X 8.	He		acts		crazy

	Subject (Noun)	—	Linking Verb	—	Adjective Complement
9.	The day		is		beautiful

	Subject (Pronoun)	—	Linking Verb	—	Adjective Complement
X 10.	They		were		excited.

A FINAL WORD TO THE STUDENT

Use the following procedure to check your exercise before you hand it in:

1. Re-read the special instructions one at a time.
2. After you re-read each separate instruction, examine your completed exercise to make certain that you have followed that particular instruction exactly.
3. Revise your work wherever necessary.
4. When you are certain that the special instruction you are considering has been observed throughout your exercise, place a check (√) to the left of that special instruction and go on to the next one until you have completed the entire list.

This process will take several minutes of your time, but failure to recheck your exercises in this manner may mean that you have wasted all of the time and effort you have spent in doing the exercise.

EXERCISE 10

REVIEW

This exercise is a review of all of the material covered thus far. Write two sentences to fit each of the indicated patterns unless your teacher specifically instructs you to write only one sentence for each pattern.

Special Instructions:

.... 1. Use *a, an,* or *the* before a noun if one of these articles is needed to avoid primer or telegraphic style, but do not use any other words which are not called for by the pattern. (Particularly guard against inserting such words as *his, her, your, their.*)

.... 2. Do not use any proper noun consisting of more than one word.

.... 3. Do not use a possessive (such as *mine, his, hers, theirs, yours, men's*) as a subject, object, or complement in any sentence.

.... 4. Do not use any noun or pronoun more than once in this exercise.

.... 5. Do not use any adjective complement more than once in this exercise.

.... 6. Do not use any verb more than once in this exercise. (After you have used one form of a verb, do not use another form of the same verb. You may repeat auxiliaries but not primary verbs. Be particularly careful not to repeat forms of the primary verb *to be* in the last three patterns.)

.... 7. Do not use *progressive* or *emphatic* verb forms unless they are specifically called for.

.... 8. Do not use the passive voice.

.... 9. Use only the indicative mode.

........10. Capitalize the first word in each sentence, and place a period at the end of each sentence.

	Subject	—	**Verb**	
	(Common noun)		(Past tense)	
1.	The glider		flew.	
2.	The rabbit		jumped.	

should'nt repetition be wrong? Surely not!

should it make this

	Subject	—	**Verb**	
	(Indefinite pronoun)		(Future tense)	
3.	Everyone		will go.	
4.	Some one		will come.	

	Subject	—	**Verb**	
	(Proper noun)		(Present perfect tense)	
5.	Mary		has arrived.	
6.	The President		has spoken.	

	Subject	—	**Verb**	—	**Object**
	(Indefinite pronoun)		(Past tense, progressive)		(Proper noun)
7.	Some		were attending		the Olympics.
8.	Everyone		was celebrating		Christmas.

181

	Subject (Personal pronoun)	—	**Verb** (Past tense)	—	**Object** (Reciprocal pronoun)
9.	They		met		each other.
10.	We		loved		one another.

	Subject (Personal pronoun)	—	**Verb** (Past perfect tense)	—	**Object** (Reflexive pronoun)
✗ 11.	I		had been teaching		myself
✗ 12.	You		had been driving		yourself.

	Subject (Proper noun)	—	**Verb** (Future tense)	—	**Object** (Common noun)
13.	James		will take		the train.
14.	Uncle Robert		will bring		the wood.

	Subject (Personal pronoun)	—	**Linking Verb** (Past tense)	—	**Substantive Complement** (Common noun)
15.	He		was		a fireman.
16.	She		remained		a friend.

	Subject (Demonstrative pronoun)	—	**Linking Verb** (Present tense)	—	**Adjective Complement**
17.	That		is		wet
18.	This		appears		fresh.

	Subject (Common noun)	—	**Linking Verb** (Past tense)	—	**Adjective Complement**
19.	The puppy		was		hungry
20.	The engine		ran		hot.

A FINAL WORD TO THE STUDENT

Use the following procedure to check your exercise before you hand it in:

1. Re-read the special instructions one at a time.
2. After you re-read each separate instruction, examine your completed exercise to make certain that you have followed that particular instruction exactly.
3. Revise your work wherever necessary.
4. When you are certain that the special instruction you are considering has been observed throughout your exercise, place a check (√) to the left of that special instruction and go on to the next one until you have completed the entire list.

This process will take several minutes of your time, but failure to recheck your exercises in this manner may mean that you have wasted all of the time and effort you have spent in doing the exercise.

EXERCISE 11

TYPES OF SUBSTANTIVE MODIFIERS

Complete each sentence by filling in the blank with a single word.

Special Instructions:

_____ 1. Use only one word in each blank.
_____ 2. Do not use any word more than once in this exercise.
_____ 3. Capitalize each word which begins a sentence.
_____ 4. Be sure that your use of the apostrophe is accurate.
_____ 5. Be sure that each sentence makes sense and is correct in every way.

Insert in each blank an adjective of the type specified.

1. The ___frightened___ thief escaped.
   Descriptive adjective

2. The ___dirty___ tramp frightened the child.
   Descriptive adjective

3. The ___beautiful___ girl is an actress.
   Descriptive adjective

4. A ___black___ cloud covered the sun.
   Descriptive adjective

5. A ___large___ lake was nearby.
   Descriptive adjective

6. ___Seven___ students were absent.
   Numeral adjective

7. ___Three___ candidates made speeches.
   Numeral adjective

8. The ___fourth___ attempt was successful.
   Numeral adjective

9. ___This___ novel is entertaining.
   Demonstrative adjective

10. ___These___ eggs are rotten.
    Demonstrative adjective

11. ___Those___ boys broke the windows.
    Demonstrative adjective

12. ___Each___ delegate wore a badge.
    Indefinite adjective

13. ___Several___ newspapermen wanted an interview.
    Indefinite adjective

14. _____Some_____ artists paint portraits.
   Indefinite adjective

15. _____Many_____ people were disappointed.
   Indefinite adjective

Insert in each blank the word called for. Each word will be a possessive functioning as an adjective.

---

16. _____My_____ brother will drive the car.
   Possessive form of pronoun *I*

17. _____Your_____ telephone is ringing.
   Possessive form of pronoun *you*

18. _____His_____ boat capsized.
   Possessive form of pronoun *he*

19. _____Its_____ leg is broken.
   Possessive form of pronoun *it*

20. _____Their_____ party was enjoyable.
   Possessive form of pronoun *they*

21. _____Someone's_____ chickens ruined my garden.
   Possessive form of pronoun *someone*

22. _____Thomas's_____ friend is an engineer.
   Possessive form of noun *Thomas*

23. The _____girl's_____ mother accompanied her.
   Possessive form of noun *girl*

24. The _____men's_____ dormitory is crowded.
   Possessive form of noun *men*

25. The _____coaches'_____ selection was Bill Green.
   Possessive form of noun *coaches*

A FINAL WORD TO THE STUDENT

Use the following procedure to check your exercise before you hand it in:

1. Re-read the special instructions one at a time.
2. After you re-read each separate instruction, examine your completed exercise to make certain that you have followed that particular instruction exactly.
3. Revise your work wherever necessary.
4. When you are certain that the special instruction you are considering has been observed throughout your exercise, place a check (√) to the left of that special instruction and go on to the next one until you have completed the entire list.

This process will take several minutes of your time, but failure to recheck your exercises in this manner may mean that you have wasted all of the time and effort you have spent in doing the exercise.

EXERCISE 12

RESTRICTIVE AND NON-RESTRICTIVE SUBSTANTIVE MODIFIERS

Write two sentences to fit each of the indicated patterns unless your teacher specifically instructs you to write only one sentence for each pattern.

Special Instructions:

_____ 1. Use *a, an,* or *the* wherever one of these articles is needed to avoid primer or telegraphic style, but do not use any other words which are not called for by the pattern.

_____ 2. Do not use *a, an,* or *the* to fulfill a requirement for a substantive modifier. In other words, disregard the presence or absence of articles in writing sentences to fit patterns.

_____ 3. Do not use a possessive (such as *mine, his, hers, theirs, yours, men's*) as a subject, object, or complement in any sentence.

_____ 4. Do not use any proper nouns in this exercise.

_____ 5. Do not use any noun or pronoun more than once in this exercise.

_____ 6. Do not use any adjective more than once in this exercise. (Exception: You may use the articles *a, an,* and *the* as many times as you wish.)

_____ 7. Do not use any verb more than once in this exercise. (After you have used one form of a verb, do not use another form of the same verb. You may repeat auxiliaries but not primary verbs.)

_____ 8. Do not use any substantive which is composed of more than one word.

_____ 9. Do not use any modifier which is composed of more than one word.

_____10. Do not use the passive voice.

_____11. Use only the indicative mode.

_____12. Capitalize the first word in each sentence, and place a period at the end of each sentence.

_____13. Be sure that your comma punctuation with non-restrictive modifiers is correct.

_____14. Be sure that each sentence is a statement, not a question.

_____15. Be sure that each sentence makes good sense.

_____16. Be certain that you follow the specified pattern exactly.

MODIFIER —*Subject*—*Verb*

(Restrictive)

1. Absent students will fail.

2. The large dogs howled.

Subject—*Verb*—MODIFIER —*Object*

(Restrictive)

3. We like fried trout.

4. The team chose dangerous missions.

185

MODIFIER →Subject—Verb—Object

(Restrictive)

5. The weary campers cooked supper.

6. A terrible wind destroyed the barn.

MODIFIER →Subject—Verb—Object

(Non-restrictive)

7. Unafraid, the boy mounted the horse.

8. Overjoyed, the climbers reached the summit.

MODIFIER →Subject—Verb—MODIFIER →Object

(Non-restrictive)   (Restrictive)

9. Nervous, the scientist continued the dangerous experiment.

10. Weary, the firemen fought the raging fire.

MODIFIER →Subject—Verb

(Non-restrictive)

11. Angry, he cursed.

12. Thankful, the people prayed.

MODIFIER →Subject—Verb—MODIFIER →Object

(Restrictive)   (Restrictive)

13. The deer jumped the fallen log.

14. Migrants picked the ripe tomatoes.

Subject—MODIFIER —Verb—Object

(Non-restrictive)

15. The captain, anxious, watched the horizon.

16. The regiment, undetered, crossed the river.

186

Exercise 12 (continued)

MODIFIER—Subject—Linking Verb—MODIFIER—Substantive Complement

(Restrictive)   (Restrictive)

17. _The defiant woman is a christian activist._

18. _wounded, The ╪soldier was an instant hero._

MODIFIER—Subject—Linking Verb—Adjective Complement

(Restrictive)

19. _The small child seemed happy._

20. _The amber stone appeared genuine._

A FINAL WORD TO THE STUDENT

Use the following procedure to check your exercise before you hand it in:

1. Re-read the special instructions one at a time.
2. After you re-read each separate instruction, examine your completed exercise to make certain that you have followed that particular instruction exactly.
3. Revise your work wherever necessary.
4. When you are certain that the special instruction you are considering has been observed throughout your exercise, place a check (√) to the left of that special instruction and go on to the next one until you have completed the entire list.

This process will take several minutes of your time, but failure to recheck your exercises in this manner may mean that you have wasted all of the time and effort you have spent in doing the exercise.

EXERCISE 13

ADJECTIVE-NOUN COMBINATIONS

Write two sentences to fit each of the indicated patterns.

Special Instructions:

_____ 1. Use *a, an,* or *the* wherever one of these articles is needed to avoid primer or telegraphic style, but do not use any other words which are not called for by the pattern.

_____ 2. Do not use *a, an,* or *the* to fulfill a requirement for a substantive modifier. In other words, disregard the presence or absence of articles in writing sentences to fit patterns.

_____ 3. Do not use a possessive (such as *mine, his, hers, theirs, yours, men's*) as a subject, object, or complement in any sentence.

_____ 4. Do not use any proper nouns in this exercise.

_____ 5. Do not use any noun or pronoun more than once in this exercise.

_____ 6. Do not use any adjective more than once in this exercise. (Exception: You may use the articles *a, an,* and *the* as many times as you wish.)

_____ 7. Do not use any verb more than once in this exercise. (After you have used one form of a verb, do not use another form of the same verb. You may repeat auxiliaries but not primary verbs.)

_____ 8. Do not use any substantive which is composed of more than one word.

_____ 9. Do not use any modifier which is composed of more than one word.

_____ 10. Do not use the passive voice.

_____ 11. Use only the indicative mode.

_____ 12. Capitalize the first word in each sentence, and place a period at the end of each sentence.

_____ 13. Note that no comma punctuation is used in any of these patterns.

_____ 14. Be sure that each sentence is a statement, not a question.

_____ 15. Be sure that each sentence makes good sense.

_____ 16. Be sure that the words you use as an adjective-noun combination are properly written as *two separate words.* Consult your dictionary if necessary.

_____ 17. Test each sentence to see whether you can insert the word *and* between the modifiers. If you *can,* you do *not* have an adjective-noun combination. (See p. 56.)

_____ 18. Be certain that you follow the specified pattern exactly.

MODIFIER— | MODIFIER—Subject | —Verb

1. ___This new sweater itches.___

2. ___That old tractor runs.___

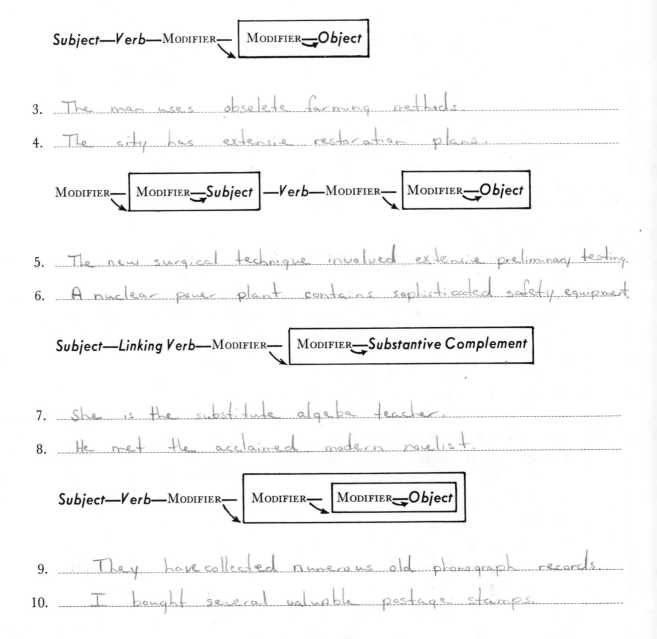

Subject—Verb—Modifier— | Modifier→Object |

3. The man uses obselete farming methods

4. The city has extensive restoration plans.

Modifier— | Modifier→Subject | —Verb—Modifier— | Modifier→Object |

5. The new surgical technique involved extensive preliminary testing.

6. A nuclear power plant contains sophisticated safety equipment.

Subject—Linking Verb—Modifier— | Modifier→Substantive Complement |

7. She is the substitute algebra teacher.

8. He met the acclaimed modern novelist.

Subject—Verb—Modifier— | Modifier— | Modifier→Object |

9. They have collected numerous old phonograph records.

10. I bought several valuable postage stamps.

A FINAL WORD TO THE STUDENT

Use the following procedure to check your exercise before you hand it in:

1. Re-read the special instructions one at a time.
2. After you re-read each separate instruction, examine your completed exercise to make certain that you have followed that particular instruction exactly.
3. Revise your work wherever necessary.
4. When you are certain that the special instruction you are considering has been observed throughout your exercise, place a check (√) to the left of that special instruction and go on to the next one until you have completed the entire list.

This process will take several minutes of your time, but failure to recheck your exercises in this manner may mean that you have wasted all of the time and effort you have spent in doing the exercise.

EXERCISE 14

MODIFIERS OF VERBS

Write two sentences to fit each of the indicated patterns.

Special Instructions:

_____ 1. Place *a, an,* or *the* before a noun if one of these articles is needed to avoid primer or telegraphic style, but do not use any other words which are not called for by the pattern.

_____ 2. Do not use a possessive (such as *mine, his, hers, theirs, yours, men's*) as a subject, object, or complement in any sentence.

_____ 3. Do not use any proper nouns in this exercise.

_____ 4. Do not use any noun or pronoun more than once in this exercise.

_____ 5. Do not use any adjective complement more than once in this exercise.

_____ 6. Do not use any adverb more than once in this exercise.

_____ 7. Do not use any verb more than once in this exercise. (After you have used one form of a verb, do not use another form of the same verb. You may repeat auxiliaries but not primary verbs.)

_____ 8. Do not use any substantive which is composed of more than one word.

_____ 9. Do not use any modifier which is composed of more than one word.

_____10. Do not use the passive voice.

_____11. Use only the indicative mode.

_____12. Capitalize the first word in each sentence, and place a period at the end of each sentence.

_____13. Be sure that each sentence is a statement, not a question.

_____14. Be sure that each sentence makes good sense.

_____15. Be certain that you follow the specified pattern exactly.

Subject—Verb—MODIFIER
(Adverb of time)

1. _____We went yesterday._____

2. _____The boy batted again._____

Subject—Verb—MODIFIER
(Adverb of manner)

3. _____The ship docked slowly._____

4. _____I showered quickly._____

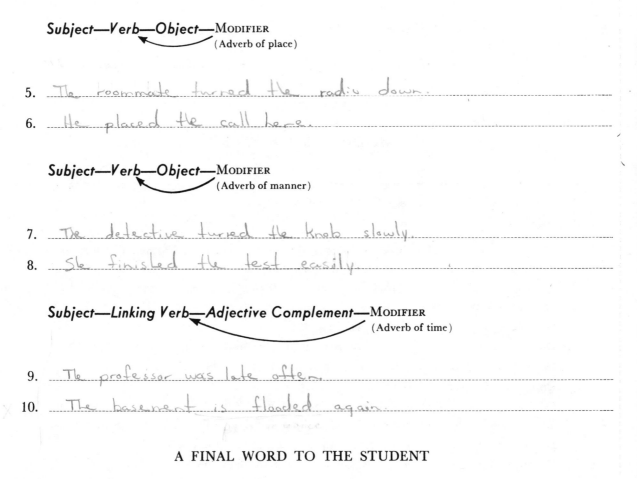

*Subject—Verb—Object—*Modifier
(Adverb of place)

5. The roommate turned the radio down.

6. He placed the call here.

*Subject—Verb—Object—*Modifier
(Adverb of manner)

7. The detective turned the knob slowly.

8. She finished the test easily.

*Subject—Linking Verb—Adjective Complement—*Modifier
(Adverb of time)

9. The professor was late often.

10. The basement is flooded again.

A FINAL WORD TO THE STUDENT

Use the following procedure to check your exercise before you hand it in:

1. Re-read the special instructions one at a time.
2. After you re-read each separate instruction, examine your completed exercise to make certain that you have followed that particular instruction exactly.
3. Revise your work wherever necessary.
4. When you are certain that the special instruction you are considering has been observed throughout your exercise, place a check (√) to the left of that special instruction and go on to the next one until you have completed the entire list.

This process will take several minutes of your time, but failure to recheck your exercises in this manner may mean that you have wasted all of the time and effort you have spent in doing the exercise.

EXERCISE 15

VERB-ADVERB COMBINATIONS

Write ten sentences containing verb-adverb combinations. Each sentence will fit the following pattern:

Pattern: **Subject—** | **Verb—**MODIFIER | **—Object**

Example: I blew out the candle.

Special Instructions:

------- 1. Place *a, an,* or *the* before a noun if one of these articles is needed to avoid primer or telegraphic style, but do not use any other words which are not called for by the pattern.

------- 2. Do not use a possessive (such as *mine, his, hers, theirs, yours, men's*) as a subject or object in any sentence.

------- 3. Do not use any proper nouns in this exercise.

------- 4. Do not use any noun or pronoun more than once in this exercise.

------- 5. Do not use any adverb more than once in this exercise.

------- 6. Do not use any verb more than once in this exercise. (After you have used one form of a verb, do not use another form of the same verb. You may repeat auxiliaries but not primary verbs.)

------- 7. Do not use any substantive which is composed of more than one word.

------- 8. Do not use any modifier which is composed of more than one word.

------- 9. Use only the indicative mode.

------10. Capitalize the first word in each sentence, and place a period at the end of each sentence.

------11. Be sure that each sentence is a statement, not a question.

------ 12. Be sure that you can move the adverb to the end of the sentence (*I blew the candle out.*) and still have a sensible sentence. If you cannot, rewrite the sentence. (See p. 38.)

1. We gave up hope.

2. The company took away the bonus.

3. The family has been through an ordeal.

4. The volunteer passed out booklets.

5. The candidate pulled down the posters.

6. The bondsman put up a deposit.

7. He handed in a resignation.

8. The storm turned out a disaster.

9. He came across the hunter.

10. The employee stopped by the office.

A FINAL WORD TO THE STUDENT

Use the following procedure to check your exercise before you hand it in:

1. Re-read the special instructions one at a time.
2. After you re-read each separate instruction, examine your completed exercise to make certain that you have followed that particular instruction exactly.
3. Revise your work wherever necessary.
4. When you are certain that the special instruction you are considering has been observed throughout your exercise, place a check (√) to the left of that special instruction and go on to the next one until you have completed the entire list.

This process will take several minutes of your time, but failure to recheck your exercises in this manner may mean that you have wasted all of the time and effort you have spent in doing the exercise.

EXERCISE 16

MODIFIERS OF MODIFIERS

Write two sentences to fit each of the indicated patterns.

Special Instructions:

_____ 1. Use *a, an,* or *the* wherever one of these articles is needed to avoid primer or telegraphic style, but do not use any other words which are not called for by the pattern.

_____ 2. Do not use *a, an,* or *the* to fulfill a requirement for a substantive modifier. In other words, disregard the presence or absence of articles in writing sentences to fit patterns.

_____ 3. Do not use a possessive (such as *mine, his, hers, theirs, yours, men's*) as a subject, object, or complement in any sentence.

_____ 4. Do not use any proper nouns in this exercise.

_____ 5. Do not use any noun or pronoun more than once in this exercise.

_____ 6. Do not use any adjective or adverb more than once in this exercise. (Exception: You may use the articles *a, an,* and *the* as many times as you wish.)

_____ 7. Do not use any verb more than once in this exercise. (After you have used one form of a verb, do not use another form of the same verb. You may repeat auxiliaries but not primary verbs.)

_____ 8. Do not use any substantive which is composed of more than one word.

_____ 9. Do not use any modifier which is composed of more than one word.

_____10. Do not use the passive voice.

_____11. Use only the indicative mode.

_____12. Capitalize the first word in each sentence, and place a period at the end of each sentence.

_____13. Be sure that each sentence is a statement, not a question.

_____14. Be sure that each sentence makes good sense.

_____15. Be certain that you follow each pattern exactly, making sure that each modifier modifies the specified sentence element.

_____16. Make all substantive modifiers *restrictive.*

Subject—Verb—Modifier—Modifier

1. _We arrived quite safely._

2. _The boy ran rather clumsily._

Modifier—Modifier—*Subject—Verb—Object*

3. _The very angry child hit the dog._

4. _The tremendously happy child opened the present._

195

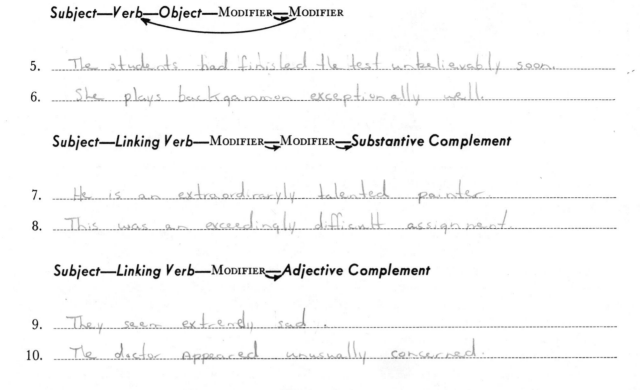

*Subject—Verb—Object—*MODIFIER—MODIFIER

5. The students had finished the test unbelievably soon.

6. She plays backgammon exceptionally well.

*Subject—Linking Verb—*MODIFIER—MODIFIER—*Substantive Complement*

7. He is an extraordinarily talented painter.

8. This was an exceedingly difficult assignment

*Subject—Linking Verb—*MODIFIER—*Adjective Complement*

9. They seem extremely sad.

10. The doctor appeared unusually concerned.

A FINAL WORD TO THE STUDENT

Use the following procedure to check your exercise before you hand it in:

1. Re-read the special instructions one at a time.
2. After you re-read each separate instruction, examine your completed exercise to make certain that you have followed that particular instruction exactly.
3. Revise your work wherever necessary.
4. When you are certain that the special instruction you are considering has been observed throughout your exercise, place a check (√) to the left of that special instruction and go on to the next one until you have completed the entire list.

This process will take several minutes of your time, but failure to recheck your exercises in this manner may mean that you have wasted all of the time and effort you have spent in doing the exercise.

EXERCISE 17

COMPARISON: ADJECTIVES AND ADVERBS

Fill in the blanks with the comparative and superlative forms of the adjectives and adverbs listed.

Special Instructions:

1. Do not use the forms showing decreasing intensity—*i.e.,* those employing *less* and *least.*
2. Do not capitalize the forms you insert.
3. Be sure that your spelling is correct.

ADJECTIVES Positive	Comparative	Superlative
1. bad	worse	worst
2. good	better	best
3. helpful	more helpful	most helpful
4. intelligent	more intelligent	most intelligent
5. large	larger	largest
6. lucky	luckier	luckiest
7. strong	stronger	strongest
8. tall	taller	tallest
9. terrible	more terrible	most terrible
10. warm	warmer	warmest

ADVERBS Positive	Comparative	Superlative
11. badly	worse	worst
12. carefully	more carefully	most carefully
13. easily	more easily	most easily
14. late	later	latest

15. near   _nearer_   _nearest_

16. quickly   _more quickly_   _most quickly_

17. recently   _more recently_   _most recently_

18. reluctantly   _more reluctantly_   _most reluctantly_

19. slow   _slower_   _slowest_

20. well   _better_   _best_

A FINAL WORD TO THE STUDENT

Use the following procedure to check your exercise before you hand it in:

1. Re-read the special instructions one at a time.
2. After you re-read each separate instruction, examine your completed exercise to make certain that you have followed that particular instruction exactly.
3. Revise your work wherever necessary.
4. When you are certain that the special instruction you are considering has been observed throughout your exercise, place a check ($\checkmark$) to the left of that special instruction and go on to the next one until you have completed the entire list.

This process will take several minutes of your time, but failure to recheck your exercises in this manner may mean that you have wasted all of the time and effort you have spent in doing the exercise.

EXERCISE 18

USE OF MODIFIERS IN THE FIRST THREE BASIC PATTERNS

Write two sentences to fit each of the indicated patterns unless your teacher specifically instructs you to write only one sentence for each pattern.

Special Instructions:

_____ 1. Use *a, an,* or *the* wherever one of these articles is needed to avoid primer or telegraphic style, but do not use any other words which are not called for by the pattern.

_____ 2. Do not use *a, an,* or *the* to fulfill a requirement for a substantive modifier. In other words, disregard the presence or absence of articles in writing sentences to fit patterns.

_____ 3. Do not use a possessive (such as *mine, his, hers, theirs, yours, men's*) as a subject, object, or complement in any sentence.

_____ 4. Do not use any proper nouns in this exercise.

_____ 5. Do not use any noun or pronoun more than once in this exercise.

_____ 6. Do not use any adjective or adverb more than once in this exercise. (Exception: You may use the articles *a, an,* and *the* as many times as you wish.)

_____ 7. Do not use any verb more than once in this exercise. (After you have used one form of a verb, do not use another form of the same verb. You may repeat auxiliaries but not primary verbs.)

_____ 8. Do not use comparative or superlative forms of adjectives or adverbs.

_____ 9. Do not use any substantive which is composed of more than one word.

_____10. Do not use any modifier which is composed of more than one word.

_____11. Do not use the passive voice.

_____12. Use only the indicative mode.

_____13. Capitalize the first word in each sentence, and place a period at the end of each sentence.

_____14. Be sure that each sentence is a statement, not a question.

_____15. Be sure that each sentence makes good sense.

_____16. Be certain that you follow each pattern exactly, making sure that each modifier modifies the specified sentence element. Be particularly careful in distinguishing *modifiers of substantive modifiers* from *modifiers of adjective-noun combinations* in sentences 15–20. If necessary, review pp. 34–35 and pp. 38–39 of this text.

_____17. Make all substantive modifiers *restrictive*.

MODIFIER—*Subject—Verb*—MODIFIER

1. The beautiful deer leaped gracefully.

2. The insurance saleman called recently.

MODIFIER→*Subject*—*Verb*—MODIFIER→*Object*

3. The old watchmaker repaired the golden clock.

4. The morning sun filled the dark glen.

MODIFIER→*Subject*—*Verb*—*Object*—MODIFIER

5. He mounted the horse wreaddklessly

6. She sang the song well.

MODIFIER→*Subject*—*Verb*—MODIFIER→*Object*—MODIFIER

7. The little puppy ate the table scraps hastily.

Loss of All credit for a misspelled word. How can it be?

X 8. The senior senator (attacked) the problem boldly.

MODIFIER→*Subject*—MODIFIER→*Verb*—MODIFIER→*Object*

9. The recent announcement greatly surprized the news reporter.

10. The ballet dancer slowly circled the outdoor stage

MODIFIER→*Subject*—*Linking Verb*—MODIFIER→*Substantive Complement*

11. The famous artist became a virtual recluse.

12. The heart surgeon remains a respected specialist.

MODIFIER→*Subject*—*Linking Verb*—MODIFIER→*Adjective Complement*

13. The rose garden looks unusually beautiful

14. The election results were rather vague.

MODIFIER—MODIFIER—*Subject*—*Verb*—MODIFIER—MODIFIER

15. The tremendously expensive car travels quite smoothly.

16. The exceptionally nervous student studies very often.

MODIFIER— | MODIFIER—*Subject* | —*Verb*—MODIFIER—MODIFIER—*Object*

17. The luxury railroad car entered the dimly lighted station.

18. The hearty mountain climber left the beautifully forested valley.

MODIFIER—*Subject*—*Verb*—MODIFIER— | MODIFIER—*Object* | —MODIFIER

19. The teenage children enjoy the mahogany pool table immensely.

20. The excited boy met the professional football player yesterday.

A FINAL WORD TO THE STUDENT

Use the following procedure to check your exercise before you hand it in:

1. Re-read the special instructions one at a time.
2. After you re-read each separate instruction, examine your completed exercise to make certain that you have followed that particular instruction exactly.
3. Revise your work wherever necessary.
4. When you are certain that the special instruction you are considering has been observed throughout your exercise, place a check (√) to the left of that special instruction and go on to the next one until you have completed the entire list.

This process will take several minutes of your time, but failure to recheck your exercises in this manner may mean that you have wasted all of the time and effort you have spent in doing the exercise.

EXERCISE 19

REVIEW

Write two sentences to fit each of the indicated patterns.

Special Instructions:

_____ 1. Use *a, an,* or *the* wherever one of these articles is needed to avoid primer or telegraphic style, but do not use any other words which are not called for by the pattern.

_____ 2. Do not use *a, an,* or *the* to fulfill a requirement for a substantive modifier. In other words, disregard the presence or absence of articles in writing sentences to fit patterns.

_____ 3. Do not use a possessive (such as *mine, his, hers, theirs, yours, men's*) as a subject, object, or complement in any sentence.

_____ 4. Do not use any noun or pronoun more than once in this exercise.

_____ 5. Do not use any adjective or adverb more than once in this exercise. (Exception: You may use the articles *a, an,* and *the* as many times as you wish.)

_____ 6. Do not use any verb more than once in this exercise. (After you have used one form of a verb, do not use another form of the same verb. You may repeat auxiliaries but not primary verbs.)

_____ 7. Do not use comparative or superlative forms of adjectives or adverbs.

_____ 8. Do not use any substantive which is composed of more than one word.

_____ 9. Do not use any modifier which is composed of more than one word.

_____10. Do not use the passive voice.

_____11. Use only the indicative mode.

_____12. Do not use progressive or emphatic verb forms.

_____13. Make all substantive modifiers restrictive.

_____14. Capitalize the first word in each sentence, and place a period at the end of each sentence.

_____15. Be sure that each sentence is a statement, not a question.

_____16. Be sure that each sentence makes good sense.

_____17. Be certain that you follow each pattern exactly.

Subject   —Verb
(Common noun)   (Past tense)

1. _The horse ran._

2. _The rabbit jumped_

Subject   —Verb   —Object
(Proper noun)   (Past perfect tense)   (Personal pronoun)

✗ 3. _The children had been visiting her._

✗ 4. _The class had been studying him._

Subject —*Linking Verb*—***Substantive Complement***
(Common noun) (Present tense) (Common noun)

5. The girl is a patient.

6. The boy became a doctor.

Subject —*Linking Verb*—***Adjective Complement***
(Personal pronoun) (Past tense)

7. He was nervous.

8. She felt sick.

MODIFIER ⟶***Subject*** —***Verb*** ⟵ MODIFIER
(Descriptive adjective) (Common noun) (Past tense) (Adverb of manner)

9. The green turtle crawled slowly.

10. The white dog approached cautiously.

MODIFIER⟶***Subject*** —***Verb*** ⟵ —***Object***—MODIFIER
(Possessive) (Common noun) (Present tense) (Adverb of time)

11. His mother bakes a cake often.

12. Their grandfather visits the family seldom.

MODIFIER ⟶***Subject*** —*Linking Verb*—MODIFIER⟶***Adjective Complement***
(Indefinite adjective) (Common noun) (Present tense)

13. Each graduate appears extremely happy.

14. The garden seems quite productive.

MODIFIER ⟶***Subject*** —***Verb*** ⟵—***Object***—MODIFIER—MODIFIER
(Demonstrative adjective) (Common noun) (Future tense) (Adverb of manner)

15. This swimmer will finish the heat very quickly.

16. That student will play the piano rather badly.

MODIFIER ⟶***Subject*** —***Verb*** —MODIFIER⟶MODIFIER ⟶***Object***
(Possessive) (Common noun) (Past perfect tense) (Descriptive adjective) (Common noun)

X 17. Her aunt had been seeking an unusually small car.

X 18. My family had been occupying an incredibly beautiful estate.

MODIFIER ⟶***Subject*** —***Verb*** —MODIFIER— MODIFIER⟶***Object***
(Descriptive adjective) (Common noun) (Past tense) (Descriptive adjective)

19. The arrogant squire surveyed the vast land holdings.

20. The nervous passenger appreciated the kind airline stewardess.

IMPORTANT NOTE

In the remaining exercises the following special instructions are to be observed whenever you write sentences to fit patterns:

1. Use *a, an,* or *the* wherever one of these articles is needed to avoid primer or telegraphic style, but do not use any other words which are not called for by the pattern.
2. Do not use *a, an,* or *the* to fulfill a requirement for a substantive modifier. In other words, disregard the presence or absence of articles in writing sentences to fit patterns.
3. Do not use a possessive (such as *mine, his, hers, theirs, yours, men's*) as a substantive in any sentence.
4. Do not use any substantive which is composed of more than one word unless you are specifically asked for such a substantive. (In other words, if you are asked to use a substantive consisting of a phrase or a clause or any of certain verbals, you will, of course, have to use a substantive composed of more than one word. However, always use a *one-word* substantive wherever such a substantive will meet the requirements of the pattern.)
5. Do not use any modifier which is composed of more than one word unless you are specifically asked for such a modifier. (In other words, if you are asked to use a modifier consisting of a phrase or a clause or any of certain verbals, you will, of course, have to use a modifier composed of more than one word. However, always use a *one-word* modifier wherever such a modifier will meet the requirements of the pattern.)
6. Capitalize the first word in each sentence, and place the proper terminal punctuation at the end of each sentence.

These instructions will not be repeated in the individual exercises, but you will be held responsible for observing them.

In some of the exercises which follow, you will be directed to refer to the instructions printed below.

A FINAL WORD TO THE STUDENT

Use the following procedure to check your exercise before you hand it in:

1. Re-read the special instructions one at a time.
2. After you re-read each separate instruction, examine your completed exercise to make certain that you have followed that particular instruction exactly.
3. Revise your work wherever necessary.
4. When you are certain that the special instruction you are considering has been observed throughout your exercise, place a check (√) to the left of that special instruction and go on to the next one until you have completed the entire list.

This process will take several minutes of your time, but failure to recheck your exercises in this manner may mean that you have wasted all of the time and effort you have spent in doing the exercise.

EXERCISE 20

INFINITIVES

Fill in each blank with an infinitive which will have the function specified below the blank.

Special Instructions:

——— 1. In every sentence, use an infinitive preceded by *to,* the "sign of the infinitive."
——— 2. Do not place anything in the blank except *to* and the infinitive.
——— 3. Use any tense form of the infinitive.
——— 4. Use either active or passive voice.
——— 5. Be sure that the sequence of tenses is correct.
——— 6. After using one infinitive form of a verb, do not use any other infinitive form of the same verb.
——— 7. Be sure that the completed sentence makes good sense.
——— 8. Do not use any infinitive contained in the examples given in the text.

1. *To dance* is her greatest desire.
   Subject

2. The soldier wished *to defect*.
   Object

3. His next step was *to apologize*.
   Substantive complement

4. I had an opportunity *to skydive*.
   Modifier of *opportunity*

5. The boy stopped *to play*.
   Modifier of *stopped*

6. The child was anxious *to return*.
   Modifier of *anxious*

7. It is time *to eat*.
   Modifier of *time*

8. The student asked *to leave*.
   Object

9. The team had no chance *to recover*.
   Modifier of *chance*

10. I plan *to attend*.
    Object

Write two sentences to fit each of the indicated patterns.

Special Instructions:

——— 1. Wherever an infinitive is called for, use an infinitive preceded by *to,* the "sign of the infinitive."

2. Do not use any proper nouns in these sentences.

　3. Do not use any noun or pronoun more than once in these sentences.

　4. Do not use any adjective complement more than once in these sentences.

　5. Do not use any verb or infinitive more than once in these sentences. (After you have used one form of a verb or an infinitive, do not use any other form of the same verb or infinitive.)

　6. Do not use a main verb in the passive voice.

　7. Use only the indicative mode.

　8. Be sure that the sequence of tenses is correct.

　9. Be sure that each sentence is a statement, not a question.

10. Be sure that you follow the specified pattern exactly.

11. Be sure that each sentence makes good sense.

12. Do not use any infinitive which you have used in the first ten sentences.

Subject　—Linking Verb—Adjective Complement
(Present active infinitive)

11.　To charge was foolish.

12.　To rent seems reasonable.

Subject—Verb—Object
(Present active infinitive)

13.　She decided to change.

14.　The felon chose to cooperate.

Subject—Verb—Object
(Present passive infinitive)

15.　The candidate hopes to be nominated.

16.　The dog chatels to be brushed.

Subject—Verb—Object—MODIFIER
(Present active infinitive)

17.　He fights opponents to win.

18.　The man flies airplanes to relax.

Subject—Verb—Object—MODIFIER
(Present passive infinitive)

19.　We separated the vegetables to be washed.

20.　They brought the furniture to be refinished.

A FINAL WORD TO THE STUDENT

Check your exercise carefully before you hand it in. (See p. 205.)

EXERCISE 21

PARTICIPLES

Fill in each blank with a participle which will function as the type of modifier indicated below the blank.

Special Instructions:

-------- 1. Do not place anything in the blank except the participle.

-------- 2. Use any tense form of the participle.

-------- 3. Use either active or passive voice.

-------- 4. Be sure that the sequence of tenses is correct.

-------- 5. After using one participial form of a verb, do not use any other participle derived from the same verb.

-------- 6. Be sure that the completed sentence makes good sense.

-------- 7. Do not use any participle contained in the examples given in the text.

1. The ____bucking____ horse threw the rider.
   Restrictive modifier of *horse*

2. The woman, ____shaking____, began to moan.
   Non-restrictive modifier of *woman*

3. ____Hurrying____, the president spoke briefly.
   Non-restrictive modifier of *president*

4. A ____flapping____ shutter made a weird noise.
   Restrictive modifier of *shutter*

5. ____Cursing____, the tackle left the game.
   Non-restrictive modifier of *tackle*

6. The man ____laughing____ is my uncle.
   Restrictive modifier of *man*

7. It was a ____thrilling____ experience.
   Restrictive modifier of *experience*

8. My brother, ____smiling____, accepted the position.
   Non-restrictive modifier of *brother*

9. The ____careening____ car struck a pedestrian.
   Restrictive modifier of *car*

10. ____Pausing____, he answered the telephone.
    Non-restrictive modifier of *he*

Write two sentences to fit each of the indicated patterns.

Special Instructions:

-------- 1. Do not use any proper nouns in these sentences.

_____ 2. Do not use any noun or pronoun more than once in these sentences.

_____ 3. Do not use any adjective complement more than once in these sentences.

_____ 4. Do not use any verb or participle more than once in these sentences. (After you have used one form of a verb or participle, do not use any other form of the same verb or participle.)

_____ 5. Do not use a main verb in the passive voice.

_____ 6. Use only the indicative mode.

_____ 7. Be sure that the sequence of tenses is correct.

_____ 8. Be sure that your comma punctuation is correct.

_____ 9. Be sure that each sentence is a statement, not a question.

_____ 10. Be sure that you follow the specified pattern exactly.

_____ 11. Be sure that each sentence makes good sense.

_____ 12. Do not use any participle which you have used in the first ten sentences.

MODIFIER ⟶ —Subject—Verb—Object
(Restrictive present active participle)

11. Dancing bears filled the stage.

12. Racing cars left the pit.

Subject—MODIFIER —Verb—Object
(Non-restrictive present perfect passive participle)

13. Having been awakened, I showered.

14. Having been recognized, they spoke.

MODIFIER ⟶ —Subject—Verb—Object
(Non-restrictive present perfect active participle)

15. Having recovered, she planned the trip.

16. Having returned, we recieved the mail.

MODIFIER ⟶ —Subject—Linking Verb—Adjective Complement
(Restrictive past passive participle)

17. The designated hitter was injured.

18. The selected individuals appeared happy.

Subject—Linking Verb—Adjective Complement
(Past passive participle)

19. The winner felt honored.

20. The father looks pleased.

A FINAL WORD TO THE STUDENT

Check your exercise carefully before you hand it in. (See p. 205.)

EXERCISE 22

GERUNDS

Fill in each blank with a gerund which will have the function specified below the blank.

Special Instructions:

_____ 1. Do not place anything in the blank except the gerund.
_____ 2. Use any tense form of the gerund.
_____ 3. Use either active or passive voice.
_____ 4. After using one gerund form of a verb, do not use any other gerund form of the same verb.
_____ 5. Be sure that the completed sentence makes good sense.
_____ 6. Do not use any gerund contained in the examples given in the text.

---

1. ____Studying____ was impossible.
   Subject

2. The old man enjoyed ____fishing____.
   Object

3. His ____riding____ astonished us.
   Subject

4. We appreciated their ____asking____.
   Object

5. Poor ____passing____ loses football games.
   Subject

6. Our favorite pastime is ____skating____.
   Substantive complement

7. ____Skiing____ is fun.
   Subject

8. He teaches ____repelling____.
   Object

9. A good outdoor sport is ____surfing____.
   Substantive complement

10. ____Hunting____ exhausts me.
    Subject

Write two sentences to fit each of the indicated patterns.

Special Instructions:

_____ 1. Do not use any proper nouns in these sentences.
_____ 2. Do not use any noun or pronoun more than once in these sentences.

-------- 3. Do not use any adjective complement more than once in these sentences.

-------- 4. Do not use any verb or gerund more than once in these sentences. (After you have used one form of a verb or gerund, do not use any other form of the same verb or gerund.)

-------- 5. Do not use a main verb in the passive voice.

-------- 6. Use only the indicative mode.

-------- 7. Be sure that each sentence is a statement, not a question.

-------- 8. Be sure that you follow the specified pattern exactly.

-------- 9. Be sure that each sentence makes good sense.

--------10. Do not use any gerund which you have used in the first ten sentences.

Subject —Linking Verb—Adjective Complement
(Present active gerund)

11. Diving is difficult.

12. Waiting proved futile.

Subject —Verb—Object
(Present passive gerund)

13. Being elected requires votes.

14. Being tested improves quality.

Subject—Verb—Object
(Present active gerund)

15. The lady loves gardening.

16. The boy enjoys swimming.

MODIFIER—Subject —Verb—Object
(Present active gerund)

17. Extensive researching improved the paper.

18. Periodic bulldozing cleared the lot.

Subject—Verb—Object
(Present perfect passive gerund)

19. The contestants regret having been selected.

20. The losers confess having been disappointed.

A FINAL WORD TO THE STUDENT

Check your exercise carefully before you hand it in. (See p. 205.)

EXERCISE 23

COMPOUNDS

Write two sentences to fit each of the indicated patterns unless your teacher specifically instructs you to write only one sentence for each pattern.

Special Instructions:

_____ 1. Do not use any proper nouns in this exercise.
_____ 2. Do not use any noun or pronoun more than once in this exercise.
_____ 3. Do not use any adjective or adverb more than once in this exercise. (Exception: You may use the articles *a, an,* and *the* as many times as you wish.)
_____ 4. Do not use any verb more than once in this exercise. (After you have used one form of a verb, do not use any other form of the same verb. You may repeat auxiliaries but not primary verbs.)
_____ 5. Do not use comparative or superlative forms of adjectives or adverbs.
_____ 6. Do not use the passive voice.
_____ 7. Use only the indicative mode.
_____ 8. Be sure that your comma punctuation is correct.
_____ 9. Be sure that each sentence is a statement, not a question.
_____10. Be sure that you follow the specified pattern exactly.
_____11. Be sure that each sentence makes good sense.

*Subject—Verb—*COMPOUND MODIFIER

(_____ and _____)
      Adverb   Adverb

1. He climbed slowly and surely.

2. The candidate spoke softly and timidly.

MODIFIER—*Subject—Compound Verb*

(_____, _____, and _____)
    Verb   Verb   Verb

3. The opera star acted, danced, and sang.

4. We joked, laughed and remembered.

213

Subject—Verb—Compound Object

(_____, _____, and _____)
  Noun   Noun   Noun

5. The campers brought food, lanterns and tents.

6. The tourists saw monuments, museums, and cathedrals.

Compound Subject —Verb—Object

(_____ or _____)
  Noun   Noun

7. The professor or the assistant taught the lesson.

8. The doctor or the nurse visited the patient.

Subject—Linking Verb—Compound Adjective Complement

(_____ but _____)
  Adjective   Adjective

9. The car seems sporty but unreliable.

10. Wool is warm but uncomfortable.

Compound Subject —Verb

(Both _____ and _____)
      Noun   Noun

11. Both the judge and jury agree.

12. Both the fox and hound disappeared.

Compound Subject —Verb—Modifier—Object

(Either _____ or _____)
        Noun   Noun

13. Either he or I will cook the sirloin steaks.

14. Either the wind or the sun blistered the summer vacationers.

Exercise 23 (continued)

Compound Subject　　　　　　**—Verb**

(Neither _____ nor _____)
　　　　　Noun　　　　　Noun

15. Neither the congressman nor senator voted.

16. Neither the tomatoes nor watermelons ripened.

Subject—Verb—Compound Object

(not only _____ but _____)
　　　　　Noun　　　　　Noun

17. The neighbor borrowed not only the rake but the mower.

✗ 18. He visited not only Scotland but Ireland.

Subject—Verb—Compound Modifier　　—Object

(_____, _____)
　　　Adjective　　　Adjective

19. They surveyed the beautiful, green pastures.

20. She purchased a rusty, old car.

A FINAL WORD TO THE STUDENT

Use the following procedure to check your exercise before you hand it in:

1. Re-read the special instructions one at a time.
2. After you re-read each separate instruction, examine your completed exercise to make certain that you have followed that particular instruction exactly.
3. Revise your work wherever necessary.
4. When you are certain that the special instruction you are considering has been observed throughout your exercise, place a check (√) to the left of that special instruction and go on to the next one until you have completed the entire list.

This process will take several minutes of your time, but failure to recheck your exercises in this manner may mean that you have wasted all of the time and effort you have spent in doing the exercise.

EXERCISE 24

COMPOUND PREDICATES

Write two sentences to fit each of the indicated patterns unless your teacher specifically instructs you to write only one sentence for each pattern.

Special Instructions:

_____ 1. Do not use any proper nouns in this exercise.
_____ 2. Do not use any noun or pronoun more than once in this exercise.
_____ 3. Do not use any adjective or adverb more than once in this exercise. (Exception: You may use the articles *a, an,* and *the* as many times as you wish.)
_____ 4. Do not use any verb more than once in this exercise. (After you have used one form of a verb, do not use any other form of the same verb. You may repeat auxiliaries but not primary verbs.)
_____ 5. Do not use comparative or superlative forms of adjectives or adverbs.
_____ 6. Do not use the passive voice.
_____ 7. Use only the indicative mode.
_____ 8. Be sure that your comma punctuation is correct.
_____ 9. Be sure that each sentence is a statement, not a question.
_____ 10. Be sure that you follow the specified pattern exactly.
_____ 11. Be sure that each sentence makes good sense.

MODIFIER—*Subject—Compound Predicate*

(_____ and _____)
  Verb—Object   Verb

1. ____ We painted the house and left. _____

2. ____ The firemen extinguished the blaze and returned. ____

Subject—*Compound Predicate*

(_____ and _____) *I meant this in the same*
  Verb—Object   Linking Verb—Adjective Complement   *sense as "was tired"*

✗ 3. ____ The boy mowed the lawn and was exhausted. ____ *past passive participle*

4. ____ The children visited the park and seemed happy. ____

217

Subject—Compound Predicate

(_____ but _____)
Verb—Object   Verb—Object

X 5. The squirrel climbed the tree but found no food.

X 6. The team rescued the boy but resieved no recognition.

MODIFIER→*Subject—Compound Predicate*

(either _____ or _____)
Verb—Object   Verb—Object

7. The girls either washed the dishes or mowed the lawn.

8. Our neighbors either cooked the casserole or brought the wine.

Subject—Compound Predicate

(not only _____ but also _____)
Verb—Object   Verb—Object

Misspelled word.

9. I not only completed the test but also finished the bonus.

X 10. They not only sent a gift but also (attened the wedding.)

Subject—Compound Predicate

(_____ and _____)
Verb—Modifier—Object→   Verb—Object

11. She fed the lost dog and bathed it.

12. His brother scrubbed the dirty grill and swept the patio.

Subject—Compound Predicate

(_____ , _____ , and _____)
Verb—Object   Verb—Object   Verb

13. The camper caught the trout, fried them, and ate.

X 14. The minister made announcements, read the liturgy, and preached.

Is this comma essential?

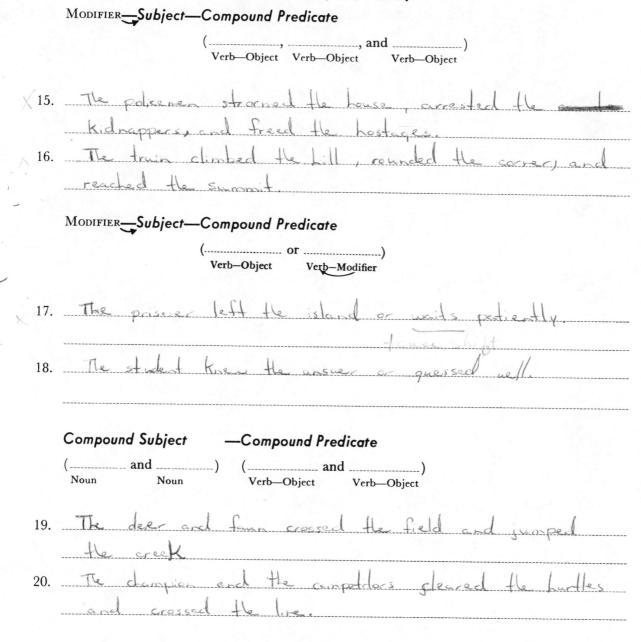

Exercise 24 (continued)

Modifier—Subject—Compound Predicate

(_____, _____, and _____)
   Verb—Object   Verb—Object   Verb—Object

15. The policemen stormed the house, arrested the ~~crooks~~ kidnappers, and freed the hostages.

16. The train climbed the hill, rounded the corner, and reached the summit.

Modifier—Subject—Compound Predicate

(_____ or _____)
   Verb—Object   Verb—Modifier

17. The prisoner left the island or waits patiently.

18. The student knew the answer or guessed well.

Compound Subject —Compound Predicate

(_____ and _____)   (_____ and _____)
   Noun   Noun   Verb—Object   Verb—Object

19. The deer and fawn crossed the field and jumped the creek.

20. The champion and the competitors cleared the hurdles and crossed the line.

A FINAL WORD TO THE STUDENT

Use the following procedure to check your exercise before you hand it in:

1. Re-read the special instructions one at a time.
2. After you re-read each separate instruction, examine your completed exercise to make certain that you have followed that particular instruction exactly.
3. Revise your work wherever necessary.
4. When you are certain that the special instruction you are considering has been observed throughout your exercise, place a check (√) to the left of that special instruction and go on to the next one until you have completed the entire list.

This process will take several minutes of your time, but failure to recheck your exercises in this manner may mean that you have wasted all of the time and effort you have spent in doing the exercise.

EXERCISE 25

APPOSITIVES

Write a sentence to fit each of the indicated patterns.

Special Instructions:

⎯⎯⎯ 1. Do not use any noun or pronoun more than once in these sentences.

⎯⎯⎯ 2. Do not use any adjective or adverb more than once in these sentences. (Exception: You may use the articles *a, an,* and *the* as many times as you wish.)

⎯⎯⎯ 3. Do not use any verb more than once in these sentences. (After you have used one form of a verb, do not use any other form of the same verb. You may repeat auxiliaries but not primary verbs.)

⎯⎯⎯ 4. Do not use comparative or superlative forms of adjectives or adverbs.

⎯⎯⎯ 5. Do not use the passive voice.

⎯⎯⎯ 6. Use only the indicative mode.

⎯⎯⎯ 7. Be sure that your comma punctuation is correct.

⎯⎯⎯ 8. Be sure that each sentence is a statement, not a question.

⎯⎯⎯ 9. Be sure that you follow the specified pattern exactly.

⎯⎯10. Be sure that each sentence makes good sense.

Subject—Appositive   —**Verb**—**Object**
    (Non-restrictive)

1. ⎯⎯⎯⎯⎯⎯⎯⎯⎯⎯⎯⎯⎯⎯⎯⎯⎯⎯⎯⎯⎯⎯

Subject—**Verb**—Modifier—**Object**—Appositive
        (Restrictive)

2. ⎯⎯⎯⎯⎯⎯⎯⎯⎯⎯⎯⎯⎯⎯⎯⎯⎯⎯⎯⎯⎯⎯

Subject—Appositive   —**Verb**—**Object**—Modifier
    (Non-restrictive)

    | Modifier—Noun |

3. ⎯⎯⎯⎯⎯⎯⎯⎯⎯⎯⎯⎯⎯⎯⎯⎯⎯⎯⎯⎯⎯⎯

Subject—Compound Appositive   —Verb—Object

(............... and ....)
　　Noun　　　　　Noun

4. ....

Subject—Appositive   —Verb—Object
(Intensive pronoun)

5. ....

Subject—Linking Verb—Adjective Complement—Appositive
(Delayed subject)

6. ....

Write four sentences containing appositives preceded by introductory words.

Special Instructions:

.... 1. Use any sentence pattern, but make the sentence relatively short.
.... 2. Be sure that your punctuation is correct.

7. ....

8. ....

9. ....

10. ....

A FINAL WORD TO THE STUDENT

Use the following procedure to check your exercise before you hand it in:

1. Re-read the special instructions one at a time.
2. After you re-read each separate instruction, examine your completed exercise to make certain that you have followed that particular instruction exactly.
3. Revise your work wherever necessary.
4. When you are certain that the special instruction you are considering has been observed throughout your exercise, place a check ($\checkmark$) to the left of that special instruction and go on to the next one until you have completed the entire list.

This process will take several minutes of your time, but failure to recheck your exercises in this manner may mean that you have wasted all of the time and effort you have spent in doing the exercise.

EXERCISE 26

INDEPENDENT SENTENCE ELEMENTS

Write a sentence to fit each of the indicated patterns.

Special Instructions:

------- 1. Do not use any noun or pronoun more than once in these sentences.
------- 2. Do not use any adjective or adverb more than once in these sentences. (Exception: You may use the articles *a, an,* and *the* as many times as you wish.)
------- 3. Do not use any verb more than once in these sentences. (Exception: You may use the verb *to be* as often as necessary.) You may, of course, repeat auxiliaries.
------- 4. Do not use comparative or superlative forms of adjectives or adverbs.
------- 5. Be sure to use the expletive *there*—not the adverb *there*—in sentences 6 and 7.
------- 6. Do not use the passive voice.
------- 7. Use only the indicative mode.
------- 8. Be sure that your punctuation is correct.
------- 9. Be sure that each sentence is a statement, not a question.
------10. Be sure that you follow the specified pattern exactly.
------11. Be sure that each sentence makes good sense.

[EXCLAMATORY ELEMENT]—*Subject—Verb*

1. _Oh! the horse escaped._

[EXCLAMATORY ELEMENT]—*Subject—Verb—Object*

X 2. _Hurrah! he crossed the finish line._

[VOCATIVE]—*Subject—Verb*

3. _Members of the board of trustees, the president resigned._

MODIFIER—*Subject*—[VOCATIVE]—*Verb—Object*

X 4. _Our main objective, George, involves a merger._

p 205. #5

223

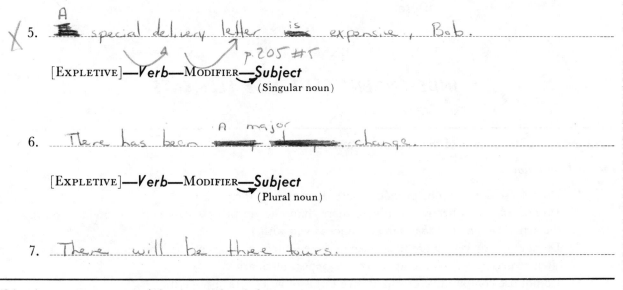

X 5. ~~A~~ *A* special delivery letter ~~is~~ is expensive, Bob.

[EXPLETIVE]—*Verb*—MODIFIER—*Subject*
(Singular noun)

6. There has been ~~A major~~ *A major* change.

[EXPLETIVE]—*Verb*—MODIFIER—*Subject*
(Plural noun)

7. There will be three tours.

Write three sentences containing interpolated elements.

Special Instructions:

_____ 1. Use any sentence pattern, but make the sentence relatively short.
_____ 2. Be sure that your punctuation is correct.

---

8. My son — he is quite a boy — made the team.

9. The cows — they are registered — will bring a high price.

10. John (you dated his sister) is on the baseball team.

A FINAL WORD TO THE STUDENT

Use the following procedure to check your exercise before you hand it in:

1. Re-read the special instructions one at a time.
2. After you re-read each separate instruction, examine your completed exercise to make certain that you have followed that particular instruction exactly.
3. Revise your work wherever necessary.
4. When you are certain that the special instruction you are considering has been observed throughout your exercise, place a check (√) to the left of that special instruction and go on to the next one until you have completed the entire list.

This process will take several minutes of your time, but failure to recheck your exercises in this manner may mean that you have wasted all of the time and effort you have spent in doing the exercise.

EXERCISE 27

TYPES OF SENTENCES

Write two sentences to fit each of the indicated patterns unless your teacher specifically instructs you to write only one sentence for each pattern.

Special Instructions:

-------- 1. In sentences 1–6, insert the understood subject *you* in parentheses, but capitalize the first word of the imperative sentence outside the parentheses. (In other words, follow the examples on p. 72.)

-------- 2. Do not use any proper nouns in these sentences.

-------- 3. Do not use any noun or pronoun more than once in these sentences. (Exception: You will, of course, repeat the understood pronoun *you* in the first six sentences.)

-------- 4. Do not use any adjective or adverb more than once in these sentences. (Exception: You may repeat the exclamatory adjective *what* and the articles *a, an,* and *the.*)

-------- 5. Do not use any verb more than once in these sentences. (You may repeat auxiliaries but not primary verbs.)

-------- 6. Do not use comparative or superlative forms of adjectives.

-------- 7. Do not use the passive voice.

-------- 8. Be sure that your punctuation is correct. Be sure to place a question mark at the end of each interrogative sentence and an exclamation point at the end of each exclamatory sentence.

-------- 9. Be sure that you follow the specified pattern exactly.

--------10. Be sure that each sentence makes good sense.

Imperative Sentences

(Subject)—Verb

1. (You) ~~Stand here~~ Wait.

2. (You) Drive.

(Subject)—Verb—Object

3. (You) Feed the horses.

4. (You) Get the paper

225

(Subject)—Linking Verb—Adjective Complement

5. _(You) Be patient._

6. _(You) Remain calm._

Interrogative Sentences

Auxiliary—*Subject*—*Verb*[?]

7. _Will he come?_

8. _Did the student pass?_

Auxiliary—*Subject*—*Verb*—*Object*[?]

9. _Did you buy groceries?_

10. _Have you bought a car?_

Subject   —*Verb*—Modifier—**Object**[?]
(Interrogative pronoun)

11. _Who bought the painting?_

12. _Which killed the sheep?_

Object   —Auxiliary—*Subject*—*Verb*[?]
(Interrogative pronoun)

13. _When did she ask?_

14. _Which did you make?_

Modifier   **Object**—Auxiliary—*Subject*—*Verb*[?]
(Interrogative adjective)

15. _Which songs did they select?_

16. _What flight shall we take?_

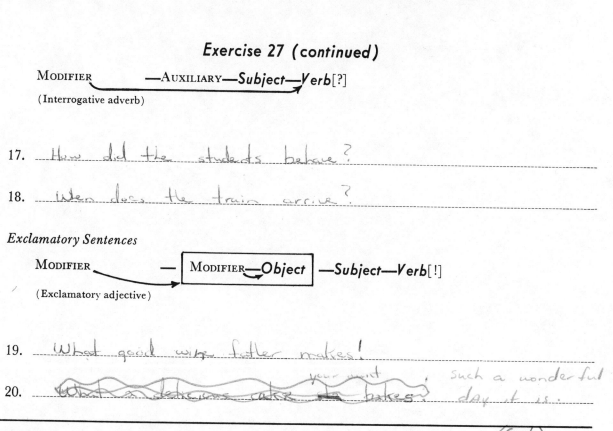

MODIFIER ——AUXILIARY—*Subject*—*Verb*[?]
(Interrogative adverb)

17. How did the students behave?

18. When does the train arrive?

Exclamatory Sentences

MODIFIER —— MODIFIER—*Object* —*Subject*—*Verb*[!]
(Exclamatory adjective)

19. What good wife father makes!

20. What a delicious cake he bakes! such a wonderful day it is.

(Such)

Insert *who* or *whom* in the blank. Be sure that you use the case form required by the function of the word in the sentence.

---

21. _____ Whom _____ does he prefer?

22. _____ Who _____ trimmed the hedge?

23. _____ who _____ is the treasurer?

24. _____ Whom _____ shall I ask?

25. _____ Whom _____ do you believe?

A FINAL WORD TO THE STUDENT

Use the following procedure to check your exercise before you hand it in:

1. Re-read the special instructions one at a time.
2. After you re-read each separate instruction, examine your completed exercise to make certain that you have followed that particular instruction exactly.
3. Revise your work wherever necessary.
4. When you are certain that the special instruction you are considering has been observed throughout your exercise, place a check (√) to the left of that special instruction and go on to the next one until you have completed the entire list.

This process will take several minutes of your time, but failure to recheck your exercises in this manner may mean that you have wasted all of the time and effort you have spent in doing the exercise.

EXERCISE 28

REVIEW

Write two sentences to fit each of the indicated patterns.

Special Instructions:

----- 1. In sentences 1 and 2, insert the understood subject *you* in parentheses, but capitalize the first word of the imperative sentence outside the parentheses.

----- 2. Be sure to use the expletive *there*—not the adverb *there*—in sentences 5 and 6.

----- 3. Do not use a proper noun unless one is called for.

----- 4. Do not use any noun or pronoun more than once in this exercise. (Exception: You will, of course, repeat the understood pronoun *you* in the first two sentences.)

----- 5. Do not use any adjective or adverb more than once in this exercise. (Exception: You may use the articles *a, an,* and *the* as many times as you wish.)

----- 6. Do not use any verb more than once in this exercise. You may repeat auxiliaries but not primary verbs. (Exception: You may use the verb *to be* in both sentence 5 and sentence 6.)

----- 7. Do not use comparative or superlative forms of adjectives.

----- 8. Do not use a main verb in the passive voice.

----- 9. Be sure that your punctuation is correct.

-----10. Be sure that you follow the specified pattern exactly.

-----11. Be sure that each sentence makes good sense.

(Subject)—Verb—Object—[Vocative]
(Proper noun)

1. (you) Buy stock , John.

2. (you) Return the records, Joel

[Exclamatory Element]—*Subject—Verb—Object*

3. Oh! he sacked the quarterback.

4. Hurrah! we won the raffle.

[Expletive]—*Verb—*Modifier—*Subject*

5. There is one solution.

6. There remains little hope.

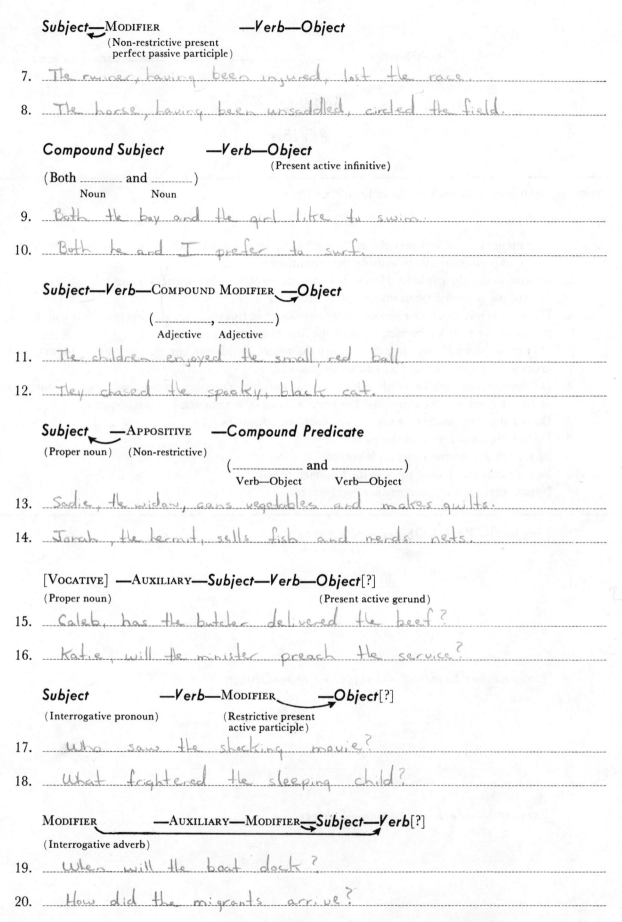

Subject—Modifier   **—Verb—Object**
        (Non-restrictive present
        perfect passive participle)

7. The runner, having been injured, lost the race.

8. The horse, having been unsaddled, circled the field.

Compound Subject   **—Verb—Object**
                  (Present active infinitive)

(Both _____ and _____)
       Noun   Noun

9. Both the boy and the girl like to swim.

10. Both he and I prefer to surf.

Subject—Verb—Compound Modifier **—Object**
           (_____, _____)
          Adjective Adjective

11. The children enjoyed the small, red ball

12. They chased the spooky, black cat.

Subject —Appositive **—Compound Predicate**
(Proper noun) (Non-restrictive)

            (_____ and _____)
           Verb—Object Verb—Object

13. Sadie, the widow, cans vegetables and makes quilts.

14. Jonah, the hermit, sells fish and mends nets.

[Vocative] —Auxiliary—**Subject—Verb—Object**[?]
(Proper noun)   (Present active gerund)

15. Caleb, has the butler delivered the beef?

16. Katie, will the minister preach the service?

Subject **—Verb—**Modifier **—Object**[?]
(Interrogative pronoun)   (Restrictive present
             active participle)

17. Who saw the shocking movie?

18. What frightened the sleeping child?

Modifier **—**Auxiliary—Modifier**Subject—Verb**[?]
(Interrogative adverb)

19. When will the boat dock?

20. How did the migrants arrive?

IMPORTANT NOTE

In the remaining exercises, the special instructions will not include specific rules forbidding the use of words contained in the examples in the text or the repetition of words within the exercise. You will be expected, nevertheless, to use your ingenuity to make each sentence as original as possible. As in previous exercises, sentences containing unnecessary repetition will not be accepted.

EXERCISE 29

PREPOSITIONAL PHRASES

Fill in each blank with a prepositional phrase which will modify the specified word.

Special Instructions:

_____ 1. Write each prepositional phrase to fit the following pattern:
  Prep.—Object
  You may use *a, an,* or *the* before the object, but do not use any other modifiers.
_____ 2. Do not insert anything in the blank except the prepositional phrase.
_____ 3. Do not use any proper nouns in these sentences.
_____ 4. Be sure that the object of each preposition is in the objective case.
_____ 5. Be sure that the prepositional phrase functions in the way specified below the blank.
_____ 6. Be sure that the completed sentence makes good sense.

1. The children played ___in the yard___.
  Modifier of *played*

2. The top ___of the dresser___ is dusty.
  Modifier of *top*

3. ___By the pond___ lay an uprooted tree.
  Modifier of *lay*

4. The boy ___on the bank___ threw the rock ___into the water___.
  Modifier of *boy*   **Modifier of** *threw*

5. We covered the floor ___of the cabin___ ___with rushes___.
  Modifier of *floor*   **Modifier of** *covered*

Write a sentence to fit each of the indicated patterns.

Special Instructions:

_____ 1. Do not use any proper nouns in these sentences.
_____ 2. Be sure that the object of each preposition is in the objective case.
_____ 3. Do not use the passive voice.
_____ 4. Use only the indicative mode.
_____ 5. Be sure that each sentence is a statement, not a question.
_____ 6. Be sure that you follow the specified pattern exactly.
_____ 7. Be sure that each sentence makes good sense.

Subject—Modifier   —*Verb*—*Object*
  | Prep.—Object |

6. ___The boy on the horse jumped the fence.___

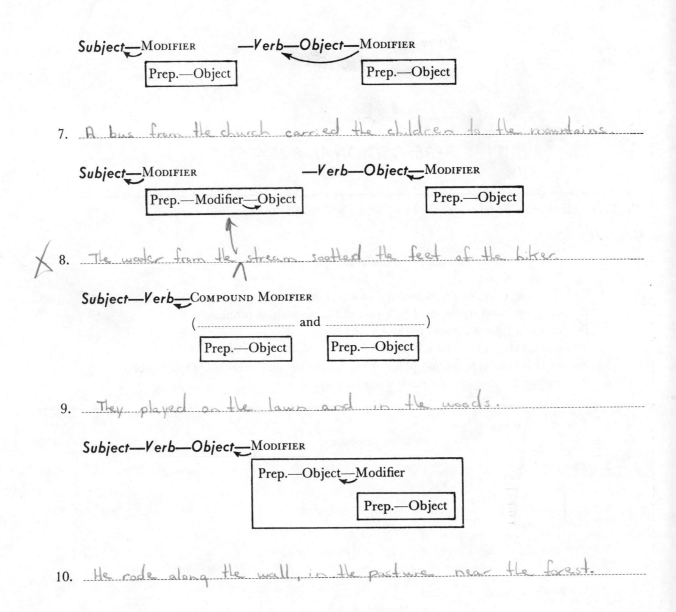

Subject—MODIFIER   —Verb—Object—MODIFIER

Prep.—Object   Prep.—Object

7. A bus from the church carried the children to the mountains.

Subject—MODIFIER   —Verb—Object—MODIFIER

Prep.—Modifier—Object   Prep.—Object

8. The water from the stream soothed the feet of the hiker.

Subject—Verb—COMPOUND MODIFIER

(_____ and _____)

Prep.—Object   Prep.—Object

9. They played on the lawn and in the woods.

Subject—Verb—Object—MODIFIER

Prep.—Object—Modifier

Prep.—Object

10. He rode along the wall, in the pasture near the forest.

A FINAL WORD TO THE STUDENT

Use the following procedure to check your exercise before you hand it in:

1. Re-read the special instructions one at a time.
2. After you re-read each separate instruction, examine your completed exercise to make certain that you have followed that particular instruction exactly.
3. Revise your work wherever necessary.
4. When you are certain that the special instruction you are considering has been observed throughout your exercise, place a check (√) to the left of that special instruction and go on to the next one until you have completed the entire list.

This process will take several minutes of your time, but failure to recheck your exercises in this manner may mean that you have wasted all of the time and effort you have spent in doing the exercise.

EXERCISE 30

INDIRECT OBJECTS

Using the indicated verbs, write sentences to fit the following pattern:

Pattern: **Subject—Verb—**Modifier **—Object**
(Indirect object)

Example: The butcher sold me a roast.

Special Instructions:

------ 1. Do not use any proper nouns in this exercise.
------ 2. Be sure that each indirect object is in the objective case.
------ 3. Do not use the passive voice.
------ 4. Use only the indicative mode.
------ 5. Be sure that each sentence is a statement, not a question.
------ 6. Be sure that you follow the specified pattern exactly.
------ 7. Be sure that each sentence makes good sense.
------ 8. Vary the *form* of the verb in the two sentences which you compose with each verb.

to give   1. She gave me the keys.

              2. The lady had given the waiter a tip.

to offer   3. The hostess offered the guest a drink.

              4. The company has offered the man a job.

to pay   5. He will pay the policeman the fine.

              spelling
✗ 6. The tenents will have paid the landlord the rent.

to bring   7. The minister has brought the church stability.

              8. I brought the patient flowers.

to send   9. We sent the girl a postcard.

              10. They will send the boy money.

to buy   11. The company bought the employees presents.

              12. The plant will bring the area income.

to assign   13. The professor assigned the students homework.

              14. The sargeant has assigned the soldiers the detail.

to make   15. The children made the teacher a present.

16. The plant makes the company money.

to tell   17. Everyone told the jury the truth.

18. Someone had told the tourists a lie.

to write   19. The protesters wrote the senator a letter.

20. The customer had written the store a check.

A FINAL WORD TO THE STUDENT

Use the following procedure to check your exercise before you hand it in:

1. Re-read the special instructions one at a time.
2. After you re-read each separate instruction, examine your completed exercise to make certain that you have followed that particular instruction exactly.
3. Revise your work wherever necessary.
4. When you are certain that the special instruction you are considering has been observed throughout your exercise, place a check (√) to the left of that special instruction and go on to the next one until you have completed the entire list.

This process will take several minutes of your time, but failure to recheck your exercises in this manner may mean that you have wasted all of the time and effort you have spent in doing the exercise.

EXERCISE 31

PASSIVE VOICE WITH AGENT EXPRESSED

Write ten sentences containing verbs in the passive voice with the agent expressed as the object of the preposition *by*. Each sentence will fit the following pattern:

Pattern: **Subject—Passive Verb—**MODIFIER

Prep.—Object

Example: The baby was scratched by the cat.

Special Instructions:

_____ 1. Do not use any proper nouns in this exercise.
_____ 2. Be sure that the object of the preposition *by* is in the objective case.
_____ 3. Use only the indicative mode.
_____ 4. Be sure that each sentence is a statement, not a question.
_____ 5. Be sure that you follow the specified pattern exactly.
_____ 6. Be sure that each sentence makes good sense.
_____ 7. Note that the statement of an idea in a sentence using a verb in the passive voice is usually weaker than a statement of the same idea in a sentence using a verb in the active voice.

1. He was struck by lightning.

2. She was adopted by a couple.

3. They were arrested by a detective.

4. The deer was shot by a hunter.

5. The crowd was entertained by a clown.

6. A champion was raised by the farmer.

7. The river was crossed by the campers.

8. The bill was killed by the council.

9. Hopes were raised by the announcement.

10. The road was built by the engineers.

237

A FINAL WORD TO THE STUDENT

Use the following procedure to check your exercise before you hand it in:

1. Re-read the special instructions one at a time.
2. After you re-read each separate instruction, examine your completed exercise to make certain that you have followed that particular instruction exactly.
3. Revise your work wherever necessary.
4. When you are certain that the special instruction you are considering has been observed throughout your exercise, place a check (√) to the left of that special instruction and go on to the next one until you have completed the entire list.

This process will take several minutes of your time, but failure to recheck your exercises in this manner may mean that you have wasted all of the time and effort you have spent in doing the exercise.

EXERCISE 32

GERUND PHRASES

Fill in each blank with a gerund phrase which will have the function specified below the blank.

Special Instructions:

_____ 1. Be sure that you insert a gerund *phrase* in each blank, not merely a gerund. The gerund phrases may fit any of the five basic gerund phrase patterns.
_____ 2. Do not place anything in the blank except the gerund phrase. (Remember that a possessive modifying a phrase is not part of the phrase.)
_____ 3. Do not use any proper nouns in these sentences.
_____ 4. Use any tense form of the gerund.
_____ 5. Use either active or passive voice forms.
_____ 6. Be sure that the completed sentence makes good sense.

1. ___Playing baseball___ is good exercise.

Subject

2. Do you like ___having children___?

Object

3. He became popular by ___making movies___.

Object of preposition

4. Her hobby was ___collecting coins___.

Substantive complement

5. After ___eating dinner___, we attended a movie.

Object of preposition

Write a sentence to fit each of the indicated patterns.

Special Instructions:

_____ 1. Do not use any proper nouns in these sentences.
_____ 2. Use any tense form of the gerund.
_____ 3. Do not use a main verb in the passive voice.
_____ 4. Use only the indicative mode.
_____ 5. Be sure that each sentence is a statement, not a question.
_____ 6. Be sure that you follow the specified pattern exactly.
_____ 7. Be sure that each sentence makes good sense.

Subject —Linking Verb—Adjective Complement
| Gerund—Object |

6. ___Shooting rapids is exciting.___

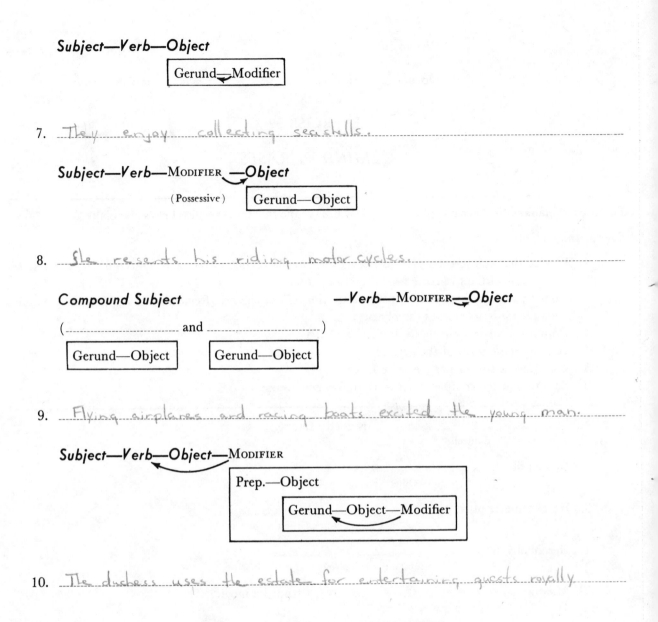

Subject—Verb—Object

Gerund—Modifier

7. They enjoy collecting seashells.

Subject—Verb—MODIFIER—Object

(Possessive)   Gerund—Object

8. She resents his riding motor cycles.

Compound Subject   —Verb—MODIFIER—Object

(_____ and _____)

Gerund—Object   Gerund—Object

9. Flying airplanes and racing boats excited the young man.

Subject—Verb—Object—MODIFIER

Prep.—Object

Gerund—Object—Modifier

10. The duchess uses the estate for entertaining guests royally

A FINAL WORD TO THE STUDENT

Use the following procedure to check your exercise before you hand it in:

1. Re-read the special instructions one at a time.
2. After you re-read each separate instruction, examine your completed exercise to make certain that you have followed that particular instruction exactly.
3. Revise your work wherever necessary.
4. When you are certain that the special instruction you are considering has been observed throughout your exercise, place a check (√) to the left of that special instruction and go on to the next one until you have completed the entire list.

This process will take several minutes of your time, but failure to recheck your exercises in this manner may mean that you have wasted all of the time and effort you have spent in doing the exercise.

EXERCISE 33

PARICIPIAL PHRASES

Fill in each blank with a participial phrase which will modify the specified word.

Special Instructions:

1. Be sure that you insert a participial phrase in each blank, not merely a participle. The participial phrases may fit any of the five basic participial phrase patterns.
2. Do not place anything in the blank except the participial phrase.
3. Do not use any proper nouns in these sentences.
4. Use any tense form of the participle, but be sure that the sequence of tenses is correct.
5. Use either active or passive voice forms.
6. Be sure that the participial phrase functions in the way specified below the blank.
7. Be sure that the completed sentence makes good sense.

1. My brother, _finishing his shower_, ran to the phone.
    Non-restrictive modifier of *brother*

2. The girl _holding the baby_ answered the question.
    Restrictive modifier of *girl*

3. The car _passing the truck_ is a new model.
    Restrictive modifier of *car*

4. His sister is the child _wearing the ribbon_.
    Restrictive modifier of *child*

5. _Catching the ball_, the fullback made a touchdown.
    Non-restrictive modifier of *fullback*

Write a sentence to fit each of the indicated patterns.

Special Instructions:

1. Do not use any proper nouns in these sentences.
2. Use any tense form of the participle, but be sure that the sequence of tenses is correct.
3. Do not use a main verb in the passive voice.
4. Use only the indicative mode.
5. Be sure that your comma punctuation is correct.
6. Be sure that you do not write any "dangling" participial phrases.
7. Be sure that each sentence is a statement, not a question.
8. Be sure that you follow the specified pattern exactly.
9. Be sure that each sentence makes good sense.

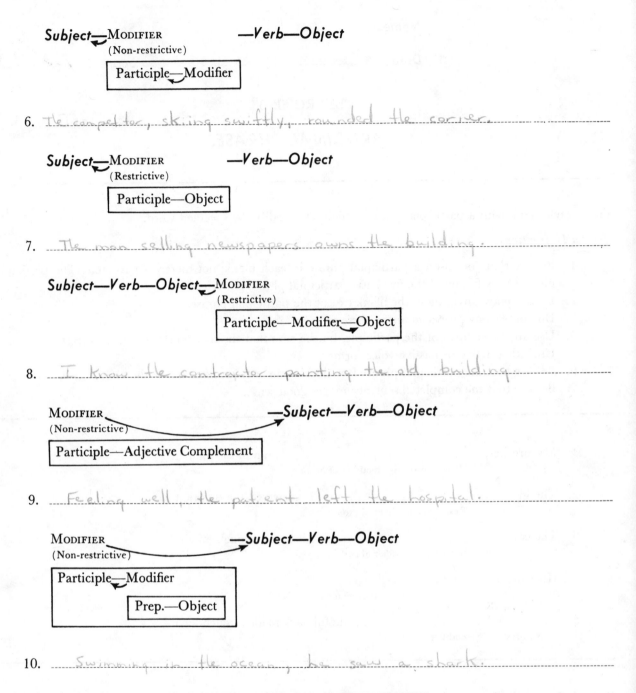

Subject—MODIFIER   —Verb—Object
(Non-restrictive)

Participle—Modifier

6. The competitor, skiing swiftly, rounded the corner.

Subject—MODIFIER   —Verb—Object
(Restrictive)

Participle—Object

7. The man selling newspapers owns the building.

Subject—Verb—Object—MODIFIER
(Restrictive)

Participle—Modifier—Object

8. I know the contractor painting the old building.

MODIFIER   —Subject—Verb—Object
(Non-restrictive)

Participle—Adjective Complement

9. Feeling well, the patient left the hospital.

MODIFIER   —Subject—Verb—Object
(Non-restrictive)

Participle—Modifier

Prep.—Object

10. Swimming in the ocean, he saw a shark.

A FINAL WORD TO THE STUDENT

Use the following procedure to check your exercise before you hand it in:

1. Re-read the special instructions one at a time.
2. After you re-read each separate instruction, examine your completed exercise to make certain that you have followed that particular instruction exactly.
3. Revise your work wherever necessary.
4. When you are certain that the special instruction you are considering has been observed throughout your exercise, place a check (√) to the left of that special instruction and go on to the next one until you have completed the entire list.

This process will take several minutes of your time, but failure to recheck your exercises in this manner may mean that you have wasted all of the time and effort you have spent in doing the exercise.

EXERCISE 34

INFINITIVE PHRASES

Fill in each blank with an infinitive phrase which will have the function specified below the blank.

Special Instructions:

———— 1. Use *to,* the "sign of the infinitive," before each infinitive.
———— 2. Be sure that you insert an infinitive *phrase* in each blank, not merely an infinitive. The infinitive phrases may fit any of the five basic infinitive patterns. (Do not use an infinitive phrase containing a subject.)
———— 3. Do not place anything in the blank except the infinitive phrase.
———— 4. Do not use any proper nouns in these sentences.
———— 5. Use any tense form of the infinitive, but be sure that the sequence of tenses is correct.
———— 6. Use either active or passive voice forms.
———— 7. Be sure that your use of case forms is correct.
———— 8. Be sure that the completed sentence makes good sense.

1. __To become a doctor__ was his ambition.
   Subject

2. Tomorrow is the day __to register for classes__.
   Modifier of *day*

3. The woman hurried __to complete the shopping__.
   Modifier of *hurried*

4. He intended __to return the watch__.
   Object

✗ 5. I expect to try __the product__.
   Object of infinitive

Write a sentence to fit each of the indicated patterns.

Special Instructions:

———— 1. Use *to,* the "sign of the infinitive," before each infinitive.
———— 2. Do not use any proper nouns in these sentences.
———— 3. Use any tense form of the infinitive, but be sure that the sequence of tenses is correct.
———— 4. Do not use a main verb in the passive voice.
———— 5. Use only the indicative mode.
———— 6. Be sure that your use of case forms is correct.
———— 7. Be sure that each sentence is a statement, not a question.
———— 8. Be sure that you follow the specified pattern exactly.
———— 9. Be sure that each sentence makes good sense.

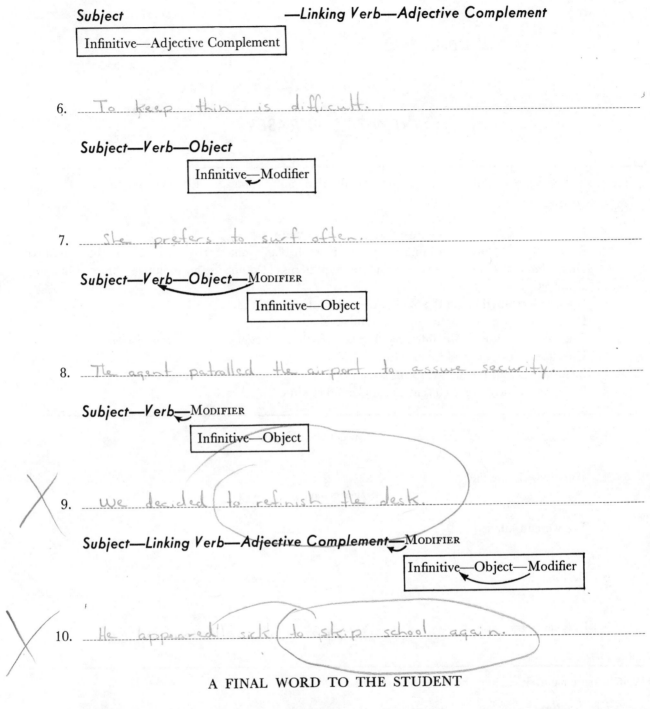

Subject   —Linking Verb—Adjective Complement

Infinitive—Adjective Complement

6. To keep thin is difficult.

Subject—Verb—Object

Infinitive—Modifier

7. She prefers to surf often.

Subject—Verb—Object—MODIFIER

Infinitive—Object

8. The agent patrolled the airport to assure security.

Subject—Verb—MODIFIER

Infinitive—Object

9. We decided to refinish the desk.

Subject—Linking Verb—Adjective Complement—MODIFIER

Infinitive—Object—Modifier

10. He appeared sick to skip school again.

A FINAL WORD TO THE STUDENT

Use the following procedure to check your exercise before you hand it in:

1. Re-read the special instructions one at a time.
2. After you re-read each separate instruction, examine your completed exercise to make certain that you have followed that particular instruction exactly.
3. Revise your work wherever necessary.
4. When you are certain that the special instruction you are considering has been observed throughout your exercise, place a check (√) to the left of that special instruction and go on to the next one until you have completed the entire list.

This process will take several minutes of your time, but failure to recheck your exercises in this manner may mean that you have wasted all of the time and effort you have spent in doing the exercise.

EXERCISE 35

MORE INFINITIVE PHRASES

Fill in each blank with an infinitive phrase containing a subject.

Special Instructions:

1. In sentences 1–5, each infinitive will be preceded by *to;* in sentences 6–7, the infinitive will not be preceded by *to.*
2. Be sure that each infinitive phrase contains a subject.
3. Do not place anything in the blank except the infinitive phrase. (In three of the sentences the expletive *for* will have to be included as part of the phrase.)
4. Do not use any proper nouns in these sentences.
5. Use any tense form of the infinitive, but be sure that the sequence of tenses is correct.
6. Use either active or passive voice forms.
7. Be sure that your use of case forms is correct.
8. Be sure that the completed sentence makes good sense.

---

1. The teacher wanted ___her to leave the room___.

Object

2. He requested ___them to buy a notebook___.

Object

3. ___For you to resign___ appears unnecessary.

Subject

4. The plan is ___for him to drive the car___.

Substantive complement

5. It would be dangerous ___to attack him___.

Delayed subject

6. The sheriff made ___the deputy arrest me___.

Object

7. I saw ___the family greet her___.

Object

Fill in each blank with an infinitive phrase containing an interrogative word.

Special Instructions:

1. Use *to,* the "sign of the infinitive," before each infinitive.
2. Be sure that each infinitive phrase contains an interrogative word.
3. Do not place anything in the blank except the infinitive phrase.
4. Do not use any proper nouns in these sentences.
5. Use any tense form of the infinitive, but be sure that the sequence of tenses is correct.
6. Use either active or passive voice forms.

_____ 7. Be sure that your use of case forms is correct.

_____ 8. Be sure that the completed sentence makes good sense.

---

8. The girl asked _____when to notify_____ .

   Object

9. We wondered _____where to find her_____ .

   Object

10. They inquired _____which road to take_____ .

    Object

A FINAL WORD TO THE STUDENT

Use the following procedure to check your exercise before you hand it in:

1. Re-read the special instructions one at a time.
2. After you re-read each separate instruction, examine your completed exercise to make certain that you have followed that particular instruction exactly.
3. Revise your work wherever necessary.
4. When you are certain that the special instruction you are considering has been observed throughout your exercise, place a check (√) to the left of that special instruction and go on to the next one until you have completed the entire list.

This process will take several minutes of your time, but failure to recheck your exercises in this manner may mean that you have wasted all of the time and effort you have spent in doing the exercise.

EXERCISE 36

NOUN CLAUSES OF DIRECT QUOTATION

Write a sentence to fit each of the indicated patterns.

Special Instructions:

----- 1. No specific clause patterns are designated for the noun clauses of direct quotation in these sentences. However, you must be sure that each is a *complete* clause of the kind indicated.
----- 2. Do not use any proper nouns in these sentences.
----- 3. Do not use the passive voice.
----- 4. Be sure that your punctuation is correct.
----- 5. Be sure that you follow the specified pattern exactly.
----- 6. Be sure that each sentence makes good sense.

Subject—Verb—Object
(Direct quotation of declarative statement)

1. ____He said, "We want justice."_____

Object —Subject—Verb—MODIFIER
(Direct quotation of declarative statement)

2. ____"I need protection," the juror said angrily._____

Subject—Verb—Object
(Direct quotation of imperative statement)

3. ____The officer demanded, "Get out of the car."_____

Object —Subject—Verb
(Direct quotation of imperative statement)

4. ____"Hand it over," she requested._____

Subject—Verb—Object
(Direct quotation of exclamatory statement)

5. ____The editor screamed, "Get out of my office!"_____

Object   *—Subject—Verb*
(Direct quotation of
  exclamatory statement)

6. "Leave us alone!" they shouted.

Subject—Verb—Object
(Direct quotation of question)

7. We asked, "Are they really coming?"

Object   *—Subject—Verb*
(Direct quotation of question)

8. "Are you sure?" the judge asked.

Write two sentences, each containing a noun clause of direct quotation which is interrupted by the subject-verb element.

       Example: "The problem," he said, "seems extremely difficult."

Special Instructions:

_____ 1. Do not use any proper nouns in these sentences.
_____ 2. Do not use the passive voice.
_____ 3. Be sure that your punctuation is correct.
_____ 4. Be sure that each sentence makes good sense.

---

9. "The dunes," he said, "protect the beach from erosion."
10. "The answers," she said, "are in the back of the book."

A FINAL WORD TO THE STUDENT

Use the following procedure to check your exercise before you hand it in:

1. Re-read the special instructions one at a time.
2. After you re-read each separate instruction, examine your completed exercise to make certain that you have followed that particular instruction exactly.
3. Revise your work wherever necessary.
4. When you are certain that the special instruction you are considering has been observed throughout your exercise, place a check (√) to the left of that special instruction and go on to the next one until you have completed the entire list.

This process will take several minutes of your time, but failure to recheck your exercises in this manner may mean that you have wasted all of the time and effort you have spent in doing the exercise.

EXERCISE 37

NOUN CLAUSES OF INDIRECT STATEMENT
AND RELATED THAT-CLAUSES

Write two sentences to fit each of the indicated patterns.

Special Instructions:

------- 1. Do not use any proper nouns in this exercise.
------- 2. Do not use the passive voice.
------- 3. Be sure that your use of the subjunctive is correct.
------- 4. Be sure that the sequence of tenses is correct.
------- 5. Use the subordinating conjunction *that* to introduce each noun clause.
------- 6. Be sure that your punctuation is correct.
------- 7. Be sure that you follow the specified pattern exactly.
------- 8. Be sure that each sentence makes good sense.

Subject—Verb—Object
Sub. Conj.—Subject—Verb—Object

1. I believe that he wrote the book.

2. The students doubted that the instructor knew the material.

Subject _____—Linking Verb—Adjective Complement
Sub. Conj.—Subject—Verb

3. That she will come is certain.

4. That the horse escaped seems possible.

Subject—Verb—Object
Sub. Conj.—Subject—Verb
(Subjunctive)

5. The committee knows that I have taught.

6. The doorman suggested that we enter.

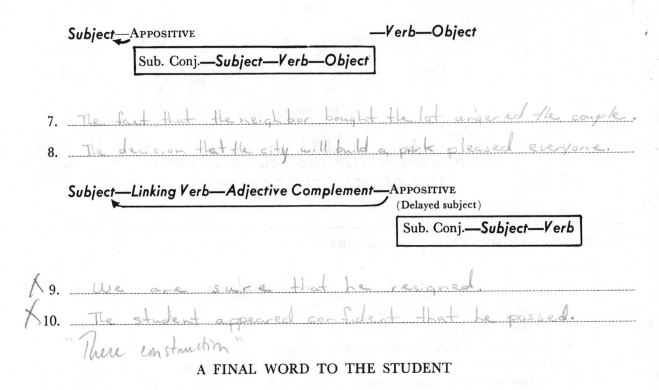

Subject—APPOSITIVE   —*Verb*—*Object*

> Sub. Conj.—*Subject*—*Verb*—*Object*

7. The fact that the neighbor bought the lot angered the couple.

8. The decision that the city will build a park pleased everyone.

Subject—*Linking Verb*—*Adjective Complement*—APPOSITIVE
(Delayed subject)

> Sub. Conj.—*Subject*—*Verb*

9. We are sure that he resigned.

10. The student appeared confident that he passed.

"There construction"

A FINAL WORD TO THE STUDENT

Use the following procedure to check your exercise before you hand it in:

1. Re-read the special instructions one at a time.
2. After you re-read each separate instruction, examine your completed exercise to make certain that you have followed that particular instruction exactly.
3. Revise your work wherever necessary.
4. When you are certain that the special instruction you are considering has been observed throughout your exercise, place a check (√) to the left of that special instruction and go on to the next one until you have completed the entire list.

This process will take several minutes of your time, but failure to recheck your exercises in this manner may mean that you have wasted all of the time and effort you have spent in doing the exercise.

EXERCISE 38

NOUN CLAUSES OF INDIRECT QUESTION
AND RELATED CLAUSES

Fill in each blank with a noun clause of indirect question or a related clause introduced by the word specified below the blank.

Special Instructions:

------- 1. Do not use any proper nouns in this exercise.
------- 2. Do not use the passive voice.
------- 3. Be sure that the sequence of tenses is correct.
------- 4. Be sure that the completed sentence makes good sense.

1. The farmer asked _____whether it will rain_____.
   Noun clause introduced by *whether*

2. ____Whether the student registered_____ was the question.
   Noun clause introduced by *whether*

3. The dean wondered ____who broke the window._____.
   Noun clause introduced by *who*

4. I know _____whom she questioned_____.
   Noun clause introduced by *whom*

5. The girl had decided _____which was appropriate._____.
   Noun clause introduced by pronoun *which*

6. We asked ____which house belonged to them_____.
   Noun clause introduced by adjective *which*

7. The mechanic discovered ____why the car engine knocked_____.
   Noun clause introduced by *why*

8. The reporter explained ____how the fire started_____.
   Noun clause introduced by *how*

9. _____Whomever we choose_____ must be well qualified.
   Noun clause introduced by *whomever*

10. She reads ____whatever she likes_____.
    Noun clause introduced by *whatever*

A FINAL WORD TO THE STUDENT

Use the following procedure to check your exercise before you hand it in:

1. Re-read the special instructions one at a time.
2. After you re-read each separate instruction, examine your completed exercise to make certain that you have followed that particular instruction exactly.
3. Revise your work wherever necessary.
4. When you are certain that the special instruction you are considering has been observed throughout your exercise, place a check (√) to the left of that special instruction and go on to the next one until you have completed the entire list.

This process will take several minutes of your time, but failure to recheck your exercises in this manner may mean that you have wasted all of the time and effort you have spent in doing the exercise.

EXERCISE 39

ADJECTIVE CLAUSES INTRODUCED BY RELATIVE PRONOUNS

Write sentences containing the specified types of adjective clauses.

Special Instructions:

...... 1. Do not use any proper nouns in this exercise.
...... 2. Do not use the passive voice.
...... 3. Be sure that the sequence of tenses is correct.
...... 4. Be sure that your punctuation is correct.
...... 5. Be sure that the adjective clause in each sentence is of the type specified.
...... 6. Be sure that the relative pronoun functions as specified.
...... 7. Be sure that each sentence makes good sense.

Restrictive adjective clause containing *who* functioning as subject of verb

1. The person who leaves last should close the window.

Non-restrictive adjective clause containing *who* functioning as subject of verb

2. My brother, who is on the motorcycle, is younger than I

Restrictive adjective clause containing *whom* functioning as object of verb

3. He will marry whom he wishes

Non-restrictive adjective clause containing *whom* functioning as object of verb

4. The city judge, whom you declared senile, has arrived

Restrictive adjective clause containing *whom* functioning as object of preposition

5. The friend with whom we toured Europe is Scottish.

Non-restrictive adjective clause containing *which* functioning as subject of verb

6. Hydrogen cloride, which is essential, serves as a precipitate.

Restrictive adjective clause containing *which* functioning as object of verb

7. The play which my sister wrote starts tomorrow.

Restrictive adjective clause containing *that* functioning as subject of verb

8. The mail that is here has been opened.

Restrictive adjective clause containing *that* functioning as object of verb

9. The coat that she wants was sold.

Restrictive adjective clause with relative pronoun omitted

10. The fence he built was damaged.

A FINAL WORD TO THE STUDENT

Use the following procedure to check your exercise before you hand it in:

1. Re-read the special instructions one at a time.
2. After you re-read each separate instruction, examine your completed exercise to make certain that you have followed that particular instruction exactly.
3. Revise your work wherever necessary.
4. When you are certain that the special instruction you are considering has been observed throughout your exercise, place a check (√) to the left of that special instruction and go on to the next one until you have completed the entire list.

This process will take several minutes of your time, but failure to recheck your exercises in this manner may mean that you have wasted all of the time and effort you have spent in doing the exercise.

EXERCISE 40

ADJECTIVE CLAUSES INTRODUCED BY RELATIVE ADJECTIVES AND RELATIVE ADVERBS

Write sentences containing the specified types of adjective clauses.

Special Instructions:

_____ 1. Do not use any proper nouns in this exercise. (Exception: You may use proper nouns indicating places in sentences 5 and 6.)
_____ 2. Do not use the passive voice.
_____ 3. Be sure that the sequence of tenses is correct.
_____ 4. Be sure that your punctuation is correct.
_____ 5. Be sure that the adjective clause in each sentence is of the type specified.
_____ 6. Be sure that each sentence makes good sense.

Restrictive adjective clause introduced by *whose*

1. The man whose car I drove is my uncle.
2. He found the bird whose wing was broken at the lake.

Restrictive adjective clause introduced by *where*

3. The house where she was born still stands.
4. The city where we want want to vacation is on the coast.

Non-restrictive adjective clause introduced by *where*

5. A tiny mountain pass, where avalanches often occur, sheltered the elk.
6. The smoke filled forest, where a single match had been dropped, continued to burn.

Restrictive adjective clause introduced by *when*

7. The day when I get my braces off will be a happy one.
8. The time when we went hiking is a pleasant memory.

255

Restrictive adjective clause with relative adverb omitted

9. 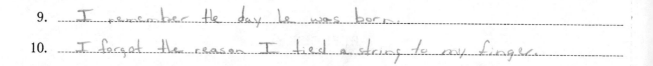 I remember the day he was born.

10. I forgot the reason I tied a string to my finger.

A FINAL WORD TO THE STUDENT

Use the following procedure to check your exercise before you hand it in:

1. Re-read the special instructions one at a time.
2. After you re-read each separate instruction, examine your completed exercise to make certain that you have followed that particular instruction exactly.
3. Revise your work wherever necessary.
4. When you are certain that the special instruction you are considering has been observed throughout your exercise, place a check (√) to the left of that special instruction and go on to the next one until you have completed the entire list.

This process will take several minutes of your time, but failure to recheck your exercises in this manner may mean that you have wasted all of the time and effort you have spent in doing the exercise.

EXERCISE 41

ADVERB CLAUSES OF TIME, PLACE, MANNER, CAUSE, PURPOSE, CONCESSION, AND CONDITION

Write two sentences to fit each of the indicated patterns unless your teacher specifically instructs you to write only one sentence for each pattern. The various headings show the specific type of adverb clause required in each group of sentences.

Special Instructions:

------- 1. Do not use any proper nouns in this exercise.
------- 2. Do not use the passive voice.
------- 3. Be sure that the sequence of tenses is correct.
------- 4. Be sure that your punctuation is correct.
------- 5. Be sure that the adverb clause in each sentence is of the type specified in the heading which precedes it.
------- 6. Be sure that each sentence makes good sense.

Adverb Clause of Time

Subject—Verb—Modifier

Sub. Conj.—*Subject—Verb*

1. _The plane flew until the wing broke_

2. _We left after the sun rose_

Modifier_____—*Subject—Verb—Object*

Sub. Conj.—*Subject—Verb—Object*

3. _As he studied physics, the boys played football._

4. _Since she failed school, her mother repossessed the car._

Adverb Clause of Place

Subject—Verb—Object—MODIFIER

Sub. Conj.—**Subject—Verb**

5. We bought tickets where the line shortened.

6. The settlers guarded the fort where the houses stood.

MODIFIER

Sub. Conj.—**Subject—Verb**

—Subject—Verb—Object

7. Everywhere the men *went*, the wolves hunted them.

8. Wherever the blight appeared, the farmer sprayed the crops.

Adverb Clause of Manner

Subject—Verb—MODIFIER

Sub. Conj.—**Subject—Verb**

9. The boy acted as though he hurt.

10. They couple talked as if they cared.

Adverb Clause of Cause

Subject—Verb—MODIFIER

Sub. Conj.—**Subject—Linking Verb—Adjective Complement**

11. He ate because he was hungry.

12. The children swam since they were hot.

MODIFIER

Sub. Conj.—**Subject—Verb—**Modifier

—Subject—Verb—MODIFIER**—Object**

13. Since the wind blew wildly, the men docked the shrimp boats.

14. Because the fight ended quickly, the crowd mocked the former champion.

Adverb Clause of Purpose

Subject—Verb—Object—MODIFIER

Sub. Conj.—**Subject—Verb—Object**

15. The explorers searched the caves in order that they might find the child.

16. I visit my relatives so that they will visit me.

Adverb Clause of Concession

MODIFIER—**Subject—Verb—Object**—MODIFIER

Sub. Conj.—**Subject—Verb—Object**

17. The young couple built a house although the bank rejected the loan.

18. The teenagers played tennis even though the rain dampened the courts.

Adverb Clause of Condition

Subject—Verb—Object—MODIFIER

Sub. Conj.—**Subject—Verb**

19. I will call you if we go.

20. The dog will bite him unless he stops.

A FINAL WORD TO THE STUDENT

Use the following procedure to check your exercise before you hand it in:

1. Re-read the special instructions one at a time.
2. After you re-read each separate instruction, examine your completed exercise to make certain that you have followed that particular instruction exactly.
3. Revise your work wherever necessary.
4. When you are certain that the special instruction you are considering has been observed throughout your exercise, place a check (√) to the left of that special instruction and go on to the next one until you have completed the entire list.

This process will take several minutes of your time, but failure to recheck your exercises in this manner may mean that you have wasted all of the time and effort you have spent in doing the exercise.

EXERCISE 42

ADVERB CLAUSES OF DEGREE

Write two sentences to fit each of the indicated patterns unless your teacher specifically instructs you to write only one sentence for each pattern. Every adverb clause will be a clause of degree. (In several of the patterns the degree clause is partly elliptical. However, both subject and verb are expressed in all of the degree clauses in this exercise.)

Special Instructions:

_____ 1. Do not use any proper nouns in this exercise.
_____ 2. Do not use the passive voice.
_____ 3. Use only the indicative mode.
_____ 4. Be sure that the sequence of tenses is correct.
_____ 5. Be sure that each sentence is a statement, not a question.
_____ 6. Be sure that you follow the specified pattern exactly.
_____ 7. Be sure that each sentence makes good sense.

Subject—Linking Verb—Adjective Complement—Modifier
(Adj. in *-er*)
| Sub. Conj.—*Subject—Verb* |

1. ___She___ is ___smarter___ than ___her sister___ guesses.

2. The river was deeper than the campers thought.

Subject—Verb—Modifier **—Object—**Modifier
(Adj. in *-er*)
| Sub. Conj.—*Subject—Verb* |

3. The farmer has larger pastures than he can cut.

4. The shaft contains deeper veins than they can mine.

Subject—Verb—Modifier **—**Modifier
(Adv. in *-er*)
| Sub. Conj.—*Subject—Verb* |

5. He works harder than you know.

6. She jumps higher than deer leap.

Subject—Linking Verb—Modifier ——**Adjective Complement**—Modifier
(Adv. *more* or *less*)

Sub. Conj.—*Subject*
—*Verb*

7. She is more athletic than the champion (is).

8. I am less nervous than he (is).

Subject—Verb—Modifier ——Modifier—Modifier
(Adv. *more* or *less*)

Sub. Conj.—*Subject*—*Verb*

9. The boy ran more quickly than a horse (runs)

10. The couple walked more slowly than a turtle crawls.

Subject—Linking Verb—Modifier—**Adjective Complement**—Modifier
(Adv. *as*)

Sub. Conj.—*Subject*—*Verb*

11. She is as pretty as they come.

12. He was as nice as anyone can be.

Subject—Verb—**Object**—Modifier—Modifier—Modifier
(Adv. *as*)

Sub. Conj.—*Subject*—*Verb*—*Object*

13. The woman sang the song as well as the accompanist played it.

14. We can work the problem as quickly as they can work it.

Subject—Linking Verb—Modifier—**Adjective Complement**—Modifier
(Adv. *so*)

Sub. Conj.—*Subject*—*Verb*

15. They were so unhappy that they cried.

16. The passengers will be so relieved that they will cheer.

Exercise 42 (continued)

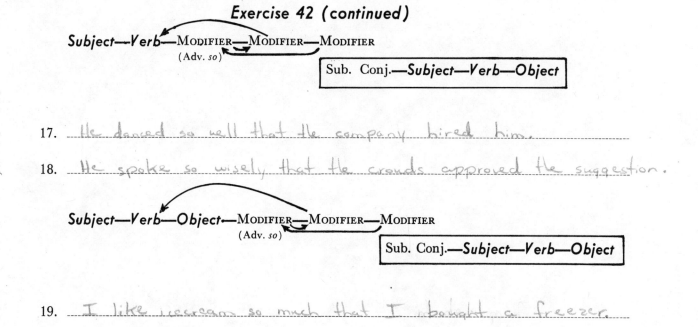

Subject—Verb—Modifier—Modifier—Modifier
(Adv. *so*)

Sub. Conj.—*Subject—Verb—Object*

17. He danced so well that the company hired him.

18. He spoke so wisely that the crowds approved the suggestion.

Subject—Verb—Object—Modifier—Modifier—Modifier
(Adv. *so*)

Sub. Conj.—*Subject—Verb—Object*

19. I like icecream so much that I bought a freezer.

20. They enjoy the beach so much that they have planned a trip.

A FINAL WORD TO THE STUDENT

Use the following procedure to check your exercise before you hand it in:

1. Re-read the special instructions one at a time.
2. After you re-read each separate instruction, examine your completed exercise to make certain that you have followed that particular instruction exactly.
3. Revise your work wherever necessary.
4. When you are certain that the special instruction you are considering has been observed throughout your exercise, place a check (✓) to the left of that special instruction and go on to the next one until you have completed the entire list.

This process will take several minutes of your time, but failure to recheck your exercises in this manner may mean that you have wasted all of the time and effort you have spent in doing the exercise.

EXERCISE 43

ELLIPTICAL ADVERB CLAUSES OF DEGREE

Write five sentences, each of which contains an elliptical adverb clause of degree consisting of a *subordinating conjunction* and a *personal pronoun in the nominative case.*

Example: Her sister was smaller *than she.*

Special Instructions:

------- 1. Be sure that the pronoun in the elliptical clause of degree functions in such a way that the nominative case is correct.

------- 2. Be sure that each sentence makes good sense.

1.   He is brighter than she.

2.   We swim better than they.

3.   He seems older than I.

4.   I worked harder than he.

5.   The foreigners live longer than we.

Write five sentences, each of which contains an elliptical clause of degree consisting of a *subordinating conjunction* and a *personal pronoun in the objective case.*

Example: The registrar notified him sooner *than me.*

Special Instructions:

------- 1. Be sure that the pronoun in the elliptical clause of degree functions in such a way that the objective case is correct.

------- 2. Be sure that each sentence makes good sense.

6.   She likes him better than me.

7.   They invited them sooner than us.

8.   He treats the cat better than her.

9.   She loves money more than him.

10. The principal expelled us sooner than them.

265

A FINAL WORD TO THE STUDENT

Use the following procedure to check your exercise before you hand it in:

1. Re-read the special instructions one at a time.
2. After you re-read each separate instruction, examine your completed exercise to make certain that you have followed that particular instruction exactly.
3. Revise your work wherever necessary.
4. When you are certain that the special instruction you are considering has been observed throughout your exercise, place a check ($\checkmark$) to the left of that special instruction and go on to the next one until you have completed the entire list.

This process will take several minutes of your time, but failure to recheck your exercises in this manner may mean that you have wasted all of the time and effort you have spent in doing the exercise.

EXERCISE 44

COMPOUND SENTENCES

Write a sentence to fit each of the indicated patterns.

Special Instructions:

_____ 1. Do not use any proper nouns in this exercise.
_____ 2. Do not use the passive voice.
_____ 3. Use only the indicative mode.
_____ 4. Be sure that your punctuation is correct.
_____ 5. Be sure that each sentence is a statement, not a question.
_____ 6. Be sure that you follow the specified pattern exactly.
_____ 7. Be sure that each sentence makes good sense.
_____ 8. Be sure that the ideas expressed in the independent clauses of each sentence have a sufficiently close relationship to justify their being in the same sentence.

Compound Pattern

(_____ , and _____ .)
         1   2

1. **Subject—Verb—Object**
2. **Subject—Verb—Object**

1. _I packed the car, and we left the cabin._

Compound Pattern

(_____ , _____ , and _____ .)
       1   2   3

1. **Subject—Verb**
2. **Subject—Verb**
3. **Subject—Verb**

2. _He plowed, the brother planted, the father watered._

Compound Pattern

(——————————————, but ——————————————.)

    1   2

1. *Subject—Linking Verb—Adjective Complement*
2. *Subject—Verb—Object*

3. The test was difficult, but the student
   passed it.

Compound Pattern

(——————————, for ——————————.)

    1   2

1. *Subject—Verb—Object*
2. *Subject—Verb—*MODIFIER*—Object*

4. The nurse brought a map , for the
   girl broke a medicine bottle.

Compound Pattern

(Not only ——————————, but ——————————.)

            1   2

1. AUXILIARY*—Subject—Verb—Object*
2. *Subject—Verb—Object*

5. Not only did the boy paint the barn, but
   he stacked the hay.

Compound Pattern

(——————————; ——————————.)

    1   2

1. *Subject—Verb—Object*
2. *Subject—Verb—Object*

6. The instructor broke a ski; I broke a
   leg.

Exercise 44 (continued)

Compound Pattern

(————————————————; so ———————————————.)

             1   2

1. MODIFIER—*Subject—Verb—Object*
2. MODIFIER —*Subject—Verb—Object*—MODIFIER
(Conjunctive adverb *so*)

7. The orchestra conductor provided the tickets; so we attended the concert gladly.

Compound Pattern

(————————————————; consequently, ————————————.)

             1   2

1. *Subject—Linking Verb—Adjective Complement*
2. MODIFIER —*Subject—Verb—Object*—MODIFIER
(Conjunctive adverb *consequently*)

what is wrong?

8. The plates were broken; consequently we returned the order promptly.

Compound Pattern

(————————————; ————————————, however, ————————.)

             1   2

1. *Subject—Verb*—MODIFIER—*Object*
2. MODIFIER—*Subject*— MODIFIER —*Verb—Object*
(Conjunctive adverb *however*)

9. I lost the office key; the janitor, however, opened the door.

Compound Pattern

(————————————; ————————————, on the other hand, ————————.)

             1   2

1. *Subject—Verb—Object*
2. *Subject*— MODIFIER —*Verb—Object*
(Conjunctive adverb *on the other hand*)

10. We dropped the course; a foreign student, on the other hand, made an A.

A FINAL WORD TO THE STUDENT

Use the following procedure to check your exercise before you hand it in:

1. Re-read the special instructions one at a time.
2. After you re-read each separate instruction, examine your completed exercise to make certain that you have followed that particular instruction exactly.
3. Revise your work wherever necessary.
4. When you are certain that the special instruction you are considering has been observed throughout your exercise, place a check ($\checkmark$) to the left of that special instruction and go on to the next one until you have completed the entire list.

This process will take several minutes of your time, but failure to recheck your exercises in this manner may mean that you have wasted all of the time and effort you have spent in doing the exercise.

EXERCISE 45

COMPOUND-COMPLEX SENTENCES

Write ten compound-complex sentences.

Special Instructions:

_____ 1. Do not use any proper nouns in this exercise.
_____ 2. Do not use the passive voice.
_____ 3. Be sure that your punctuation is correct.
_____ 4. Be sure that each sentence is a statement, not a question.
_____ 5. Be sure that each sentence makes good sense.
_____ 6. Be sure that there are at least *two* independent clauses and at least *one* dependent clause in each sentence.

1. We found the camp ground which you suggested, but there were no vacancies.

2. I returned the watch that she bought for me; however she would not accept it.

3. They know that you are sorry; yet they are still angry.

4. The girl left before the dance ended; yet her date did not leave.

5. He is the man who was seen at the scene of the crime; nevertheless he was released.

6. I thought that he was right, but my friend wasn't sure.

7. He is the student who wants to be an architect; however his grades are not high enough.

8. I knew that she wanted to go, but I didn't know that she wanted to go with me.

9. The clouds which he hoped would bring rain disappeared, and there are no others in sight.

10. The flight that I booked has been canceled; nevertheless I will wait for another flight.

A FINAL WORD TO THE STUDENT

Use the following procedure to check your exercise before you hand it in:

1. Re-read the special instructions one at a time.
2. After you re-read each separate instruction, examine your completed exercise to make certain that you have followed that particular instruction exactly.
3. Revise your work wherever necessary.
4. When you are certain that the special instruction you are considering has been observed throughout your exercise, place a check (√) to the left of that special instruction and go on to the next one until you have completed the entire list.

This process will take several minutes of your time, but failure to recheck your exercises in this manner may mean that you have wasted all of the time and effort you have spent in doing the exercise.

EXERCISE 46

COORDINATION AND SUBORDINATION

Write five compound sentences, making certain that the ideas expressed in the independent clauses of each sentence are *of equal importance.*

Special Instructions:

——— 1. Use two independent clauses to form each compound sentence.
——— 2. Be sure that there is no dependent clause in any of your sentences.
——— 3. Do not use any proper nouns in these sentences.
——— 4. Do not use the passive voice.
——— 5. Be sure that your punctuation is correct.
——— 6. Be sure that each sentence is a statement, not a question.
——— 7. Be sure that each sentence makes good sense.
——— 8. Be sure that the ideas expressed in the independent clauses of each sentence have a sufficiently close relationship to justify their being in the same sentence.

1. ——

   ——

2. ——

   ——

3. ——

   ——

4. ——

   ——

5. ——

   ——

Write five complex sentences, making certain that in each sentence the idea expressed in the dependent clause is *of less importance* than the idea expressed in the independent clause.

Special Instructions:

——— 1. Use either an adjective clause or an adverb clause as the dependent clause of each complex sentence.
——— 2. Do not use more than one dependent clause in each sentence.
——— 3. Do not use more than one independent clause in each sentence.
——— 4. Do not use any proper nouns in these sentences.
——— 5. Do not use the passive voice.
——— 6. Be sure that your punctuation is correct.
——— 7. Be sure that each sentence is a statement, not a question.
——— 8. Be sure that each sentence makes good sense.

6. _____

_____

7. _____

_____

8. _____

_____

9. _____

_____

10. _____

_____

A FINAL WORD TO THE STUDENT

Use the following procedure to check your exercise before you hand it in:

1. Re-read the special instructions one at a time.
2. After you re-read each separate instruction, examine your completed exercise to make certain that you have followed that particular instruction exactly.
3. Revise your work wherever necessary.
4. When you are certain that the special instruction you are considering has been observed throughout your exercise, place a check ($\checkmark$) to the left of that special instruction and go on to the next one until you have completed the entire list.

This process will take several minutes of your time, but failure to recheck your exercises in this manner may mean that you have wasted all of the time and effort you have spent in doing the exercise.

APPENDIX

PUNCTUATION AND MECHANICS

A. THE COMMA

1. **Commas are used to separate the units of certain types of compounds.**

Compounds consisting of single-word units, compounds consisting of predicates, compounds consisting of phrases, and compounds consisting of dependent clauses follow identical punctuation patterns.

Punctuation patterns:

```
_____ and _____

_____, _____

_____, _____, and _____
_____ and _____ and _____
_____, _____, _____
```

See pp. 52–53.

2. **Commas are used to separate the independent units of certain compound and compound-complex sentences.**

a. If there is no internal comma punctuation near a break between independent units, a sentence containing independent units connected by a single coordinating conjunction normally follows one of two punctuation patterns.

Punctuation patterns:

```
                    { and }
                    { but }
_____, {  or  } _____.
                    { for }
                    { nor }

_____, _____, { and } _____.
                                     { or  }
```

See p. 150.

b. If there is no internal comma punctuation near the break between independent units, a sentence containing independent units connected by a pair of conjunctions normally has a comma separating the units.

Punctuation patterns:

Not only _____, but (also) _____.
Either _____, or _____.

See p. 151.

3. **Commas are used to set off non-restrictive modifiers.**

a. Adjectival modifiers

(1) Non-restrictive adjectives are set off by commas.
   See pp. 33–34.
(2) Non-restrictive participles and participial phrases are set off by commas.
   See pp. 49, 90.
(3) Non-restrictive adjective clauses are set off by commas.
   See p. 127.

b. Adverbial modifiers

(1) Non-restrictive adverbs are set off by commas.

> Example:
>
> He climbed the stairs, slowly and painfully.

(2) Non-restrictive adverbial phrases are set off by commas.

> Example:
>
> The motion was carried, despite his opposition.

(3) Non-restrictive adverb clauses are set off by commas.
See pp. 135, 137, 138.

4. **Commas are used to set off certain non-restrictive appositives.**
See pp. 64–65, 67.

5. **A comma usually follows an introductory expression used with an appositive.**
See p. 67.

6. **Commas are used to set off certain independent sentence elements.**

a. Mild exclamatory expressions are often set off by commas.
See p. 68.

b. Vocatives are set off by commas.
See p. 69.

7. **Commas are used to set off most sentence modifiers.**

a. Commas are used to set off most single-word sentence modifiers.

> Example:
>
> Honestly, I do not know what he said.

See pp. 39–40.

b. Commas are used to set off phrases functioning as sentence modifiers.

> Example:
>
> To tell the truth, he has already written the letter.

See p. 84.

c. Commas are used to set off clauses functioning as sentence modifiers.

> Example:
>
> Mary, you know, was the person who invited him.

d. Commas are used to set off certain conjunctive adverbs.
See p. 152.

e. Commas are used to set off nominative absolute constructions.

> Example:
>
> The bell having rung, the teacher ended his lecture.

See Note on p. 92.

8. **Commas are used to set off certain elements when they occur in specified positions in the sentence.**

a. A long prepositional phrase preceding the subject is set off by comma punctuation.
See p. 84.

b. An infinitive or an infinitive phrase functioning as an adverb is set off by comma punctuation when it precedes the element it modifies.
See pp. 46, 100.

c. An adverb clause preceding or falling within the independent clause to which it belongs is set off by comma punctuation.
See p. 135.

9. **Commas are used to set off a short direct quotation functioning as the object of a verb of** *saying, commanding, exclaiming, asking, etc.*
   See pp. 106–07.

10. **Commas are used to set off parts of dates and addresses.**

   Examples:

   > On Wednesday, February 23, 1949, the preliminary agreement was signed.
   > She lives at 4515 East 25th Avenue, Denver, Colorado.

11. **Commas are used to prevent misreading.**
   Example:

   > *Confusing:* Below the football players were practicing.
   > *Clarified:* Below, the football players were practicing.

B. PARENTHESES

1. **Parentheses may be used to enclose certain types of appositives.**
   See pp. 64–65, 67.
2. **Parentheses may be used to enclose interpolated elements.**
   See p. 69.

C. THE DASH

1. **A dash is used to mark sudden shifting or interruption of thought in a sentence.**

   Examples:

   > He said—I won't tell you what he said.
   > I wonder what they—

2. **Dashes may be used to enclose certain types of appositives.**
   See pp. 64–65, 67.

3. **Dashes may be used to enclose interpolated elements.**
   See p. 69.

D. BRACKETS

Brackets are used to enclose explanatory notes or additions inserted in quoted material.

   Example:

   > Byron said: "He [Colonel Stanhope] leaves nothing untouched from the general government to the schools for children."

E. THE SEMICOLON

1. **Semicolons are used to separate the independent units of certain compound and compound-complex sentences.**

a. If there is no conjunction connecting the independent units, a semicolon is used to separate the units.

   Punctuation patterns:

   > ----------------------------------; ----------------------------------.
   > ----------------------------------; ----------------------------------; ----------------------------------.

See pp. 151–53.

b. If there is internal comma punctuation near a break between independent units, a semicolon is used to separate the units even though they are connected by a conjunction.
   See pp. 150–51.

2. **Semicolons are used instead of commas to separate the units of compounds containing internal comma punctuation.**

> Example:
>> We invited Jones, the banker; Smith, the merchant; and Johnson, the editor.

F. THE COLON

1. **A colon is used before a direct quotation which is formally introduced.** Usually such a quotation will be relatively long.

> Example:
>> George Washington said: "A slender acquaintance with the world must convince every man that actions, not words, are the true criterion of the attachment of friends and that the most liberal professions of good-will are very far from being the surest marks of it."

2. **A colon may be used before certain types of appositives.**
See p. 65.

G. THE PERIOD

1. **A period is used to close a declarative sentence.**
See p. 71.

2. **A period is used to close an imperative sentence, unless the sentence is also exclamatory.**
See p. 71.

3. **A period is used after an abbreviation.**

> Examples:
>> Mr., Mrs., Dr., a.m., N.Y.

H. THE QUESTION MARK

1. **A question mark is used to close an interrogative sentence.**
See p. 72.

2. **A question mark is used after an interrogative element which stands alone as a non-sentence.**

> Examples:
>> When? Day after tomorrow?

I. THE EXCLAMATION POINT

1. **An exclamation point is used to close an exclamatory sentence.**
See p. 76.

2. **An exclamation point is used after an exclamatory element.**
See p. 68.

J. QUOTATION MARKS

1. **Quotation marks are used to enclose titles of relatively short literary compositions, such as essays, articles, short stories, and lyrics.**

Titles of subordinate parts of long works are also enclosed in quotation marks.

> Examples:
>> We read Shelley's "Ozymandias."
>> The first chapter is "The Tennyson Legend."

2. **Quotation marks are used to enclose direct quotations.**

Note the use of quotation marks and other marks of punctuation in the following examples:

a. Direct quotations of sentences containing no punctuation

Examples:

Original sentence

Your method of working is entirely wrong.

Direct quotations

He said, "Your method of working is entirely wrong."
"Your method of working is entirely wrong," he said.
"Your method of working," he said, "is entirely wrong."

Punctuation patterns:

He said, "＿＿＿＿＿＿＿＿＿＿＿＿＿＿＿＿＿＿＿＿＿."
"＿＿＿＿＿＿＿＿＿＿＿＿＿＿＿＿＿＿＿＿＿," he said.
"＿＿＿＿＿＿＿＿＿＿＿＿," he said, "＿＿＿＿＿＿＿＿＿＿."

See pp. 106–07.

b. Direct quotations of sentences containing comma punctuation

Examples:

Original sentence

I waited at the office, but the doctor did not come.

Direct quotations

He said, "I waited at the office, but the doctor did not come."
"I waited at the office, but the doctor did not come," he said.
"I waited at the office," he said, "but the doctor did not come."

Punctuation patterns:

He said, "＿＿＿＿＿＿＿＿＿＿＿, but ＿＿＿＿＿＿＿＿＿＿＿."
"＿＿＿＿＿＿＿＿＿＿＿, but ＿＿＿＿＿＿＿＿＿＿＿," he said.
"＿＿＿＿＿＿＿＿＿＿＿," he said, "but ＿＿＿＿＿＿＿＿＿＿＿."

c. Direct quotations of sentences containing semicolon punctuation

Examples:

Original sentence

Our opponents have weight; we have skill and speed.

Direct quotations

He said, "Our opponents have weight; we have skill and speed."
"Our opponents have weight; we have skill and speed," he said.
"Our opponents have weight," he said; "we have skill and speed."

Punctuation patterns:

He said, "＿＿＿＿＿＿＿＿＿＿＿; ＿＿＿＿＿＿＿＿＿＿＿."
"＿＿＿＿＿＿＿＿＿＿＿; ＿＿＿＿＿＿＿＿＿＿＿," he said.
"＿＿＿＿＿＿＿＿＿＿＿," he said; "＿＿＿＿＿＿＿＿＿＿＿."

d. Direct quotations of more than one sentence

Examples:

Original sentences

She must be here. Her car is in the driveway.

Direct quotations

He said, "She must be here. Her car is in the driveway."
"She must be here. Her car is in the driveway," he said.
"She must be here," he said. "Her car is in the driveway."

Punctuation patterns:

He said, "_____. _____."
"_____. _____," he said.
"_____," he said. "_____."

3. **The position of various marks of punctuation in relation to the final set of a pair of quotation marks may be determined by the following rules:**

a. Commas and periods are placed *inside* the quotation marks.

Examples:

"I misplaced my notes," she explained.
The man replied, "I have not completed the work."

b. Colons and semicolons are placed *outside* the quotation marks.

Example:

I selected Poe's "The Raven"; she preferred Coleridge's "Kubla Khan."

c. Question marks and exclamation points are placed *inside* the quotation marks when they refer to the quotation itself.

Examples:

She asked, "When did you arrive?"
"What a surprise!" the girl exclaimed.

d. Question marks and exclamation points are placed *outside* the quotation marks when they refer to the entire sentence in which the quotation occurs.

Example:

Who said, "A little learning is a dangerous thing"?

4. **Single quotation marks are used to enclose a quotation within a quotation.**

Example:

Mary replied, "I'm sure the teacher said, 'We *may* have an exam.' "

K. THE APOSTROPHE

1. **The apostrophe is used in forming certain possessives.**
See pp. 31–33.

2. **The apostrophe is used to indicate omitted letters in contractions.**

Examples:

don't, doesn't, I'm, you're

3. **The apostrophe is used in forming the plural of letters, figures, and words used as words.**

Examples:

There are two *m*'s in *committee.*
There are too many *and*'s in this paragraph.

L. THE HYPHEN

1. The hyphen is used to divide compound words.

Consult a good dictionary to determine whether a word is hyphenated.
See Note 1 on p. 35.

2. The hyphen is used to divide a word which is carried over from one line to another.

A word may be divided only between syllables. Consult a good dictionary to determine the proper syllabication of a word.

M. ITALICS

Underlining is used in handwritten and typewritten material to indicate italics.

1. Italics are used for titles of works of art, newspapers, magazines, and relatively long literary compositions, such as books, plays, and long poems.

> Examples:
>
> > He always reads the *Saturday Review of Literature.*
> > Did you see *Green Pastures?*

2. Italics are used for names of ships, trains, and airplanes.

> Example:
>
> > She arrived on the *Queen Mary.*

3. Italics are used for letters used as letters and words used as words.

> Example:
>
> > The word *across* is spelled with one *c.*

4. Italics are used for foreign words occurring in English sentences.

> Example:
>
> > They believed in the doctrine of *laissez faire.*

5. Italics are used for emphasized words.

> Example:
>
> > I am certain that he *did* go.

N. CAPITAL LETTERS

1. A capital letter is used at the beginning of a sentence.

> Example:
>
> > The car struck the wall.

2. A capital letter is used at the beginning of a quoted sentence.

> Example:
>
> > The boy replied, "You should turn at the next corner."

3. A capital letter is normally used at the beginning of every line of poetry.

> Example:
>
> > That time of year thou mayst in me behold
> > When yellow leaves, or none, or few, do hang
> > Upon those boughs which shake against the cold,
> > Bare ruin'd choirs where late the sweet birds sang.

4. **Proper nouns and adjectives derived from proper nouns begin with capital letters.** If a proper noun consists of several words, the important words are capitalized.

See pp. 4, 29.

5. **The important words in titles are capitalized.**

Example:

Cooper wrote *The Last of the Mohicans.*

6. **The pronoun *I* is always capitalized.**

7. **Words which refer to Deity are always capitalized.**

Examples:

God, Jehovah, the Almighty, Christ, the Saviour.

SECTION II

A LIST OF PRINCIPAL PARTS OF TROUBLESOME VERBS

Present Infinitive	Past Tense	Past Participle	Present Infinitive	Past Tense	Past Participle
accompany	accompanied	accompanied	bore	bored	bored
ache	ached	ached	break	broke	broken
agree	agreed	agreed	breathe	breathed	breathed
apply	applied	applied	bring	brought	brought
argue	argued	argued	build	built	built
arise	arose	arisen	burn	burned or burnt	burned or burnt
ask	asked	asked			
attack	attacked	attacked	burst	burst	burst
awake	awoke or awaked	awoke or awaked	bury	buried	buried
			buy	bought	bought
awaken	awakened	awakened	carry	carried	carried
bathe	bathed	bathed	cast	cast	cast
be	was (were)	been	catch	caught	caught
bear	bore	borne or born (passive)	choose	chose	chosen
			climb	climbed	climbed
beat	beat	beat or beaten	cling	clung	clung
			close	closed	closed
become	became	become	clothe	clothed or clad	clothed or clad
begin	began	begun			
behold	beheld	beheld	comb	combed	combed
bend	bent	bent	come	came	come
benefit	benefited	benefited	compel	compelled	compelled
bet	bet or betted	bet or betted	consider	considered	considered
			continue	continued	continued
bid (offer to purchase)	bid	bid	copy	copied	copied
			cost	cost	cost
bid (command)	bade	bidden or bid	creep	crept	crept
			cry	cried	cried
bind	bound	bound	curse	cursed or curst	cursed or curst
bite	bit	bitten or bit			
			cut	cut	cut
bleed	bled	bled	deal	dealt	dealt
blow	blew	blown	defy	defied	defied

Present Infinitive	Past Tense	Past Participle	Present Infinitive	Past Tense	Past Participle
deny	denied	denied	know	knew	known
deposit	deposited	deposited	lay	laid	laid
develop	developed	developed	lead	led	led
die	died	died	leap	leaped or leapt	leaped or leapt
dig	dug or digged	dug or digged	leave	left	left
dine	dined	dined	lend	lent	lent
dive	dived	dived	let	let	let
do	did	done	lie (recline)	lay	lain
drag	dragged	dragged	lie (tell a falsehood)	lied	lied
draw	drew	drawn			
dream	dreamed or dreamt	dreamed or dreamt	light	lighted or lit	lighted or lit
drink	drank	drunk	lose	lost	lost
drip	dripped	dripped	make	made	made
drive	drove	driven	marry	married	married
drop	dropped	dropped	mean	meant	meant
drown	drowned	drowned	meet	met	met
dry	dried	dried	owe	owed	owed
dwell	dwelt or dwelled	dwelt or dwelled	pass	passed	passed
			pay	paid	paid
eat	ate	eaten	plan	planned	planned
fall	fell	fallen	prove	proved	proved
feed	fed	fed	raise	raised	raised
feel	felt	felt	read	read	read
fell	felled	felled	ride	rode	ridden
fight	fought	fought	ring	rang	rung
find	found	found	rise	rose	risen
fit	fitted	fitted	run	ran	run
flee	fled	fled	saw	sawed	sawed
fling	flung	flung	say	said	said
flow	flowed	flowed	seat	seated	seated
fly	flew	flown	see	saw	seen
forbid	forbade or forbad	forbidden or forbid	seek	sought	sought
			seem	seemed	seemed
forget	forgot	forgotten or forgot	sell	sold	sold
			send	sent	sent
forgive	forgave	forgiven	set	set	set
freeze	froze	frozen	shake	shook	shaken
get	got	got or gotten	shine (give forth light)	shone	shone
give	gave	given			
go	went	gone	shine (polish)	shined	shined
grind	ground	ground	shoot	shot	shot
grow	grew	grown	show	showed	shown or showed
hang (suspend)	hung	hung			
hang (kill by suspending)	hanged	hanged	shrink	shrank or shrunk	shrunk
have	had	had	shut	shut	shut
hear	heard	heard	sing	sang or sung	sung
help	helped	helped			
hide	hid	hidden or hid	sink	sank or sunk	sunk
hit	hit	hit	sit	sat	sat
hold	held	held	sleep	slept	slept
hurry	hurried	hurried	slide	slid	slid
hurt	hurt	hurt	sow	sowed	sown or sowed
keep	kept	kept	speak	spoke	spoken
kill	killed	killed	spend	spent	spent

Present Infinitive	*Past Tense*	*Past Participle*	*Present Infinitive*	*Past Tense*	*Past Participle*
spin	spun	spun	take	took	taken
spread	spread	spread	teach	taught	taught
spring	sprang or sprung	sprung	tear	tore	torn
			tell	told	told
stand	stood	stood	think	thought	thought
steal	stole	stolen	throw	threw	thrown
stick	stuck	stuck	tie	tied	tied
sting	stung	stung	try	tried	tried
stink	stank or stunk	stunk	understand	understood	understood
			wake	waked or woke	waked
stop	stopped	stopped			
strike	struck	struck	wear	wore	worn
string	strung	strung	weave	wove	woven
strive	strove	striven	weep	wept	wept
study	studied	studied	win	won	won
swear	swore	sworn	wind	wound	wound
sweep	swept	swept	wring	wrung	wrung
swim	swam	swum	write	wrote	written
swing	swung	swung			

SECTION III

A SPELLING LIST

absence	agreement	apostrophe	autumn	breath	carrying
absorb	agriculture	apparatus	auxiliary	breathe	casualties
absurd	aisle	apparently	average	bridal	cavalry
accept	all right	appearance	bachelor	bridle	ceiling
acceptable	alley	appetite	balanced	brilliance	cemetery
accident	ally	appositive	balloon	Britain	century
accidentally	almost	appreciate	bargain	British	certainly
accommodate	already	approach	bath	Briton	changeable
accompaniment	altar	architect	bathe	budget	characteristics
accompany	alter	arctic	beautiful	build	chauffeur
accomplish	although	aren't	becoming	bulletin	chief
account	altogether	argument	beggar	bureau	children
accumulate	always	arrangement	beginning	bury	chimney
accustomed	amateur	arrival	belief	business	choice
achievement	amendment	article	believe	busy	choose
acquainted	among	ascend	beneath	calendar	chose
acre	amount	ashamed	benefiting	campaign	chosen
across	analysis	asked	berth	canal	circumstances
actually	analyze	assassin	bicycle	candidate	cite
address	ancient	astonish	birth	cannot	citizen
adjective	angel	athlete	biscuit	can't	climate
advantageous	angle	athletics	bishop	capital	climbed
adverb	announce	atmosphere	blossom	capitol	clothes
advice	answer	attached	born	captain	clothing
advise	antecedent	attacked	borne	carburetor	cloths
affect	anticipate	attendance	boundaries	career	coarse
afraid	anticipatory	attorney	brake	carefully	coffee
aggravate	anxious	audience	break	carriage	colonel
aggressive	apartment	author	breakfast	carried	column

comedy	delegate	equipment	gradually	knowledge	occurrence
comfortable	demonstrative	equipped	grammar	laboratories	o'clock
coming	depth	equivalent	grief	laid	officer
commission	descended	especially	guarantee	lazy	official
committee	describe	establish	guard	lead	often
comparative	description	etc.	guess	led	omitted
comparatively	desert	Europe	guidance	leisure	oneself
comparison	desperation	evening	gymnasium	length	opinion
compel	dessert	exaggeration	handkerchief	liable	opponent
competition	destroy	exceed	haphazard	library	opportunity
complement	develop	excelled	happiness	license	opposite
completely	development	excellent	height	lightning	optimistic
complex	diamond	except	hindrance	literary	originally
compliment	diary	exclamatory	hoping	literature	pageant
compulsory	difference	exercise	hopping	lonely	paid
concede	dilapidated	exhausted	huge	loose	pamphlet
conceivable	dine	exhibition	hundred	lose	paragraph
condemn	dining	existence	hungry	losing	parallel
conferred	disappeared	expensive	hurriedly	luxury	parentheses
confident	disappointed	experience	hygiene	lying	parliament
conjunction	discipline	experiment	hypocrisy	machinery	participle
conquering	discussion	explanation	icicle	magazine	particularly
conscience	disease	expletive	illicit	maintain	partner
conscious	dissatisfied	extraordinary	imagination	maneuver	pastime
consequence	dissipation	extremely	immediately	marriage	peace
consider	divide	faculty	imperative	material	peculiar
consistent	divine	fallacy	impromptu	mathematics	perceive
conspicuous	division	familiar	incidentally	measure	performance
contempt	doctor	fascinating	indefinite	medal	perhaps
continue	doesn't	favorite	independent	medicine	permanently
control	don't	February	indispensable	melancholy	personal
convenient	dormitory	field	individual	merely	personnel
coordinating	doubt	fiery	inevitably	miniature	perspiration
corps	dozen	fifth	infinitive	minute	persuaded
corpse	drowned	finally	infinity	miscellaneous	philosophy
couldn't	dumb	financial	influential	mischievous	phrase
council	during	finish	initiative	misspell	physical
counsel	dyeing	forehead	innocent	model	physician
country	dying	foreigner	inquire	momentous	physiology
courageous	ecstasy	forest	intelligence	mortgage	picnicking
course	editor	forgotten	intensive	mosquito	piece
courteous	effect	formally	intercede	murmuring	plain
cousin	efficiency	formerly	interesting	muscle	plane
cried	eight	forth	interpolated	mysterious	pleasure
criticism	eighteen	forty	interrogative	mystery	poem
criticize	eighth	four	interrupt	necessary	politician
crowd	either	fourth	intransitive	neighbor	possession
curiosity	eligibility	freshman	introduction	neither	possessive
curriculum	eliminated	freshmen	invite	nevertheless	possible
dairy	embarrassment	friend	irresistible	nickel	potatoes
daughter	emphasis	fruit	island	niece	potential
debt	emphatic	fundamentally	isle	nineteen	practical
deceive	employ	furniture	isn't	ninety	practice
decency	employee	garage	its	nominative	prairie
decision	empty	generally	it's	noticeable	precede
declarative	encourage	genius	itself	nowadays	precedence
deferred	enemies	gerund	jewelry	obedient	preceding
definite	entirely	giant	journey	occasion	predicate
definition	environment	government	judgment	occur	prefer
definitive	equal	governor	kindergarten	occurred	preference

preferred	ready	sacrilegious	stopped	there	valuable
prejudiced	realize	safety	straight	therefore	variety
preparation	really	salary	strategy	they're	vegetable
preposition	receipt	sandwich	strength	thorough	vengeance
prerequisite	receive	scene	studying	though	view
presence	recipe	scenery	subjunctive	through	vigilant
pretty	reciprocal	schedule	subordinating	to	villain
primitive	recognize	scholar	substantive	together	vocative
principal	recommended	seized	subtle	too	weather
principle	refer	separately	successful	tournament	Wednesday
prisoner	reference	sequence	sufficient	toward	weight
privileges	referred	sergeant	superlative	tragedy	weird
probably	reign	shepherd	supersede	tragic	welfare
proceed	rein	shine	supplementary	transferred	where
profession	relieve	shining	sure	treachery	wherever
professor	religious	siege	surprise	tried	whether
prominent	remedy	sight	suspect	truly	which
pronounce	remember	significance	suspicion	twelfth	wholly
pronunciation	repeat	similar	sword	twelve	witch
propaganda	repetition	sincerely	syllables	tyranny	women
propeller	restaurant	site	sympathy	unanimous	won't
psychology	review	society	system	undoubtedly	write
punctuation	rhetoric	sophomore	temperamental	unnecessary	writing
pursuit	rhythm	speak	temperature	until	written
quality	ridicule	speeches	than	unusual	yacht
quantity	ridiculous	stationary	their	usual	your
quiet	sacrifice	stationery	then	usually	you're
quite	sacrilege	stop			

SECTION IV

THE OBJECTIVE COMPLEMENT

The *objective complement* completes the meaning of a predicate consisting of a verb and a direct object. In the following sentences, the italicized words are *objective complements:*

> They elected John *president.*
> We consider her *intelligent.*
> The letter made me *angry.*

Note that each of these objective complements gives additional information about the direct object. Note also that the objective complement may be either a substantive or an adjective.

The construction can best be explained by pointing out its similarity to two other constructions: (1) the infinitive phrase containing a subject, a linking-verb infinitive, and a complement, and (2) the verb-adverb combination.

Usually a linking-verb infinitive can be inserted between a direct object and an objective complement without appreciably changing the meaning of the sentence. The resulting construction is, of course, an infinitive phrase containing a subject. Note the following examples:

> They elected John president.
> They elected John to be president.

> We consider her intelligent.
> We consider her to be intelligent.

> The letter made me angry.
> The letter made me become angry.

Besides having this similarity to an infinitive phrase construction, the objective complement construction in some ways resembles the verb-adverb combination. Like the combined verb-adverb, the combined verb-objective complement has the force of a single verb.

Examples:

Verb-adverb combination
They turned the proposition down.

They   turned down   the proposition.

Objective complement
They elected John president.

They   elected-president   John.

We consider her intelligent.

We   consider-intelligent   her.

The letter made me angry.

The letter   made-angry   me.

Note that in the last example a single verb can be substituted for the verb-objective complement combination:

The letter *angered* me.

SECTION V

MODIFIERS HAVING BOTH ADJECTIVAL AND ADVERBIAL FUNCTIONS

A non-restrictive modifier of the subject of a sentence sometimes seems to perform an adverbial function in addition to its obvious adjectival one. Note the following examples:

> The girl returned home completely *well*. [The adjective *well*, in addition to modifying *girl*, indicates a condition under which the *returning* took place.]

> The child came *running*. [The participle *running*, in addition to modifying *child*, indicates a condition under which the *coming* took place.]

> The boy stood *gazing out the window*. [The participial phrase *gazing out the window*, in addition to modifying *boy*, indicates a condition under which the *standing* took place.]

In such constructions, the element performing the dual function may be considered to be equivalent to an elliptical adverb clause. Compare the following sentences:

The man walked away   while he was stunned.

The man walked away stunned.

Note that in the first sentence *stunned* performs an adjectival function and the entire clause *while he was stunned* performs an adverbial function. Omission of the words *while he was* leaves only the word *stunned* to perform both the adjectival and the adverbial functions. (See the treatment of the appositive and the adjective clause on pp. 131–32.)

Throughout this text, modifiers of the sort considered in this section have been treated as if their function were entirely adjectival, since it is their adjectival function which is most important and obvious.

SECTION VI

THE PRESENT GERUND AND THE PRESENT AND PAST PARTICIPLES

The gerund usually functions as a substantive, and the participle as an adjective. However, the present gerund may also function as an adjective, and the present and past participles may serve as substantives.

The following constructions involve the use of a present gerund to modify a noun:

diving board	playing field
sleeping porch	drinking glass

Note that in these examples the noun names something which is *involved in* the action indicated by the gerund but is *not* actually *performing* the action. Usually the thing named by the noun is used *for* the performance of the action: a board *for* diving; a porch *for* sleeping; a field *for* playing; a glass *for* drinking. Such rephrasing, however, does not always work. For instance, *a typing mistake* is obviously not "a mistake *for* typing" but "a mistake *in* typing." Still, it is clear that the *mistake* is *not performing* the action of *typing.*

The same modifying words which are classified as gerunds in the examples above must be classified as participles if they indicate an action which is actually performed by the thing indicated by the noun:

diving boy	(The boy *is* diving.)
sleeping baby	(The baby *is* sleeping.)
playing children	(The children *are* playing.)

Sometimes, of course, the expression is ambiguous unless clarified by context or (in speech) by tone of voice:

rocking chair (a chair *for* rocking or a chair which *is* rocking)
singing teacher (a teacher *of* singing or a teacher who *is* singing)
spinning wheel (a wheel *for* spinning or a wheel which *is* spinning)

It is important to remember that an *-ing* word modifying a noun is not necessarily *either* a gerund *or* a participle:

handwriting expert
plumbing display
building inspector

The difference between these constructions and those previously discussed is that the *-ing* word indicates an *object* rather than an *action*: the *expert* judges an o*bject*, not an *action*; the display presents *objects*, not *actions*; and the *inspector* inspects an *object*, not an *action*. In such constructions, the *-ing* word is simply an adjectival use of a word which normally appears as a noun.

To classify an *-ing* word modifying a noun, then, you should first determine whether the word names an action. If it does not name an action, it is an adjective based upon a noun. If it does name an action, it is an adjectival use of a participle or a gerund—a particple if it indicates an action *performed* by the noun it modifies, a gerund if it does *not.*

Just as a present gerund may function as an adjective, a present participle or a past participle may function as a noun:

We must first of all rescue the *living*. (Present participle)
The *injured* will be flown to the hospital. (Past participle)

Note that a participle functioning in this way may be modified by the sort of adverb which modifies a verb or verbal:

He treats the *mentally* disturbed.
The doctors examined the *badly* injured.

INDEX